This book belongs to

Pauline Nelson

EXPERIENCING GOD

DAILY DEVOTIONALS

HENRY T. BLACKABY
AND
RICHARD BLACKABY

**CHURCH
STRENGTHENING
MINISTRY**

Experiencing God Daily Devotionals
© 1998 by Henry Blackaby and Richard Blackaby
All rights reserved.

Dewey Decimal Classification 242.64
Subject Heading: DEVOTIONAL EXERCISES / GOD

This edition cover design by Berlin Bondoc

Printed and published with permission in the Philippines by:

Church Strengthening Ministry
of Foreign Mission Board, SBC, Inc.
P.O. Box 2656 MCPO
1266 Makati City, Philippines
Email: direct@csm-publishing.com
Website: www.csm-publishing.net

ISBN 971-717-833-X

For sale in the Philippines only

Preface

Certain people have significantly enhanced my walk with God over the years. The positive influence of my godly parents continues to shape my life, especially my desire for integrity before God and others.

Oswald Chambers's devotional book, *My Utmost for His Highest*, has been a companion to my life, challenging me to an ever-deepening relationship with Jesus Christ my Lord. The pages of my copy are filled with dates and personal notes about special events in my life. These notes record how special a truth, a Scripture, or a statement has been to me; the pages of Chambers's book have become a spiritual journal that I treasure. My prayer is that *Experiencing God Day-by-Day* will become a source of encouragement, as you walk with God through the years.

Henry Blackaby

I was privileged to be raised by godly parents. They did not just tell me about the Christian life; they lived it out before me. One of my most treasured possessions is the worn-out Bible my father passed down to me. (My father is hard on Bibles!) He has given a well-used Bible to each of his five children over the years. As I browse through his Bible, I find notes written in the margin, verses underlined and highlighted, and dates beside verses recording times when my father experienced the truth of that passage. I have also found his tattered copy of *My Utmost for His Highest*. In the margins are his comments and dates when key events occurred in our family. Could there be any greater family heirloom than a journal of the parents' spiritual pilgrimage? We hope that this devotional guide will provide a similar opportunity for you.

Richard Blackaby

The devotional thoughts presented in this book reflect a lifetime of seeking God in Scripture each day. Many of the thoughts reflect insights God has graciously shared with us over the years, and it is our pleasure to share them with you. Nothing can replace the life-changing experience of reading Scripture. This book is designed not to take the place of God's Word in your life, but to introduce verses for you to consider and meditate upon. The Holy Spirit is your Teacher, and He will impress things upon your heart as you read the devotional thoughts. One verse is usually presented each day. You will want to have your Bible at hand to read the context of the verse and to read the further revelation God gives in the larger Scripture passage.

We appreciate those who have graciously assisted us in putting these thoughts together. Richard's wife, Lisa, spent many hours editing this material. Marilynn Blackaby has, as always, been wholly supportive. Phyllis Lincer and Anne White, as well as John Landers at Broadman & Holman, gave valuable technical assistance. It is our desire that this devotional guide will bless you as much as these truths have enriched our lives as we have experienced them in our time walking with the Lord.

The Authors

Resolutions

*So when they had eaten breakfast, Jesus said to Simon Peter,
"Simon, son of Jonah, do you love Me more than these?"*

JOHN 21:15

esus has a wonderful way of restoring us when we fail
Him! He does not humiliate us. He does not criticize us.
He does not ask us to make a resolution to try harder. Rather, He
takes us aside and asks us to reaffirm our love for Him.

Peter miserably failed his Lord when he fled with the other disciples from the Garden of Gethsemane. Later, he publicly denied
that he even knew Jesus. Peter must have wondered if he had
been capable of being Jesus' disciple when he was unfaithful to
Jesus in His most crucial hour.

As you begin a new year, you may be painfully aware that you
have failed your Lord in many ways. Perhaps you were not faithful. Perhaps you disobeyed His word to you. Perhaps you denied
Him by the way you lived. Jesus will take you aside, as He did
Peter. He will not berate you. He will not humiliate you. He *will*
ask you to examine your love for Him. He asked Peter, "Do you
love Me?" If your answer, like Peter's, is "Yes, Lord," He will
reaffirm His will for you. If you truly love Him, you will obey
Him (John 14:15). Jesus does not need your resolutions, your
recommitments, or your promises to try harder this year. If your
resolve to obey God last year did not help you to be faithful, it
will not make you successful this year. Jesus asks for your love. If
you truly love Him, your service for Him in the new year will be
of the quality that He desires.

Woe Is Me!

So I said: "Woe is me, for I am undone!
Because I am a man of unclean lips,
And I dwell in the midst of a people of unclean lips;
For my eyes have seen the King,
The Lord of hosts."

ISAIAH 6:5

An exalted view of God brings a clear view of sin and a realistic view of self. A diminished view of God brings a reduced concern for sin and an inflated view of self. Isaiah may have been satisfied with his personal holiness until he saw the Lord in His unspeakable glory. Isaiah's encounter with holy God made him immediately and keenly aware of his own unholiness and the sinfulness of those around him. It is impossible to worship God and remain unchanged. The best indication that we have truly worshiped is a changed heart.

Have we so conformed ourselves to a sinful world that we are satisfied with unholy living? Have we sunk so far below God's standard that when someone does live as God intended, we consider that person "superspiritual"? If we only compare our personal holiness to those around us, we may be deceived into believing that we are living a consecrated life. Yet when we encounter holy God, our only response can be "Woe is me!"

You will not see those around you trusting Jesus until they recognize a clear difference between you and the rest of the world. God wants to sanctify you as He is holy. When God deals with you, there will be a radical degree of purity about your life that is absolutely different from what the world can produce. The world, including those closest to you, will be convinced you serve a holy God by your consecrated life.

Making a Difference

But Daniel purposed in his heart that he would not defile himself with the portion of the king's delicacies.

DANIEL 1:8

Would you dare to believe that God, who called you to Himself and equipped you with His Spirit, could work mightily through you? Have you made the connection between the time and place in which you live and God's call upon you? World events never catch God by surprise. He placed you precisely where you are for a purpose.

Daniel did not let the temptations of his day interfere with his relationship to the Lord. He knew that to make his life useful to God he must be obedient in all things. Regardless of what the most powerful king in the world commanded, Daniel refused to compromise what he knew God required of him.

History is replete with examples of Christian men and women who believed that God would work through them to make a significant difference for His kingdom. God placed Esther strategically in the king's court at a crucial time when she could save the lives of God's people (Esther 4:14). God placed Joseph strategically to become the most powerful adviser to the pharaoh in Egypt and to save Jacob and his family from a devastating drought (Gen. 41:39–40).

Are you allowing your surroundings to determine how you invest your life? Or are you letting God use you to make a difference in your generation? Ask God to reveal His purposes for you and His will for your life today.

Trembling at God's Word

But on this one will I look:
On him who is poor and of a contrite spirit,
And who trembles at My word.

ISAIAH 66:2

Do you tremble when God speaks? When was the last time you were physically affected by the reality that almighty God just spoke directly to you? John lost all physical strength when God spoke to him (Rev. 1:17); Paul fell to the ground when Christ met him on the road to Damascus (Acts 9:4); Moses trembled when God spoke to him (Acts 7:32); and Peter, when he realized who Jesus was, "fell down at Jesus' knees, saying, 'Depart from me, for I am a sinful man, O Lord!'" (Luke 5:8).

Have you lost your sense of awe that the Creator still chooses to speak to you, His creation? Do you approach the reading of your Bible with a holy expectation, listening for the life-changing words that God has for you that day? Scripture says that "The fear of the Lord is the beginning of wisdom" (Prov. 9:10). There are things you will see and hear out of your fear and reverence for God that you will not experience in any other way.

As you study your Bible, you may sense that God has something to say directly to you through the verses you are reading. Take a moment to consider the awesome reality that the God who spoke and created a universe is now speaking to you. If Jesus could speak and raise the dead, calm a storm, cast out demons, and heal the incurable, then what effect might a word from Him have upon your life? The possibilities should cause you to tremble! The next time you open God's Word, do so with a sense of holy expectation.

Ritual or Relationship?

Neither did they say, "Where is the Lord,
Who brought us up out of the land of Egypt,
Who led us through the wilderness?"

JEREMIAH 2:6

Christianity is an intimate, growing relationship with the person of Jesus Christ. It is not a set of doctrines to believe, habits to practice, or sins to avoid. Every activity God commands is intended to enhance His love relationship with His people.

God designed worship for us to see Him in His glory and to respond appropriately; for many it has degenerated into "religion," one more meeting to attend out of habit. God established the sacrificial system so that we, His people, could express our love to Him; but we often diminish our gifts to our Lord into futile attempts to appease Him and to pacify our guilty conscience. God gave us prayer so we could have conversation with Him, but we often distort this by "saying prayers" and hurrying off without ever listening to what is on our Father's heart. God instituted His commandments as a protection for those He loves, but the commandments can become a pathway to legalism rather than an avenue for a relationship with our Father in which He protects us from harm.

Religious activity apart from fellowship with God is empty ritual. The people of Jeremiah's day were satisfied to have the ritual without the manifest presence of God. They became so comfortable with their "religion" that they didn't even notice God's absence. Is it possible to pray, to attend a worship service, or to give an offering yet not to experience the presence of God? It certainly is possible! And that has been the sad commentary on many a Christian experience. Don't settle for a religious life that lacks a vital relationship to Jesus Christ. When God is present, the difference will be obvious.

5

God Looks for Clay

"O house of Israel, can I not do with you as this potter?"
says the Lord. "Look, as the clay is in the potter's hand,
so are you in My hand, O house of Israel!"

JEREMIAH 18:6

God knows how to bring salvation to your family, your friends, your community, and your world. Accordingly, He looks for those who will allow Him to shape them into the instruments He requires to do His divine work. Clay has no plans of its own, no aspirations for service, nor reluctance to perform its given task. It is just clay. Moldable, pliable, totally submissive to the will of its master.

At times we excitedly announce to God: "I've discovered my strengths and gifts, and now I know how I can best serve You!" At other times we inform Him, "I am aware of what my weaknesses are, so I know which tasks I'm not capable of doing for You." Yet this is not characteristic of clay. God is not limited to working with our strengths (2 Cor. 12:9–10). He can mold us into whatever kind of instrument He requires. When God's assignment demands humility, he finds a servant willing to be humbled. When His work requires zeal, He looks for someone He can fill with His Spirit. God uses holy vessels, so He finds those who will allow Him to remove their impurities. It is not a noble task, being clay. There is no glamour to it, nothing boast-worthy, except that it is exactly what almighty God is looking for. Compliant, moldable, yielded clay.

If your tendency is to tell the Father what you can and cannot do for Him, submit to *His* agenda and allow Him to shape you into the person He wants you to be. Like clay.

We Live by Revelation

Where there is no revelation, the people cast off restraint;
But happy is he who keeps the law.

PROVERBS 29:18

T he world operates on *vision*. God's people live by *revelation*. The world seeks grand and noble purposes and goals to achieve. People dream up the greatest and most satisfying things in which they can invest their lives. Institutions establish goals and objectives and then organize themselves to achieve them. God's people function in a radically different way. Christians arrange their lives based on the revelation of God, regardless of whether it makes sense to them. God does not ask for our opinion about what is best for our future, our family, our church, or our country. He already knows! What God wants is to get the attention of His people and reveal to us what is on His heart and what is *His* will, for God's ways are not our ways! (Isa. 55:8–9).

Whenever people do not base their lives on God's revelation, they "cast off restraint." That is, they do what is right in their own eyes. They set their goals, arrange their agendas, and then pray for God's blessings. Some Christians are living far outside the will of God, yet they have the audacity to pray and ask God to bless their efforts!

The only way for you to know God's will is for Him to reveal it to you. You will never discover it on your own. When you hear from the Father, you have an immediate agenda for your life: obedience. As the writer of Proverbs observed: "*Happy* is he who keeps the law."

Exceedingly Abundantly

Now to Him who is able to do exceedingly
abundantly above all that we ask or think,
according to the power that works in us.

EPHESIANS 3:20

At times we feel as if we could impress God with all we are trying to do for Him and His church. Yet God has yet to be impressed with even the most grandiose human aspirations (Ps. 8:3–4). You will never set a goal so big or attempt a task so significant that God does not have something far greater that He could do in and through your life. Saul of Tarsus worked harder than anyone else to impress God with his efforts, only to discover that his greatest achievements were but rubbish compared to God's will for his life (Phil. 3:7–8).

Our problem is that we become too easily enamored with our own plans. If we are attempting to do noble or difficult things, we assume that we must be experiencing the maximum potential for our lives and that God must, therefore, be pleased with us. Until we have heard from God, we cannot even imagine all that our lives could become or all that God could accomplish through us.

We need to remind ourselves that the Father sees the "big picture," that His power far exceeds our limited imagination. We *must* set aside our own agenda, however lofty. We must never become satisfied with our own dreams, for they are finite at best. When we follow God's direction we will witness things happening in our lives that can only be explained by His powerful presence. How could we be satisfied with anything less?

Prayer Discovers God's Agenda

Now in the morning, having risen a long while before daylight,
He went out and departed to a solitary place;
and there He prayed.

MARK 1:35

It was common knowledge among the disciples that they would find Jesus praying during the early morning hours. When they needed Him, they knew to go to the place of prayer. When Judas betrayed Jesus, he led his cohorts to Jesus' place of prayer.

Every time the Lord Jesus faced an important decision, He prayed. When He was being tempted to do things by the world's methods instead of the Father's, He prayed (Matt. 4). When it was time to choose His disciples, He prayed the entire night (Luke 6:12). If the Son of God required a night of prayer in order to determine the Father's mind, how long might it take us in prayer to clearly determine our Father's will?

Because Jesus was so often surrounded by crowds, He knew He must find a quiet place so He could clearly hear His Father's voice. Jesus had many people seeking to influence the direction of His life. His disciples wanted Him to go where the crowds were (Mark 1:37). The crowds wanted to crown Him king (John 6:15). Satan tempted Him to make compromises in order to draw a following (Matt. 4:3, 6, 9). Jesus knew that His mission was not to attract a crowd, but to remain obedient to His Father. It was prayer that set the agenda for Jesus' ministry (Luke 6:12). Prayer preceded the miracles (John 11:42–43); prayer brought Him encouragement at critical moments (Luke 9:28–31); prayer enabled Him to go to the cross (Luke 22:41–42); and prayer kept Him there despite excruciating pain (Luke 23:46). Follow the Savior's example, and let your time alone with God, in prayer, set the agenda for your life.

When God Speaks, It Is So

So shall My word be that goes forth from My mouth;
It shall not return to Me void,
But it shall accomplish what I please,
And it shall prosper in the thing for which I sent it.

ISAIAH 55:11

When God speaks, nothing remains the same. At the beginning of time, God spoke, and a universe was created out of nothing. God followed a pattern when He created the earth: He spoke; it was so; it was good (Gen. 1:3–4). This pattern continued throughout the Bible. Whenever God revealed His plans, things happened just as He said, and God considered the result "good" (Phil. 2:13). God doesn't make suggestions. He speaks with the full determination to see that what He has said will come to fruition.

Whenever Jesus spoke, what He said came to pass. Lepers found that a word from Jesus meant healing (Luke 5:13; 17:14). The blind man discovered that a word from Jesus meant sight (Luke 18:42). Through a barren fig tree the disciples saw that a curse from Jesus meant destruction (Mark 11:20). The sinner experienced forgiveness through a word from Jesus (John 8:11). How many attempts did it take Jesus to raise Lazarus from the dead? Only one (John 11:43). There was never a time that Jesus spoke that what He said did not happen.

What happens when Jesus speaks to you? Have you been reading the words of Jesus in your Bible without experiencing His word that transforms everything around you? Jesus condemned the Pharisees because they assumed that knowledge of the written Scriptures would give them life. They were satisfied with having the words instead of experiencing the person who spoke the words (John 5:39). How powerful a word from God is to your life! As you read your Bible and pray, listen to what God has to say to you about His will for your life.

Sowing Seeds of Righteousness

But he who sows righteousness will have a sure reward.

PROVERBS 11:18b

There are many ways to invest our lives, but none offers greater reward than devoting ourselves to the pursuit of righteousness. Every area of our lives should reflect the holiness of God that is ours by salvation: our thoughts, so that nothing we think about would be inappropriate for a child of God; our actions, so that our lives demonstrate that we serve a holy God; our integrity, so that we are above reproach in all our relationships.

Are you taking God's righteousness in your life for granted? Righteousness is something you must allow the Holy Spirit to work in your life. Instead of sowing holy thoughts, are you allowing evil and sinful thoughts to grow in your mind? Are you allowing lust to grow unchecked within you? Does enmity, bitterness, jealousy, or unforgiveness remain in your life? Jesus said if we seek first God and His righteousness, everything else will follow (Matt. 6:33).

There is great reward in sowing righteousness. What are you presently doing to plant holiness in your life? (1 Pet. 1:15). How are you putting righteousness in your mind so that your thoughts are holy? How are you cultivating righteousness in your relationships so that you maintain your integrity? Are you instilling righteousness in your activities so that your life is above reproach? If you want to harvest righteousness in your life tomorrow, you must plant seeds of righteousness today.

11

The Key to God's Redemptive Mission

"That they all may be one, as You, Father, are in Me,
and I in You; that they also may be one in Us,
that the world may believe that You sent Me."

JOHN 17:21

G od often speaks of human relationships as a part of His mission to redeem a lost world (John 13:20; Matt. 25:40). One reason He gives for a husband and wife to live in unity is so they can produce a "godly seed," that is, children who love and obey God, who can be used in God's mission to bring redemption to a lost world (Mal. 2:14–15). Similarly, the church is the body of Christ. A church cannot be on mission with the Father in our world if its members are waging war with one another (1 Cor. 12:12). There is a crucial connection between our relationships with others and the salvation of those around us.

We might assume that during Jesus' prayer before His crucifixion, He would have prayed that His disciples would have courage, or would remain faithful, or would remember what they had been taught. Yet He asked that His followers would remain united in their love for one another. Jesus understood that it is spiritually impossible to love God but not love others.

A test of your love for God is to examine your love for others. Our tendency is to say, "Heavenly Father, the problem is not between You and me. I love You with all my heart. I just don't love my brother." And God says, "That is an impossibility. You cannot love Me without loving the ones for whom My Son died" (John 13:34–35). Your life will not convince those around you of the reality of Jesus if you cannot live in unity with your fellow Christians.

The Penetrating Word of God

*For the word of God is living and powerful, and sharper than
any two-edged sword, piercing even to the division of soul
and spirit, and of joints and marrow, and is a discerner
of the thoughts and intents of the heart.*

HEBREWS 4:12

Does God's Word ever cause you discomfort? When you read the Bible, does what you read make you uneasy? Do you find, when you listen to sermons, that the Scripture seems aimed directly at you? You are experiencing the reality that the word of God is alive and can read your thoughts and judge your intentions.

When God's Word speaks to you it is always for a purpose. God knows your heart and knows what you need to do to bring your life into conformity to Christ. If you have a problem with sinful talk, the word that comes to you will address the tongue. If you are struggling to forgive, God's Word will confront you with His standard for forgiveness. If pride has a stronghold in your life, God's Word will speak to you about humility. Whatever sin needs addressing, you will find you are confronted by God's Word on the matter.

One way you can escape the discomfort of conviction is to avoid hearing God speak to you. You may neglect reading your Bible and stay away from places where it is taught. You may avoid those whom you know will uphold the truths of Scripture. The best response, however, is to pray as the psalmist did: "Search me, O God, and know my heart" (Ps. 139:23). Regularly allow the word of God to wash over you and find any sin or impurity (Eph. 5:26). Always make the connection between your life and what God is saying to you through His word. Make a habit of taking every word from God seriously, knowing that it is able to judge your heart and mind.

Warfare . . . or Discipline?

For whom the Lord loves He chastens,
And scourges every son whom He receives.

HEBREWS 12:6

There is a tendency among Christians to view anything unpleasant that happens to them as the result of "spiritual warfare." When a difficulty arises, many immediately ask God to remove their distress. The problem is that their predicament may have nothing to do with Satan or with spiritual warfare. It may appear far more glorious for us to explain our hardships as Satan's determined attacks against us, rather than admitting that we are merely reaping what we have sown and are being disciplined by our heavenly Father (Gal. 6:7).

What is often mistaken as Satan's attack may actually be chastisement from our loving Father. If you have neglected your role as spiritual teacher to your children, God may allow them to fall into sin. If you have been dishonest at work, God may correct you by letting you face the consequences. It would be foolish to pray that God would ease your discomfort. God is disciplining you in order to gain your attention and bring necessary change to your life. How tragic never to make the connection between your problems and God's discipline. God's discipline will not help you if you dismiss it as Satan's doing or spiritual warfare. Not every hardship you face is the chastisement of God, but Scripture indicates that God *will* discipline you.

If you misunderstand God's chastening, you may actually blame Him for not answering your prayers or failing to protect you from Satan. Meanwhile, God is warning you of the danger you face because of your sin. Are there difficult circumstances in your life? Could it be the discipline of God? God, whose nature is perfect love, will correct you because He has your ultimate good in His heart.

Compelled to Serve

Your people shall be volunteers
In the day of Your power.

PSALM 110:3

One mark of revival, during which God comes to His people in power, is that God's people are compelled to offer their lives for His service. Many churches lack people who are willing to get involved in carrying out God's redemptive work. The mission fields are crying out for Christians to go and share the gospel with those who've never heard it. What we need is not more pleas for volunteers, but an outpouring of the power of God. When God comes among His people in power, there is never a shortage of volunteers or resources for His work!

When Christians today are asked what aspects of the Christian life are most important to them, missions is not usually ranked as a priority. This is because we have lost track of why God called us in the first place. We were not saved from our sin simply so that we would qualify for heaven. God delivered us so we would have a relationship with Him through which He could carry out His mission to redeem a lost world.

Only the power of God can free us from our natural self-centeredness and reorient us toward the *mission* of God. There is no need to pray that God would come in power. That is the only way He ever comes. We need hearts that are so responsive to Him that He will choose to demonstrate His power through us. Is your heart so filled with love for God that you are watching for the first opportunity to say with Isaiah, "Here am I. Send me!"?

God's Eternal Perspective

I will make you a great nation; I will bless you
And make your name great;
And you shall be a blessing.

GENESIS 12:2

Big assignments require big characters. God will give you a
responsibility in proportion to the size of your character.
In Bible times, a person's name represented his character; to know
someone's name was to know what the person was like. That's
why God changed the name of some when He transformed their
character. For example, the Lord wanted to bless all the nations of
the earth through Abram, yet Abram's character was too weak for
such a great task. God said He would make Abram's name great
so that He could make him a blessing to future generations. Then
over the next twenty-five years, God developed Abraham's character to match the name He had given him.

God sees your life from His eternal perspective. He will take
whatever time is necessary to grow your character to match His
assignment for you. If you have not received a divine commission
lately, it may be that your character needs maturing. Are you
impatient to begin your work before God has refined your character? A small character will fail in a large responsibility every
time. Don't be too hasty to get to the work. Character-building
can be long and painful. It took twenty-five years before God
entrusted Abraham with his first son and set in motion the estab-
lishment of the nation of Israel. Yet God was true to His word,
and thousands of years later people continue to be blessed by the
account of Abraham's life and by his descendant, Jesus.

How is God building your character? Do you sense He has a
task for you that will require a far greater man or woman than
you presently are? Will you yield to God as He works in your life
to prepare you for your next assignment?

Be Reconciled!

"Leave your gift there before the altar, and go your way.
First be reconciled to your brother,
and then come and offer your gift."

MATTHEW 5:24

It is useless to give offerings to God while you are at enmity with your brother. Jesus said that His followers should be reconciled with anyone who has something against them. The world seeks reconciliation on limited terms. Christians are to be reconciled, *whatever it takes.*

You say, "But you don't know how deeply he hurt me! It's unreasonable to ask me to restore our relationship." Or, "I tried but she would not be appeased." Jesus did not include an exception clause for our reconciliation. If the person is an enemy, Jesus said to love him (Matt. 5:44). If he persecutes you, you are to pray for him (v. 44). If she publicly humiliates you, you are not to retaliate (v. 39). If someone takes advantage of you, you are to give even more than he asks (v. 41). The world preaches "Assert yourself." Jesus taught, "Deny yourself." The world warns that you will be constantly exploited. Jesus' concern was not that His disciples be treated fairly but that they show unconditional love to others regardless of how they are treated. Men spat upon Jesus and nailed Him to a cross. His response was our model: "Father, forgive them, for they do not know what they do" (Luke 23:34).

If there were ever a command that is constantly disobeyed, it is this mandate to be reconciled. We comfort ourselves with the thought, "God knows that I tried to make things right, but my enemy refused." God's Word does not say "*Try* to be reconciled," but "*Be* reconciled." Is there someone with whom you need to make peace? Then do what God tells you to do.

17

New Life

Therefore, if anyone is in Christ, he is a new creation;
old things have passed away; behold,
all things have become new.

2 CORINTHIANS 5:17

You do not become a Christian by asking Jesus into your heart. You become a Christian when you are born again. Jesus said, "Unless one is born again, he cannot see the kingdom of God" (John 3:3). Saying a prayer or making a public commitment or signing a decision card will not save you. Only being born again will do that. The apostle Paul said that when you are "in Christ," the old things pass away. In the moment of your salvation, every sin you ever committed is forgiven. Healing for every hurt you have ever suffered is available. Love and acceptance are yours despite every failure you have ever experienced. Your past, no matter how difficult or painful, is completely and thoroughly provided for.

Some will seek to diminish the awesome reality of your spiritual rebirth. You will hear them say, "Even though you're now a Christian, you must still undergo years of counseling to overcome the hurts you've experienced" or "You may be born again, but you'll continue to struggle with your sin, and hopefully you will eventually gain victory in areas of your weakness."

The problem is that we seek changes by our own will rather than by turning our lives over in faith to the One who has given us new life. The profound testimony of Scripture is that the blood of Jesus Christ and the death of the Son of God is sufficient to completely free you from your sin. Satan will seek to convince you that it is not. Whom will you believe?

Discipleship Is
Christ in You

To them God willed to make known what are the riches
of the glory of this mystery among the Gentiles:
which is Christ in you, the hope of glory.

COLOSSIANS 1:27

The heavenly Father's plan from the beginning of time was to place His eternal Son in every believer. If you are a Christian, all the fullness of God dwells in you. Christ's life becomes your life. When Christ lives in you, He brings every divine resource with Him. Every time you face a need, you meet it with the presence of the crucified, risen, and triumphant Lord of the universe inhabiting you. When God invites you to become involved in His work, He has already placed His Son in you so that He can carry out His assignment through your life.

This has significant implications for your Christian life. Discipleship is more than acquiring head knowledge and memorizing Scripture verses. It is learning to give Jesus Christ total access to your life so He will live His life through you. Your greatest difficulty will be believing that your relationship with Christ is at the heart of your Christian life. When others watch you face a crisis, do they see the risen Lord responding? Does your family see the difference Christ makes when you face a need? What difference does the presence of Jesus Christ make in your life?

God wants to reveal Himself to those around you by working mightily through you. He wants your family to see Christ in you each day. God wants to express His love through your life. There is a great difference between "living the Christian life" and allowing Christ to live His life through you.

Royal Priests

But you are a chosen generation, a royal priesthood,
a holy nation, His own special people, that you
may proclaim the praises of Him who called you
out of darkness into His marvelous light.

1 PETER 2:9

If you are a Christian, you are a priest, chosen by God. As a member of the royal priesthood you have constant access to the King. If there is ever a need in your life, you don't have to find an intermediary or enlist another priest in order to gain a hearing from the King. Your position as a royal priest allows you direct access. This privilege describes your *position* as a priest.

However, priests also have a *function*. It is the responsibility of a priest to work within a *priesthood*. Scripture does not promote the practice of individual priests, each with a separate ministry. Rather, priests function together (Lev. 9:1). An unbiblical sense of individualism can isolate you from functioning within God's royal priesthood as He intended.

The priest represents God to the people, but he also takes the people's concerns to God. Is there someone around you who desperately needs the intercession of one of God's priests? Perhaps someone will only come to know God by seeing Him in your life. Our world hungers for an expression of Christ as He really is, living out His life through His people. It is dangerous to put our job above our calling by God. We are called to be priests first, and to hold a job second. When we get these out of order, everyone around us is denied access to the Father through us. God may have called you into a secular job as a vocation, but more importantly He has appointed you to be one of His royal priests.

Sanctified and Then Sent

"Sanctify them by Your truth. Your word is truth.
As You sent Me into the world,
I also have sent them into the world."

JOHN 17:17–18

Gd will always sanctify you before He sends you. The Father set aside the twelve disciples and made them holy by the Truth, His Son. As they related to Jesus, the Truth (John 14:6), the disciples were refined by that Truth and were prepared to be sent out to preach the gospel. Jesus challenged their ambitions (Luke 9:46–48), chastised their lack of faith (Matt. 17:19–20), refuted Satan's influence (Matt. 16:23), and denounced their pride (Matt. 26:33–35). When Jesus had finished preparing them, the disciples were sent out in such power that their world was never the same again.

Satan will try to convince you that your sin renders you useless to God. That is a lie from the author and father of lies. As soon as you sin, the Deceiver will whisper, "You failure! You are now of no use to God." This can bring a deep sense of defeat and hopelessness to a Christian. Yet, there is no freedom that compares to a soul set free by God's grace. When God's people allow God's truth to realign them to God's will and God's standard, then the power of God will be released through them the same way it was through the first disciples.

The Truth will set you free. The Truth is: "If we confess our sins, He is faithful and just to forgive us our sins and to cleanse us from all unrighteousness" (1 John 1:9), and we are restored to usefulness to God.

Our Motivation of Love

*"O righteous Father! The world has not known You, but I have
known You; and these have known that You sent Me. And I
have declared to them Your name, and will declare it, that the
love with which You loved Me may be in them, and I in them."*

JOHN 17:25–26

You do not "organize" the kingdom of God; you "agonize" the kingdom of God. You cannot be close to God without being affected by His love. The heavenly Father loved His Son with an eternal love. Everything in the heart and life of the Father was released to His Son. As the Father expressed His love for a broken and sinful world, this passion was manifested through the life of His Son. The Father initiated His plan to save mankind, and out of a heart of devotion, the Son accepted the assignment that took Him to the cross.

As Jesus walked among people, the Father's love filled His Son. Jesus recognized that no ordinary love could motivate Him to go to the cross. No human love could keep Him perfectly obedient to His Father throughout His life. Only His Father's love was powerful enough to compel Him to commit His life to the saving purpose of His Father.

Jesus prayed that God would place this same love in His disciples. He knew that no other motivation would be sufficient for the assignments God had for them. God's answer was to place His Son in them. It is impossible for a Christian to be filled with this measure of love and not to be on mission with God.

You will be incapable of ministering to everyone God sends you unless you have His love. You cannot forgive others or go the extra mile with others or sacrifice for others unless you have first been filled with the boundless love of God. Seek to know the Father and His immeasurable love; then allow His Son to love others through you!

Truth Sets You Free

*"And you shall know the truth,
and the truth shall make you free."*

JOHN 8:32

God's truth never restricts you; it always sets you free! Are you discouraged? Is there a sense of bondage in a particular area of your life? A lack of victory over a certain sin? A harmful addiction? It is possible that you do not yet understand a truth about God that can release you.

If you feel powerless to meet the challenges before you, take encouragement from the promise of Philippians 4:13: "I can do all things through Christ who strengthens me." If you are defeated by circumstance, hold on to the truth of Romans 8:28 that God can work your most difficult situation into His good. If you are enslaved to a particular sin, work the truth of 1 John 1:9 into your life, which promises that if you confess your sin, God is faithful to cleanse you from *all* unrighteousness. All of these truths await the Holy Spirit's implementation into your life.

It is one thing to know *about* the truth. It is yet another thing to experience the truth of God being worked out in your life. God's truth will have no effect upon you unless you accept it and believe it. Perhaps you have already read and heard accounts of God working mightily in the lives of others. But have you allowed God to implement those truths into your life? What truth about God would you like to be experiencing in your life? Ask Him to implement that truth into your life today.

Come and See

They said to Him, "Rabbi . . . where are You staying?"
He said to them, "Come and see." They came and saw where
He was staying, and remained with Him that day.

JOHN 1:38b–39

There comes a time for each of us when merely talking about the Christian pilgrimage is not sufficient. We must actually set out on the journey! We can spend many hours debating and discussing issues related to the Christian life, but this means little if we never actually step out and follow Christ!

For generations, the coming of the Messiah had been pondered and predicted by the nation of Israel. Perhaps no topic garnered more discussion among Jews than the nature and work of the Messiah. Andrew had listened to John the Baptist and had heard of the coming Messiah. Now, suddenly, he was face to face with the One he had yearned to see! Andrew's mind was filled with questions he longed to ask. Instead of entering into a theological dialogue with Andrew, however, Jesus turned and began to walk. Andrew's questions would not be answered by discussion alone, but by walking with Him.

Christianity is not a set of teachings to understand. It is a Person to follow. As he walked with Jesus, Andrew watched Jesus heal the sick, teach God's wisdom, and demonstrate God's power. Andrew not only learned *about* God; he actually experienced Him!

Moments will come when you stand at a crossroads with your Lord. You will have a hundred questions for Him. Rather than answering the questions one by one, Jesus may say, "Put on your shoes, step out onto the road, and follow Me." As you walk daily with Him, Jesus will answer your questions, and you will discover far more than you even knew to ask.

The Father Draws You

*And He said, "Therefore I have said to you that
no one can come to Me unless it has been
granted to him by My Father."*

JOHN 6:65

Throughout Jesus' ministry on earth, He never seemed intimidated by the crowds. Instead, He looked into the multitudes and focused on those whom His Father was sending to Him. Jesus knew that because of sin, no one naturally seeks after God. Sinful man's inclination is to hide from God, rather than to come to Him (Gen. 3:8; Ps. 14:1–3). Therefore, whenever Jesus saw that the Father was drawing a person to Himself, Jesus immediately began relating to that person.

Jesus observed the great lengths to which the despised tax collector, Zacchaeus, had gone in order to see Him pass by. In response, Jesus immediately left the crowd and spent time with this man in whom the Father was obviously working (Luke 19:1–10). When Jesus noticed a man following after Him, Jesus spoke to Andrew, "Come!" (John 1:39). Every time the disciples experienced a new insight into the truths of God, Jesus recognized that it was the Father who had been at work in their lives (Matt. 16:17).

As the multitudes gathered around Jesus, He spoke some truths that were difficult for the people to grasp (John 6:60). So challenging were His words that many of His listeners departed, but Jesus did not become discouraged. He saw that the Father was working in the lives of His disciples, and that is where Jesus invested His time.

As you desire to spend time alone with Jesus, recognize that this is the Father drawing you to His Son. You do not seek quiet times with God *in order* to experience Him. The fact that He has brought you to a place of fellowship with Him is evidence that you are *already* sensing His activity. As you read the Scriptures and pray, trust that God will honor your response to His leading by teaching you more about Himself.

Praying with Tears

*Who, in the days of His flesh, when He had offered up
prayers and supplications, with vehement cries and tears to
Him who was able to save Him from death,
and was heard because of His godly fear.*

HEBREWS 5:7

The life of Jesus provides the model for our prayer lives. God is seeking to mold us into the image of His Son (Col. 1:27–28). If we are to act like Christ, our prayer lives must be conformed to His. Many Christians are unwilling to pay the price that Jesus paid when it comes to interceding with God. Jesus' prayers came with vehement cries and tears and, "because of His godly fear," He was heard by the Father.

Why, then, did the Father refuse His request? It was not due to any sin in Jesus' life, nor was it because the Father did not love His Son. The Father said no, despite the unfathomable love He had for His Son, because He knew He could not spare His Son and save a world. Likewise, the Lord cannot always spare you and your family and complete His redemptive work in those around you.

Are you willing for God to deny your pleadings? Will you intercede with the Father so deeply and intimately that even in the midst of your tears you are able to say, "Nevertheless, not my will but thine be done?" The Father will always relate to you out of the context of His love for a lost world. Has God said no to one of your requests recently? Accept His answer. Have you been learning obedience through what you have been suffering (Heb. 5:8)? If you have, God may choose to make you a source of salvation to others even as He did with His Son.

Are You Being Made Perfect?

Though He was a Son, yet He learned obedience by the things which He suffered. And having been perfected, He became the author of eternal salvation to all who obey Him.

HEBREWS 5:8–9

There is a positive aspect to suffering. We all endure suffering to some degree, but the good news is that through it we can become like Jesus. Are you willing to pay whatever price is necessary in order to become like Christ? There are some things that God can build into your life only through suffering. Even Jesus, the sinless Son of God, was complete only after He had endured the suffering His Father had set before Him. Once He had suffered, He was the complete, mature, and perfect Savior through whom an entire world could find salvation.

If you become bitter over your hardships, you close some parts of your life from God. If you do this, you will never be complete. Some places in your soul can be reached only by suffering. The Spirit of God has important things to teach you, but you can only learn these lessons in the midst of your trials. King Saul was made king without ever enduring hardship, but he never developed the character or maturity to handle God's assignment. David spent years in suffering and heartache. When he finally ascended the throne, he was a man after God's own heart.

Don't resent the suffering God allows in your life. Don't make all your decisions and invest everything you have into avoiding hardship. God did not spare His own Son. How can we expect Him to spare us? Learn obedience even when it hurts!

God Is Looking for Intercessors

So I sought for a man among them who would make a wall,
and stand in the gap before Me on behalf of the land,
that I should not destroy it; but I found no one.

EZEKIEL 22:30

God looks for those whose hearts are prepared to be intercessors before Him. Intercessors have hearts in tune with God's heart. They are so acutely aware of what is at stake, for their land, that they will stay before God as long as necessary in order to obtain God's answer. That is why you do not volunteer to be an intercessor. God enlists you.

Why do we not intercede as we should? Perhaps we are afraid to put God to the test. We worry that God might not answer our prayers. Yet God promises that if we ask, we *will* receive (Matt. 7:7). We may fail to intercede because we believe the busyness of our everyday lives is more effective than prayer. Jesus warned that apart from Him, we can do *nothing* (John 15:5). Without being intimately acquainted with God and His will, all of our labors are futile. Perhaps we fail to intercede because we misunderstand the heart of God. Jesus wept over the city of Jerusalem as He interceded for it (Matt. 23:37). If we truly have God's love within us, we will feel compelled to plead with God on behalf of those who face His imminent judgment.

Intercession is a lonely business. There may be many days or even years when there appear to be few results for your labor. Yet intercessors can be the only ones standing between a family and God's judgment, or between an individual or nation and God's wrath.

Prepare to Meet
Your God!

*Then the Lord said to Moses, "Go to the people and conse-
crate them today and tomorrow, and let them wash their
clothes. And let them be ready for the third day.
For on the third day the Lord will come down upon Mount
Sinai in the sight of all the people."*

EXODUS 19:10–11

Meeting with God requires preparation. God is awesome
and perfectly holy. Barging into His presence unprepared
is an affront. When the children of Israel were to meet with Him,
God commanded them first to take two full days to prepare.
Once the people were ready, however, God spoke to them with
thunder and lightning, with fire and smoke and the sound of
loud trumpets (Exod. 19:16–25). It was through this encounter
that God revealed such marvelous truths as the Ten Commandments, establishing the standard by which God expected His people to live.

You cannot spend day after day in the world without its affect-
ing your mind and will and heart. It doesn't take long to become
disoriented to the ways of God. The world has a dulling effect on
your spiritual sensibilities. God established the Sabbath so His
people could take an entire day to refocus on Him and His will
for them after spending six days in the world.

How do you prepare for your times of worship? What fills your
mind the night before? Often the last thing you put into your
mind at night is still on your mind the next morning. Genuine
worship requires spiritual preparation. Your experiences of worship reflect your spiritual preparation. Prepare yourself now for
your next encounter with God.

Do Not Prove Disobedient

*Therefore, King Agrippa, I was not disobedient
to the heavenly vision.*

ACTS 26:19

God does everything for a reason. God met Saul of Tarsus on the Damascus road for a purpose (Acts 9:1–9). Saul had planned to persecute Christians, but his encounter with Christ changed him forever. God did more in that encounter than save Saul from his sin. God began to reveal His will for Paul's life. God's assignment for Paul was clear: "He is a chosen vessel of Mine to bear My name before Gentiles, kings, and the children of Israel. For I will show him how many things he must suffer for My name's sake" (Acts 9:15–16).

God's plan for Paul, revealed through a vision, involved both testifying before kings and suffering persecution. Paul was to enjoy the thrill of performing miracles, preaching to large crowds, and starting churches. But Paul was also to be stoned, shipwrecked, whipped, mocked, conspired against, and imprisoned (2 Cor. 11:23–28). Would we accept this part of his assignment as readily as the first? We never hear of Paul complaining about his commission from God. He never asked that he be given a role like Peter's, or James's, or John's (Gal. 2:9–10). It was enough for Paul that he be given any task in the kingdom of God. As he neared the end of his ministry, Paul could boldly state to King Agrippa, "I was not disobedient to the heavenly vision."

Oh, to have Paul's tenacity and devotion to the Father's will! What joy there is not only to *begin* well in our Christian faith, but also to *end* faithfully! It is God's desire that each of us could say at the end of our lives, "I was not disobedient."

Where Are You Looking?

Then Peter, turning around, saw the disciple whom
Jesus loved following. . . . Peter, seeing him, said to Jesus,
"But Lord, what about this man?"

JOHN 21:20–21

The first thing you do after God speaks to you is critical. Jesus was telling Peter what type of ministry he would have and what type of death he would suffer (vv. 18–19). It was a sacred moment in Peter's life, as his Lord pulled back the curtain to his future. His was not to be an easy life but a life ordained and blessed by his Lord and Master.

Rather than responding to what Jesus told him, Peter looked around at his fellow disciples. His glance fell upon John, the disciple whom Jesus loved. "But Lord, what about *this* man?" Peter asked. Peter had just been given the somber news of his future death. How natural to compare his assignment with that of the others! This is the great temptation of God's servants: to compare our situation with that of others. Did God give my friend a larger house? Did God heal my friend's loved one and not mine? Did God allow my friend to receive appreciation and praise for his work while I remain anonymous? Did God allow another Christian to remain close to her family while I am far removed from mine?

Jesus assigned Peter and John to walk two different paths, but both Peter and John have enriched our lives. Jesus knew how dangerous it is when a servant takes his eyes off the master to focus on a fellow servant. Where is your focus? Have you become more concerned with how God is treating someone else than you are with how He is relating to you?

Firmly Planted

Blessed is the man
Who walks not in the counsel of the ungodly,
Nor stands in the path of sinners,
Nor sits in the seat of the scornful;
But his delight is in the law of the Lord,
And in His law he meditates day and night.

He shall be like a tree
Planted by the rivers of water,
That brings forth its fruit in its season,
Whose leaf also shall not wither;
And whatever he does shall prosper.

PSALM 1:1-3

It is possible to spend your whole life knowing about the truths of God and never experiencing any of them. Simply knowing *about* the truths of God does not mean that they have become a part of your life. Here is the important question: What are you doing with the word of God? Some people allow themselves to come under the influence of ungodly thinking to the point that God's Word makes no difference to them. If you seek your counsel from ungodly persons, you will find yourself moving away from the direction God's Word commands. If you intentionally seek out sinners as your companions, they will lead you down paths that take you far from God. If you choose to join those who are scornful, you will eventually become cynical.

The righteous man does not find encouragement in the opinions of others but in God's Word. He is not content with a surface knowledge of Scripture but meditates on it day and night until he is satisfied that what he reads reflects his own experience. He becomes like a fruit tree standing firmly on the bank of the river. The tree is well nourished and produces delicious fruit and bountiful leaves. People come from miles around to sit in its shade and eat its fruit.

If you allow God to implement His Word in your life, others will draw encouragement from you. The more you grow in God's righteousness, the stronger you will become. Some people would look in vain to find anyone they were encouraging, but not so the righteous person. A constant stream of people will seek you out because they know that your life will be a blessing.

Life's Seasons

To everything there is a season,
A time for every purpose under heaven.

ECCLESIASTES 3:1

The beauty in the way God designed the four seasons is that, though each one is distinct, they all work together to bring life and growth. Spring is a period of freshness and new life. Summer sees growth and productivity. Autumn is a time for harvesting the rewards of past labors. Winter is the season of dormancy and closure. Each season has its own unique beauty and makes a significant contribution to life.

Just as God planned seasons in nature, He planned seasons in life as well. Life has its springtime, when we begin new things and look excitedly toward the future. Summer comes and we work diligently in the heat of the day at all that God has assigned to us. With autumn comes the fruition of things begun at an earlier time in our lives. Winter brings an end to a particular period in our lives. Sometimes winter brings hardship, but we remain hopeful, for another spring is just around the corner!

In God's perfect design for our lives, He has planned for times of fruitfulness and activity. He will also build in times of quiet and rest. There will be times when He asks us to remain faithful doing the same work day after day. But there will also be periods of excitement and new beginnings. By God's grace, we will enjoy seasons of harvesting the fruit of our faithfulness. By God's grace, we will also overcome the cold winters of heartache and grief, for without winter there would be no spring. Just as it is with the seasons of nature, these seasons in our lives work together to bring about God's perfect will for each one of us.

Power, Not Fear

For God has not given us a spirit of fear,
but of power and of love and of a sound mind.

2 TIMOTHY 1:7

The only fear that God encourages in a Christian's life is the fear of God (2 Cor. 5:10–11; Heb. 10:31). Fear of people does not come from God. The problem is that many Christians fear people more than they fear God. Their fear hinders them from pleasing God because they waste their efforts appeasing other people.

Timothy was a young man, timid by nature, and probably not strong physically (1 Tim. 5:23). He knew of Paul's frequent trials and persecutions. He knew that he, too, might suffer those same persecutions. Paul reminded his young colleague that fear of others does not come from God.

Fear causes us to stop and question what God has clearly told us to do. Perhaps we were confident in our obedience until persecution came; now we doubt whether we heard God correctly. Most fear is fear of the unknown. We do not know what lies ahead of us, so we become apprehensive. Our imaginations can magnify problems until they seem insurmountable. We need a sound mind to see things in proper perspective. That is why God gave us His Holy Spirit, to enable us to see things as God sees them.

Fear is no excuse to disobey God. There is no reason to live in fear when you have the mighty presence of the Holy Spirit within you. Fear will enslave you, but Christ has come to set you free. Ask God to free you from any fear you are experiencing and to open your eyes. As He reveals the reality of your situation, He will enable you to continue in obedience.

The Living Word

*And they said to one another, "Did not our heart burn
within us while He talked with us on the road,
and while He opened the Scriptures to us?"*

LUKE 24:32

esus joins those who are earnestly seeking Him. Two
men walked along the road to Emmaus discussing the
confusing events that had just occurred in Jerusalem. They
thought they had understood the happenings of their day, but
the death of Jesus had left them disoriented to God and His activity in their world. They had hoped that Jesus was the Messiah,
but His death had left them perplexed and discouraged. They
needed answers.

God reads the heart and knows the honest pursuit of His will
by His children. Jesus drew near to these men, walked with them,
and opened their minds to what the Scriptures said about Him
and about the events of their day. As Jesus was speaking, their
hearts burned within them! As they listened to Jesus relate the
Scriptures to what they were experiencing, they knew in their
hearts that they were hearing God's truth. Their doubts vanished, excitement overcame them, and they raced back to share
the truth with their friends!

If you become bewildered by circumstances in your life, Jesus
can reorient you to Himself through the Scriptures just as He did
for these two men. From your human perspective, the situation
may be confusing and discouraging. It takes the presence of
Christ to open your eyes to the truth of the Scriptures. Have your
circumstances confused you? You need Jesus to give you His perspective. Once you've heard from Him, you'll be like these two
men, excited to join God in what He is doing around you and
eager to include others in the experience.

Seeking Jesus

*And Simon and those who were with Him
searched for Him.*

MARK 1:36

Simon Peter is well known to us for his foolish, extemporaneous statements throughout the Gospels (Matt. 16:22; 17:4; 26:33). But Peter was always seeking after Jesus. Peter followed Jesus from afar during the night of Jesus' crucifixion (Matt. 26:58). Peter ran to the tomb when he heard Jesus had risen (Luke 24:12). Peter swam in the sea in his haste to get to Jesus (John 21:7) and even walked on water in order to join Jesus (Matt. 14:29). Peter did not always say or do the right things, but he *did* constantly seek to be with Jesus. Because of this, he was continually encountering his Lord and growing to be a more faithful disciple.

Whenever we see Peter coming to Jesus he is always accompanied by others. Because Peter was seeking Jesus, others sought Him too. What are you known for by those who know you best? Do they see you searching for fame, power, success, or happiness? Are you known as a person who seeks after Jesus? God promises: "And you will seek Me and find Me, when you search for Me with all your heart" (Jer. 29:13).

Did you begin today intent on encountering Jesus? Is your search for Him halfhearted, or are you seeking Him with all your heart? Have others grown closer to Jesus because they followed your example and sought Jesus? If your heart is set on pursuing Jesus, you will always find Him. "And the Spirit and the bride say, 'Come!' And let him who hears say, 'Come!' And let him who thirsts come" (Rev. 22:17).

Sin That Entangles Us

Therefore, since we are surrounded by such a great cloud of witnesses, let us throw off everything that hinders and the sin that so easily entangles, and let us run with perseverance the race marked out for us.

HEBREWS 12:1 (NIV)

Sin is our most persistent, determined, and pernicious enemy. Sin seeks to rob us of every good thing God has designed for us. Paul tells us that sin brings death (Rom. 7:11). Yet it is very subtle. Sin creeps into our lives when and where we least expect it. It packages itself so attractively that we are lulled into thinking that it cannot really harm us (2 Cor. 11:14–15).

Sin stealthily and relentlessly entangles our lives. We will never be able to run the race marked out for us as long as we are entrapped in sin. We can free ourselves from sin's bondage only if we recognize it for what it is. If we call sin a "mistake," a "bad habit," or a "weakness," we will never escape its grasp. We must not blame our sins on others. We must not allow pride to convince us it is too humiliating to admit the sin in our lives. Sin can blind us to its presence. It does not always command our attention but rather, it subtly and pervasively robs us of the spiritual power and victory that could be ours. The good news is that there is no extent to which sin can entangle us that God's grace does not abound still more to free us (Rom. 5:20).

Has sin robbed your joy? Has it prevented you from being the best husband, wife, son, daughter, or friend you could be? Is it keeping you from spiritual maturity? If you have become entangled with sin, God can release you immediately, no matter how desperately entangled you may have become!

Without Faith

*But he who doubts is condemned if he eats, because he does
not eat from faith; for whatever is not from faith is sin.*

ROMANS 14:23

The writer of Hebrews reminds us that without faith it is
impossible to please God (Heb. 11:6). Whenever God
reveals something, He expects us to believe Him and adjust our
lives accordingly. What does this mean? It means we trust Him
implicitly for all of our needs because He says He will provide
(Phil. 4:19). It means we approach crises with the assurance that
God will bring good from them (Rom. 8:28). It means we overcome anxiety during stressful situations because God instructs us
to bring our requests to Him (Phil. 4:6). It means that we never
worry that we are alone because God said He would never leave
us or forsake us (Deut. 31:6). It means that, despite what happens in our lives, we will never doubt God's love because He has
told us that He loves us with an everlasting love (Jer. 31:3).

At times we try to justify our lack of faith! We know what God
has promised, but we doubt that He will make a practical difference in our life. We are filled with anxiety and excuse ourselves by
saying: "I am just a worrier!" We become bitter during a crisis
and reason that "God could not possibly bring anything good
out of this pain!" We appeal for help from everyone around us
when we have a need; then we explain: "I know God can provide
for my needs, but I think I should do everything I can, just in
case." God calls this faithlessness. Faithlessness is sin. "But without faith it is impossible to please Him" (Heb. 11:6).

Be Anxious for Nothing

Be anxious for nothing, but in everything by prayer and
supplication, with thanksgiving, let your requests be made known
to God; and the peace of God, which surpasses all understanding,
will guard your hearts and minds through Christ Jesus.

PHILIPPIANS 4:6

Don't be anxious! Paul said there is *nothing* that should cause a child of God to worry. He was well aware of things that cause anxiety. His nation was occupied by a foreign army and ruled by corrupt leaders. He was writing from prison, where he was being held as a result of false accusations. He was separated from those he loved; his motives had been questioned; and he had been misrepresented. Some were trying to undermine all that he had accomplished in starting churches. He suffered physically and faced imminent execution (2 Cor. 11:23–29). Yet Paul said there would never be a crisis so troubling that God could not bring peace in the midst of it!

God will not necessarily take your problems away, but He will carry the load for you. He wants you to experience His peace, which is beyond human comprehension. You will never fully understand how God could give you peace in some of the situations you face, but you do not have to understand it in order to experience it. This peace is not just for those who "handle stress well"; it is for everyone! You may know that God wants you to experience peace but wonder how this is possible, given what you are presently facing. Yet, Scripture says to be anxious for *nothing*. God's Word clearly indicates that there is nothing you can face that is too difficult, too troubling, or too fearful for God. No matter what your circumstances are, turn your anxiety over to God and let His perfect peace guard your heart.

Encounters with God

*"But rise and stand on your feet; for I have appeared
to you for this purpose, to make you a minister
and a witness both of the things which you have seen
and of the things which I will yet reveal to you."*

ACTS 26:16

G od was working in your life long before you began
working with Him. The Lord knew you before time
began, and He knew what He wanted to do with your life
(Jer. 1:5; Ps. 139:13). Before the apostle Paul's conversion experience on the road to Damascus, Jesus already knew Paul and had
a specific assignment for him. But Jesus only revealed this assignment after Paul's conversion (Acts 9:15). So misguided was Paul
that in his sincere efforts to serve God, he had actually been waging war against Christians! Although God knew what He wanted
for Paul, He waited to reveal it to him until He gained his attention and became his Lord.

Our Lord does not come to us to discover what we would like
to accomplish for *Him*. He encounters us in order to reveal His
activity and invite us to become involved in *His* work. An
encounter with God requires us to adjust ourselves to the activity of God that has been revealed. God never communicates with
us merely to give us a warm devotional thought for that day. He
never speaks to us simply to increase our biblical knowledge. Our
Lord has far more significant things to reveal to us than that!
When God shows us what He is doing, He invites us to join Him
in the work He is doing.

Are you prepared to meet God today? Don't seek to hear
from God unless you are ready to ask, as Paul did, "What shall I
do, Lord?"

God's Promises Are Yes

*For all the promises of God in Him are Yes, and in Him
Amen, to the glory of God through us.*

2 CORINTHIANS 1:20

G od keeps every promise He makes. When we walk in intimate fellowship with Christ, we have the assurance that every *promise* God has made in Scripture is available to us. This truth should motivate us to search the Scriptures for each promise in order to meditate upon its potential for our life.

Jesus promised that when you ask for something in His will, He will give you what you ask (John 16:23b). This *promise* is available to every Christian. If you ask God if this *promise* applies to your life, His answer is yes. If you are not now experiencing this promise, it does not change the fact that God has said it. You may need to seek God's answer for why His promise has not yet reached maturity in you.

Paul claimed he had tested each of these promises in his own life and found them all to be abundantly true. That's why he could speak of the "exceeding riches of His grace in His kindness toward us in Christ Jesus" (Eph. 2:7b) and the "unsearchable riches of Christ" (Eph. 3:8b). Paul had found a wealth of God's promises and enjoyed them all in abundance.

Don't become discouraged or impatient if you are not experiencing to the fullest all of God's promises in your life. God may want to prepare you to receive some of the great truths He has made available to you. Walk closely with your Lord and, in time, you will see Him bring His promises to fruition in your life.

Love Brings Obedience

"He who has My commandments and keeps them,
it is he who loves Me. And he who loves Me will be loved by
My Father, and I will love him and manifest Myself to him."

JOHN 14:21

Obedience to God's commands comes from your heart. When you begin struggling to obey God, that is a clear indication that your heart has shifted away from Him. Some claim: "I love God, but I'm having difficulty obeying Him in certain areas of my life." That is a spiritual impossibility. If I were to ask you, "Do you love God?" you might easily respond, "Yes!" However, if I were to ask you, "Are you obeying God?" would you answer yes as quickly? Yet I would be asking you the same question! Genuine love for God leads to wholehearted obedience. If you told your spouse that you loved her at certain times but that you struggled to love her at others, your relationship would be in jeopardy. Yet we assume that God is satisfied with occasional love or partial obedience. He is not.

Obedience without love is legalism. Obedience for its own sake can be nothing more than perfectionism, which leads to pride. Many conscientious Christians seek to cultivate discipline in their lives to be more obedient to Christ. As helpful as spiritual disciplines can be, they never can replace your love for God. Love is the discipline. God looks beyond your godly habits, beyond your moral lifestyle, and beyond your church involvement and focuses His penetrating gaze upon your heart.

Has your worship become empty and routine? Have you lost your motivation to read God's Word? Are you experiencing spiritual lethargy? Is your prayer life reduced to a ritual? These are symptoms of a heart that has shifted away from God. Return to your first love. Love is the greatest motivation for a relationship with God and for serving Him.

Sin Is Lawlessness

Whoever commits sin also commits lawlessness,
and sin is lawlessness.

1 JOHN 3:4

I t is a dangerous thing to live your life without a spiritual "plumb line," or standard, by which you determine right from wrong. God's Word is that plumb line. Spiritual laws, like physical laws, are meant to protect you, not restrict you. You may exercise your freedom to challenge the laws of electricity, but to do so can bring you death. Likewise, you will not break God's laws, they will break you. God established absolute moral and spiritual laws that we are free to ignore, but we do so at our own peril. These laws are timeless. Culture does not supersede them. Circumstances do not abrogate them. God's laws are eternal, and they will save you from death if you follow them.

You may feel that God's laws restrict and bind you. On the contrary, God's Word *protects* you from death (Rom. 6:23). For example, when God said that you are not to commit adultery, He wanted to free you to experience the fullest pleasure of a marriage relationship. Furthermore, He knew the devastating heartache that would come to you, your spouse, your children, your relatives, your friends, and your church family if you broke this law. How important the laws of God are for your life! Without them, you would be robbed of the delights God has in store for you. Sin is choosing a standard other than God's law on which to base your life. If you are measuring your life by that of your neighbors, or society at large, then you are basing your life on lawlessness, and lawlessness is sin.

Love Assumes the Best

*Love . . . bears all things, believes all things,
hopes all things, endures all things.*

1 CORINTHIANS 13:7

Love has no limits. Love never says, "You've gone too far. I can't love you now." "All things" means *everything* is included. Christlike love leaves no doubt in the mind of another that you will continue to love steadfastly. Do those close to you know that they can fail and do foolish things, yet you will not falter in your love for them? Are others assured that, even when they hurt you, you still love them, holding nothing against them?

Love assumes the best about others. If someone inadvertently offends you, you choose to believe the offense was unintentional. If someone seeks to harm you, you "bear all things," forgiving unconditionally. If a positive light can be shed on a difficult encounter, you grasp it. If someone continually provokes you, you "endure all things." You never lose hope in the ones you love. You practice the same unconditional love toward others that Christ gives to you.

Paul said that he was nothing if he had the faith to move mountains, the tongue of an angel, and the gift of prophecy to understand all mysteries, yet did not have God's love. It is unacceptable to say, "Well, I just can't love people that way!" When God loves people through you, this is the only kind of love He has! Read 1 Corinthians 13 with gratitude that God has already expressed this complete and selfless love to you. Pray and ask Him to express it *through* you now, to others.

Relentless Love

Then the Lord said to me, "Go again, love a woman who is
loved by a lover and is committing adultery, just like the love of
the Lord for the children of Israel, who look to other gods
and love the raisin cakes of the pagans."

HOSEA 3:1

No human can comprehend God's love for His children!
Our limited experience of human love hinders us from
understanding God's unconditional love for us. We can see a picture of this love in the life of Hosea.

Hosea was a righteous man, but God told him to marry a sinful woman. Hosea obeyed and took Gomer as his wife. He cherished her and treated her with dignity and respect. Never before
had Gomer experienced this kind of love, but she soon grew dissatisfied. She began giving her affections to other men. She
became so involved in adulterous pursuits that finally she abandoned Hosea altogether. Other men used her until she had nothing left to give. Then they sold her into slavery. After this, God
gave Hosea an amazing command: "Go and buy her back."
Despite the intense pain and hurt that Gomer had inflicted on
him, God told Hosea to forgive her and to pay any price to bring
her back into his home.

God's message is clear: When we reject Him and turn our
devotion elsewhere, our rejection carries the same pain as an
adulterous betrayal. After all God has done for us, it is incomprehensible that we should reject Him. It is even harder to fath-
om that God could love us even after we have rejected, ignored,
and disobeyed Him. Yet God's love is completely different from
ours. His love follows us to the depths of our sinfulness until He
has reclaimed us. His love is undaunted when we run from Him,
and He continues to pursue us. What incredible love He has
demonstrated to us!

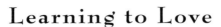

Learning to Love

*And may the Lord make you increase and abound in love
to one another and to all, just as we do to you . . .
But concerning brotherly love you have no need that I should write
to you, for you yourselves are taught by God to love one another.*

1 THESSALONIANS 3:12; 4:9

God is love (1 John 4:16). His very nature is perfect love, but because of sin love does not always come freely and naturally to His children. You may have been raised in a home where love was not expressed. Perhaps you were hurt by someone you loved, and your heart became hardened as a defense against further pain. You may love others but not know how to express your love in words or actions. You may feel frustrated because you have been called by God to love, yet you do not understand *how* to love others.

Paul wrote to the Christians in Thessalonica to encourage them not to become disheartened as they learned to love each other (1 Thess. 3:7). They did not need Paul to explain to them how to love, for God Himself would teach them how to love one another. God would give them His love, and as they followed Him, He would cause that love to multiply. If they found someone who was difficult to love, God would enable them to love through His Holy Spirit.

God in His grace has made provision for our human weakness, and He is prepared to teach us how to love one another. There are no exceptions. God can teach us to love even that especially difficult person.

Are you struggling to love someone? God will help you. He will enable you to love your parents, your spouse, your children, your friends, or your enemy in a deeper way than you could ever love them on your own. If you do not know how to express your love in a meaningful way, God will teach you how to do this. God is the authority on love. As you relate to others, ask God to make His love overflow to them through your life.

Forgive to Be Forgiven

*"And forgive us our debts,
As we forgive our debtors."*

MATTHEW 6:12

Few things are more precious to receive than forgiveness. After carrying the burden of our sin, it is wonderfully freeing to know that the one we have wronged has completely forgiven us. Jesus told His disciples to ask God for forgiveness every time they prayed. Jesus knew that we would daily incur debts against God, as we inevitably fall short of God's standard. A day does not go by that we do not need to ask God to remove our debt against Him.

Jesus warned that we should expect forgiveness from God as we forgive those who sin against us, for God will forgive us in the same way we forgive others (Matt. 6:15). God's nature is forgiveness (Exod. 34:6–7). If we are to be His disciples, we must follow His example. If God will forgive our most relentless enemy, we can do nothing less. Jesus did not say that certain offenses are unworthy of our forgiveness. We have no biblical excuse for allowing unforgiveness in our hearts.

If you choose to withhold forgiveness from someone, your worship and prayers are futile (Matt. 5:23–24). Ask God to make you aware of those dark corners in your life where you are harboring resentment. A keen awareness of your own need for forgiveness will put the offenses of others in their proper light. Ask God to make you like Christ so that, even when you are being persecuted, you can pray, "Father, forgive them."

Deny Yourself

Then Jesus said to His disciples, "If anyone desires to come after Me, let him deny himself and take up his cross, and follow Me."

MATTHEW 16:24

Sin causes us to be self-centered, shifting our hearts from God to self. The essence of salvation is an about-face from self-centeredness to God-centeredness. The Christian must spend a lifetime denying self. Our great temptation will be to affirm ourselves while we follow Jesus. James and John did this when they chose to follow Jesus but asked for the two most prominent positions in Jesus' kingdom (Mark 10:35–37). James and John wanted a discipleship that would not impede their personal desires and aspirations. Like them, we say, "Lord, I want to be pleasing to you, but I want to stay where I am."

Self-centered people try to keep their lives unruffled and undisturbed, safe and secure. Our temptation is to give our time and effort to the goals of this world. Then, when we are successful in the world's eyes, we seek to bring God into our world by honoring Him with our success. We may say, "Now that I have succeeded in business [or sports, or politics, or with my family, or even Christian ministry], I want to give God the glory for it!" God is not interested in receiving secondhand glory from our activity. God receives glory from *His* activity through our lives.

The world will entice you to adopt its goals and to invest in temporal things. Resist the temptation to pursue your own goals, asking God to bless them. Rather, deny yourself and join the activity of God as He reveals it to you.

Take up Your Cross

*Then Jesus said to His disciples, "If anyone desires
to come after Me, let him deny himself,
and take up his cross, and follow Me."*

MATTHEW 16:24

Your "cross" is God's will for you, regardless of the cost. Taking up your cross is a choice; it is not beyond your control. You may have health problems or a rebellious child or financial pressures, but do not mistake these as your "cross to bear." Neither circumstances you face nor consequences of your own actions are your cross. Your cross will be to voluntarily participate in Christ's sufferings as He carries out His redemptive purposes (Phil. 3:10). Paul said he *rejoiced* in his sufferings because he knew that by them he was able to participate in the suffering required to bring others into Christian maturity (Col. 1:24).

We tend to want to go immediately from "denying ourselves" to "following Jesus." But you can never follow Jesus unless you have first taken up your cross. There are aspects of God's redemptive work that can be accomplished only through suffering. Just as Christ had to suffer in order to bring salvation, there will be hardships you may have to endure in order for God to bring salvation to those around you. Jesus did not talk with His disciples about the cross until they had come to know He was the Christ (Matt. 16:21). You will never be able to endure the suffering of the cross unless you have first been convinced that Jesus is the Christ. Once you have settled your relationship with Christ, He will introduce you to your cross.

There is no Christianity without a cross. If you are waiting for a relationship with God that never requires suffering or inconvenience, then you cannot use Christ as your model. God's will for you involves a cross. First, take up your cross; then you can follow Him.

Follow Me

*Then Jesus said to His disciples, "If anyone desires to come
after Me, let him deny himself, and take up his cross,
and follow Me."*

MATTHEW 16:24

We can take God's presence for granted. We can assume that because Jesus said He would be with us *always*, He will follow us wherever we go (Matt. 28:20). Jesus does not follow us; we are to follow *Him*. You do not invite God to join you in your activity. He invites you to become involved in *His* activity. Jesus said: "You did not choose Me, but I chose you" (John 15:16). Following Jesus requires absolute obedience. He does not seek our counsel about which direction we think is suitable. God already knows what is best without ever having to consult with us.

Following Jesus will lead you into experiences you never dreamed of! You will be with Jesus as He weeps over those trapped in sin. You will feel the pain that Jesus feels. You will see those who were spiritually blind experience the joy of coming to see God for the first time. You will see lives that were broken, made whole. You will see marriages restored; those in bondage, released; and those who mourn, comforted. At times it will be easy to follow Jesus. At other times, you will be tempted to abandon Him. Following Jesus can mean going through a storm or standing on a mountaintop.

You may have stopped following Jesus, but now you want to follow again. When you stopped following Jesus, you did so on your terms. But the *returning* to Jesus is strictly under His conditions. He is God, and you are not. Are you willing to follow Jesus anywhere, at any time, under any condition? That is the only way you can follow Him.

You Are Salt

*"You are the salt of the earth; but if the salt loses its flavor,
how shall it be seasoned? It is then good for nothing
but to be thrown out and trampled underfoot by men."*

MATTHEW 5:13

God's people are His preserving agents for a world that is corrupted and degenerating because of sin. Your life is designed and commissioned by God to enhance a community and to preserve what is good and right. There is deep significance today for a godly life that is involved in its community. The presence of Christ in you makes all that He is available to others. His salvation can free an addict, mend a broken home, heal the pain of the past, restore a wayward child, and comfort a grieving heart. All of this is available to those around you as Christ expresses *His* life through you.

If we are not in a right relationship with our Lord, however, Jesus said we are like salt that has lost its saltiness and is, therefore, good for nothing. None of God's saving grace and power can be dispensed through us to others. How do we test the "saltiness" of our life? Look at our family. Are we preserving it from the destructive influences that surround it? Examine our workplace. Are the sinful influences in our work environment being halted because we are there? Observe our community. Is it a better place because we are involved in it? What about our church? The evidence that we have been used by God as a preserving agent is that things are becoming spiritually better around us instead of worse. If people around us are deteriorating spiritually, we need to go to our Lord and allow Him to adjust our lives so that we can be used to preserve others.

You Are Light

*"Let your light so shine before men, that they may see your
good works and glorify your Father in heaven."*

MATTHEW 5:16

There is no mistaking the effect of light upon a darkened place. Light boldly and unabashedly announces its presence and vigorously dispels darkness. God's desire is to fill you with His light. He wants you to shine as a brilliant testimony of His presence and power in your life, so that the darkness in the lives of those around you will be displaced by the light of God's glory.

If, however, you notice the world around you becoming darker and darker, don't blame the darkness! It is simply doing what darkness does. The only remedy for darkness is light. If the world is becoming darker, the problem is not with the darkness. The problem is with the light. Jesus said His disciples should be the "light of the world" (Matt. 5:14). What an awesome responsibility—to be the ones through whom God would shine His divine light and dispel the darkness from around others! In announcing His own coming, Jesus said, "The people who sat in darkness have seen a great light, / And upon those who sat in the region and shadow of death / Light has dawned" (Matt. 4:16).

There was no ignoring Jesus' arrival upon earth! Darkness was dispelled! Everywhere Jesus went, God's truth was boldly proclaimed, people were healed, hypocrisy was exposed, and sinners found forgiveness. The world was never the same once the Father introduced His light through His Son. Can that be said of you as well? Do your coworkers recognize the light that is within you? Does the presence of Christ radiate from your home into your community? When God's light is allowed to shine unhindered through your life, the darkness around you *will* be dispelled.

Whom Is God Sending to You?

"So I brought him to Your disciples, but they could not cure him." Then Jesus answered and said, "O faithless and perverse generation, how long shall I be with you? How long shall I bear with you? Bring him here to Me."

MATTHEW 17:16–17

Jesus gave His disciples the power to cast out demons and to perform miracles of healing (Matt. 10:8). He gave them His authority to minister to people, yet they became so self-centered that they lost the power to do the work of God. When God sent a father with his epileptic son to them for healing, they failed miserably. They were so concerned with position and status (Mark 9:32–35) that they lost their focus on what God wanted to do through them.

Jesus' response to His disciples included some of the harshest words ever to come from His mouth. He called His own disciples "unbelieving" and "perverse" and questioned how much longer He had to endure them! Why? Because they were supposed to be on mission with Him to bring salvation to others, but they had become so disoriented to Him that they were spiritually powerless, lacking the faith to bring physical and spiritual comfort to those God had sent to them.

God ought to be able to send hurting persons to any child of His and expect that they will be helped. Like the disciples, we can become so preoccupied with our own ambitions and distracted by the busyness of our lives that we become ineffective in ministering to those whom God sends to us. It is even possible to become so involved in religious activity that we are of no help to anyone. Regularly take inventory of your life to see if you are being a faithful steward of every life God sends to you.

An Exchanged Life

I have been crucified with Christ and I no longer live, but Christ lives in me. The life I live in the body, I live by faith in the Son of God, who loved me and gave himself for me.

GALATIANS 2:20 (NIV)

The Christian life is an exchanged life: Jesus' life for your life. When Christ takes control, your life takes on dimensions you would never have known apart from Him. When you are weak, then Christ demonstrates His strength in your life (2 Cor. 12:9–10). When you face situations that are beyond your comprehension, you have only to ask, and the infinite wisdom of God is available to you (James 1:5). When you are faced with humanly impossible situations, God does the impossible (Luke 18:27). When you encounter people whom you find difficult to love, God expresses His unconditional love through you (1 John 4:7). When you are at a loss as to what you should pray for someone, the Spirit will guide you in your prayer life (Rom. 8:16). When Christ takes up residence in the life of a believer, "all the fullness of God" is available to that person (Eph. 3:19).

It is marvelously freeing to know that God controls your life and knows what it can become. Rather than constantly worrying about what you will face, your great challenge is to continually release every area of your life to God's control. The temptation will be to try to do by yourself what only God can do. Our assignment is to "abide in the vine" and to allow God to do in and through us what only He can do (John 15:5). Only God can be God. Allow Him to live out His divine life through you. He is the only One who can.

"This Is My Beloved Son . . . Hear Him!"

While he was still speaking, behold, a bright cloud
overshadowed them; and suddenly a voice came out
of the cloud, saying, "This is My beloved Son,
in whom I am well pleased. Hear Him!"

MATTHEW 17:5

Peter and the other disciples were continually disoriented to God. While Jesus was concerned about one thing, it seems that the disciples were always distracted by something else. In order to help his three closest disciples better focus on His imminent sacrifice on the cross, Jesus took them up to the Mount of Transfiguration. There, Jesus was transfigured into a glorious state and was joined by Moses and Elijah, two of history's mightiest men of God. The disciples, however, were asleep! At one of the most profound moments in history, the disciples were more interested in sleep than they were in praying with the Son of God.

When the disciples awakened, they became distracted again. This time, Peter announced his plans to build three tabernacles. The disciples were more concerned with what they could do for God than the incredible work of redemption God was about to accomplish through His Son. Finally, God removed everything from the disciples' sight but Jesus. "This is My Beloved Son, in whom I am well pleased. Hear Him!"

It is so easy to become spiritually distracted. Do you find yourself focusing on everything else but Christ and the work He is doing around you? Are you so eager to "get to the work" that you have not yet clearly heard what is on God's heart? Does the Father need to remove from your life those things that are proving to be a distraction to you? Do you need to refocus on Jesus?

Do Not Forbid Him!

Now John answered Him, saying, "Teacher, we saw someone
who does not follow us casting out demons in Your name,
and we forbade him because he does not follow us."

MARK 9:38

At first glance, it appears a noble thing that Jesus' disciples kept such careful guard over the orthodoxy of Jesus' ministry. They found someone casting out demons in Jesus' name who was not a part of their group and not under their control, and they demanded that he stop. Yet Jesus saw through His disciples' hypocrisy. The disciples themselves had been given the power to drive out demons as well (Matt. 10:8), yet they had failed miserably (Mark 9:28).

How it must have embarrassed the disciples to have publicly failed to cast out a demon from a young boy. Yet, here was someone successfully exorcising demons who was not even regularly with Jesus as they were. They should have been concerned with their own lack of spiritual power and vitality. They should have felt convicted by their Lord's stinging rebuke at their lack of faith (Matt. 17:20). Instead, they focused on others. Rather than repenting of their sin and grieving over their spiritual impotence, the disciples attempted to hinder someone who was enjoying spiritual success.

At times, it is easier to diminish others' spiritual victories than to honestly confront our own failures. Jesus' response to His disciples must have surprised them as He said, "Do not forbid him" (Mark 9:39). He assured them that "he who is not against us is on our side" (v. 40). Have you learned this vital lesson? Are you able to genuinely rejoice in the spiritual victories of others? Are you encouraging those who serve the Lord in a different way or who belong to a different group than you do?

Life with the Shepherd

The Lord is my shepherd; I shall not want.
He makes me to lie down in green pastures;
He leads me beside the still waters.

PSALM 23:1–2

Living like a sheep can bring you incredible peace of mind! The biblical shepherd knew everything about his sheep. He understood what foods were best for them and what would harm them. He knew when they should eat and when they needed their thirst quenched. The shepherd was an expert of the terrain and was aware of the best places for food and water. As long as the sheep trusted and followed their shepherd, they would always have their needs met at the right time. Their shepherd would give them the best that he had.

Do you have absolute trust in your Good Shepherd? Do you value the nourishment that comes from Him more than any you might obtain from the world? Do you ever worry that God might be withholding from you something that you need? The psalmist was convinced that he would "want" for nothing. By his very nature, the Good Shepherd cares for His sheep and would lay down His life for them (John 10:11).

Have you allowed your focus to shift from the Shepherd to what the Shepherd gives you? If you find yourself "wanting," it is not that your Shepherd is unable or unwilling to perfectly meet your needs. It may be that you lack the faith to receive all that He has to give. Could it be that you have become dissatisfied with what your Shepherd has been providing? Are you missing the joy that comes from having a Shepherd who cares for you? Return to Him and trust Him to meet the needs in your life that only He can.

Comfort from the Shepherd

Yea, though I walk through the valley of the shadow of death,
I will fear no evil; For You are with me;
Your rod and Your staff, they comfort me.

PSALM 23:4

As a child of God you are never alone! Your Shepherd is with you at all times. You never have to call Him into your situation. You never have to wonder where He is. You never have to fear that if things become too difficult, He will abandon you. He goes before you; He walks beside you; He comes behind you. He protects you securely. Just as He sees every sparrow and knows every hair that is on your head, so His gaze is constantly upon you (Luke 12:6–7). Even when you cannot see Him, He always keeps His eyes upon you. He comforts you with His strong presence in times of sorrow and grief. He leads you through the valley of the shadow of death. He does not necessarily lead you around the valley as you might wish. There are times when your Shepherd knows that the only way to get you where He wants to take you is to lead you down the path that passes *through* the dark valley. Yet, at those times He walks closely with you, reassuring you throughout the journey that He still loves you and is with you. It is during those times that you experience His love and compassion in a deeper dimension than you ever have before.

You never need to fear evil. As intimidating as evil can be, there is nothing you will ever face that intimidates your Shepherd. He has seen it all and soundly defeated every form of wickedness. Evil never catches Him by surprise. Your Shepherd is always prepared and knows exactly when and where you will experience difficulty. Place your absolute trust in your Good Shepherd that He will protect you and demonstrate His love for you through the darkest valley.

Restoration from the Shepherd

He restores my soul;
He leads me in the paths of righteousness
For His name's sake.

PSALM 23:3

Your Shepherd knows your every need. He knows you will grow weary in your pilgrimage with Him. He knows there are times when you need rest. Your Shepherd knows just what you need to be refreshed. At times you need to lie in lush meadows or beside quiet streams. Sometimes you need to be held by your Shepherd. At other times you need to enjoy the pleasures the Shepherd provides. The Shepherd will not always replenish you in the same way; His response to you will always perfectly correspond to your present need.

As you follow your Shepherd there will be times when your soul becomes exhausted, perhaps because of trials you are experiencing or temptations you are resisting. The persecution you face or the burdens you are carrying for others may be wearing you down. You may be weary from the discipline the Shepherd has brought upon you. There will be times when you feel you can go no further in your Christian pilgrimage. Your Shepherd knows when you have reached this point, and He always has a remedy! There are many ways He can strengthen you: through His word, through others, or through your circumstances. He knows what you need even better than you do.

Have you grown weary? Does your soul need to be refreshed? Don't attempt to recover on your own. Only God knows how to heal and rejuvenate a soul (Isa. 40:28–31; Matt. 11:28–30). He will do it perfectly, sometimes in surprising ways. Ask Him to restore you, and then be prepared to respond to what He does next.

Godly Pursuits

*Therefore let us pursue the things which make for peace
and the things by which one may edify another.*

ROMANS 14:19

A mark of spiritual maturity is a willingness to sacrifice personal comfort in order to strengthen other believers. Paul urges Christians to pursue only activities that promote peace and behavior that builds up others.

To *pursue* means to passionately focus one's undistracted effort toward a goal. This is not a casual matter. It involves using all the resources God has given us to ensure growth and peace in the life of a fellow Christian. To the Colossian church, Paul said he labored, "striving . . . to present every man perfect in Christ" (Col. 1:28–29). This took concentration and effort!

For Paul, choosing to edify Christians meant refraining from any activity that caused others to stumble. He did not concern himself with his own rights or comforts because his greater priority, over his personal freedom, was to lead others to Christian maturity (1 Cor. 14:12, 26). This is how Jesus related to His disciples. He taught them that they could express no greater love than to lay down their lives for one another (John 15:13). As Christians, we ought to be so devoted to strengthening one another's faith that we pursue this goal relentlessly, even if it means laying down our own lives. This behavior characterized the early churches (Acts 2:40–47). This is what love is like among God's people (Gal. 6:9–10).

As God reveals to you what those around you need in order to grow in their faith, be prepared to make the necessary sacrifice on behalf of your fellow Christians (Col. 1:29).

Eyes That See,
Ears That Hear

*"But blessed are your eyes for they see
and your ears for they hear."*

MATTHEW 13:16

When you became a Christian, God gave you spiritual sight and hearing so you could begin experiencing His presence and activity all around you. The Holy Spirit helps you to develop these spiritual senses as you walk with Him. Spiritual sensitivity to God is a gift that must be accepted and exercised. Scripture indicates that those who are spiritually dead cannot see or understand spiritual things (Matt. 13:14–15). Without spiritual eyes, you can be right in the midst of a mighty act of God and not recognize it.

There is a radical difference between seeing your surroundings from a human perspective and seeing life through spiritual eyes. Non-Christians will see world events around them and become confused. You will look at the same events, recognize the activity of God, and adjust your life to Him. When you meet a person who is seeking God, you will recognize the convicting work of the Holy Spirit and adjust your life to God's activity (Rom. 3:11). Someone without spiritual perception will encounter that same person and not grasp the eternal significance of what is happening in that person's life. Others will hear of new philosophies and trends in society and not know how to discern the truth. You will hear God's voice over the din of the world's voices, and you will keep your bearings in the midst of the confusing circumstances.

Sin dulls your senses, ultimately leaving you spiritually blind and deaf. Do not be content with merely seeing with physical eyes and hearing with natural ears but not sensing what God is doing. Ask God, through the power of the Holy Spirit, to sensitize you to His activity all around you.

Now Is the Acceptable Time

The Spirit of the Lord God is upon Me
Because the Lord has anointed Me
To preach good tidings to the poor;
He has sent Me to heal the brokenhearted,
To proclaim liberty to the captives,
And the opening of the prison to those who are bound;
To proclaim the acceptable year of the Lord,
And the day of vengeance of our God;
To comfort all who mourn.

ISAIAH 61:1–2

God's timing is perfect! When He speaks, the time to respond in obedience is now. We often act as if we have all the time in the world to obey Him, but history doesn't wait on our commitments. There is no such thing as postponing a decision with God. Either we obey, or we disobey. It is either faith or unbelief, obedience or disobedience.

When God announces that *now* is the acceptable time, what you do next is critical. How often people have been unprepared when a word came to them from the Lord. God said, "Now is the time for you to respond to Me" and their response was, "But I'm not ready. I have some things I need to do first. I'm too busy!" (Matt. 8:21). God's timing is *always* perfect. He knows you, and He is fully aware of your circumstances. He knows all that He has built into your life until now, and He extends His invitation knowing that His resources are more than adequate for any assignment He gives you.

That is why Scripture tells us God is concerned with our heart. If we do not keep our heart in love with Jesus, our disobedience when God speaks could affect the lives of others. When God speaks it is always out of the context of eternity. We don't have to know all the implications of what He is asking. We just have to know that it is a word from almighty God. "Now" is always the acceptable time to respond to the Lord!

62

Faith Pleases God

*But without faith it is impossible to please Him, for he who
comes to God must believe that He is, and that He is a
rewarder of those who diligently seek Him.*

HEBREWS 11:6

Your relationship with God is largely determined by your
faith. When you come to Him, you must believe that He
exists and that He is exactly who He has revealed Himself to be
in Scriptures. You must also believe that He will respond to you
when you earnestly seek Him. Without this kind of faith, you
cannot please God. Regardless of the morality of your life, the
good works you perform, the words you speak, or the sacrifices
you make for His sake, if you do not have faith, you will not
please Him. It can be tempting to substitute religious activity
for faith in God. Christians may claim they are being "good
stewards" of their resources when, in fact, they are wanting to
walk by sight rather than by faith (Hob. 11:1). They may refuse
to do what God tells them unless they can see all the resources
in place first.

You may say, "I love God, but I just have difficulty trusting
Him." Then you are not pleasing to Him. You cannot struggle
at the core of your relationship with God and still enjoy a vibrant
fellowship with Him! Faith does not eliminate problems. Faith
keeps you in a trusting relationship with God *in the midst of* your
problems. Faith has to do with your relationship with God, not
your circumstances. Some may say, "I'm not much of a person
of faith. I am more of a *practical* person!" Yet you will never do
anything more practical than to place your trust in the Lord!
Nothing is more secure or certain than that which you entrust
to God.

Meditate on These Things

*Finally, brethren, whatever things are true, whatever things
are noble, whatever things are just, whatever things are pure,
whatever things are lovely, whatever things are of good report,
if there is any virtue and if there is anything praiseworthy—
meditate on these things.*

PHILIPPIANS 4:8

What you think about in your unguarded moments reflects
what your mind dwells upon. What you speak about
when your guard is down is a good gauge of what is in your heart
(Matt. 12:34). Your mind needs exercise just as your physical
body does. To keep your body healthy, you must be careful what
you put into it, and you must exercise regularly. To keep your
thoughts pure, you must guard what goes into your mind. To
exercise your mind, you must contemplate things that are noble
and truths that stretch your mind.

Some Christians allow the world to fill their minds with
ungodly thinking. Some people seem drawn to concentrate on
the negative, choosing to be pessimistic about everything. Some
remain satisfied with thinking of the mundane. Others fail to
intentionally place Scripture in their thoughts, choosing instead
to adopt human reasoning. Others, however, choose to expose
their minds to the truths of God—to that which is true, noble,
just, pure, lovely, and good.

The things you allow your mind to dwell on will be revealed by
the way you live. If you focus on negative things, you will inevitably
be a negative person. If you allow unholy thoughts to fill your
mind, ungodliness will become common in your life. If you fill
your mind with thoughts of Christ, you will become Christlike.

What you fill your mind with is a matter of choice. Choose to
concentrate on the magnificent truths of God, and they will create in you a noble character that brings glory to God.

Knowing God

"And this is eternal life, that they may know You, the only true God, and Jesus Christ whom You have sent."

JOHN 17:3

Knowing God through experience is radically different than knowing about God from a theology textbook. According to the Bible, you cannot say you know God unless you have experienced Him (Phil. 3:8, 10). Biblical knowledge always involves experience. You may become discouraged because the truths you read about in the Bible are much richer than the reality of your own experience.

If you have not experienced God's power at work in and through your life, do not settle for a secondhand knowledge of God's power, rejoicing in what He has done in others. Jesus' prayer was that you would come to know God and His presence in your life and experience. Don't discount the power of God as described in Scripture simply because you have not experienced it. Bring your experience up to the standard of Scripture; never reduce Scripture to the level of your experience. Don't settle for a head knowledge of God's love. Jesus prayed that you would experience the depth and width and height of His love and that you would enjoy God's full and unending love in the day-to-day experiences of your life.

If you sense there are biblical truths that you are not experiencing, keep that truth before you and ask God to bring it into your everyday experience. Ask God if there are any adjustments you need to make in order to receive His promise. Don't give up on the promises of God; stay with them until you are fully experiencing them.

The Extraordinary in the Midst of the Ordinary

And the Angel of the Lord appeared to him in a flame of fire
from the midst of a bush. So he looked, and behold, the bush
was burning with fire, but the bush was not consumed. Then
Moses said, "I will now turn aside and see this great sight,
why the bush does not burn." So when the Lord saw that he
turned aside to look, God called to him from the midst of the
bush and said, "Moses, Moses!" And he said, "Here I am."

EXODUS 3:2–4

Moses was going through the routine of his day when he noticed an ordinary thing: a burning bush. Moses also noticed something extraordinary. Although the bush was burning, it was not consumed. Moses turned aside to look more closely. When the Lord saw Moses turning aside from the routine of his day, He spoke to him. Everything God had been doing for forty years in Moses' life was culminating in this moment. So much of God's redemptive plan waited for Moses to notice the uncommon in the midst of the common.

There will be times when, immersed in the ordinary details of life, you may be oblivious to the extraordinary that is right next to you. You can be in the midst of a common moment, only this time the activity is filled with the presence of God. There may be times when, in the middle of your harried day, you notice something unusual. Your first reaction might be "I'm too tired to go aside to investigate this!" or "I'm not going to disrupt my life for this." Yet, in that moment you may have the opportunity for a unique encounter with God.

God usually speaks out of the ordinary experiences of life. Often, it is not while you are worshiping at church. Many of God's most profound and history-changing encounters come during the ordinary experiences of life. When you see the unusual in the midst of the mundane, don't continue business as usual. It may be that God has ordained that moment to be a life-changing time for you and those around you.

Where Has the Spirit Placed You?

*But the manifestation of the Spirit
is given to each one for the profit of all.*

1 CORINTHIANS 12:7

The moment you are born again you receive the Holy Spirit. The Holy Spirit is the gift. God doesn't give you some *thing,* He gives you *Himself.* The Holy Spirit is God. As He lives out His life through you, you have almighty God dwelling within you, carrying out His purposes. The Spirit will manifest Himself through your life, not for your good alone, but for the benefit of those around you.

The Spirit will lead you to a church body where He can minister through you to each person in that body (1 Cor. 12:18). God does not add you to a church body so you can be an observer. The Spirit has an assignment for you within the body, and He will equip you by His presence for this work.

In the Old Testament, God gave specific assignments to His servants and then placed His Spirit upon them to enable them to accomplish their work. In the New Testament, God placed each member as a vital part of a living body. He placed His Spirit within each believer and manifested Himself through the believer to encourage and equip every other member of the body. What an exciting commission from God! Today the Holy Spirit equips believers because He has given each of His servants a task.

How is the presence of the Holy Spirit in your life benefiting those around you? God has equipped you with exactly what is needed for the edification of the body in which He has placed you. If you allow the Holy Spirit to work freely within you, others will be blessed as a result.

The Certainty of God's Supply

*And my God shall supply all your need
according to His riches in glory by Christ Jesus.*

PHILIPPIANS 4:19

This verse is one of the most practical we will ever encounter in the Bible. Every one of us faces needs in our lives; at times, they are beyond our own means. Those are not the times to become anxious or to panic. Nor should we give up in defeat. It is at these times that God wants to draw from His unlimited storehouse to meet our need as only He can.

Do you believe God can meet the needs of your finances? Your health? Your children? Your parents? Your church? Scripture says you will never face a need for which God's provision is not more than adequate. This promise appears over and over again in the Scriptures (Ps. 116:6; Heb. 4:16; Matt. 6:8; Ps. 69:33). If you are not experiencing God's bountiful provision, what is the problem? Is the difficulty with God? Or could it be that you do not really believe that God stands ready to meet your every need?

Every resource of God is available to any child of God who will believe Him. No one has ever exhausted God's supply nor suffered a shortfall when trusting Him. Unfortunately, some Christians live as if God's abundant resources were not available to them. They are children of the King, but they live like beggars! Would the people close to you affirm that your life gives evidence of an unwavering belief that God will do what He said?

Reverence

*Therefore, brethren, having boldness to enter the Holiest
by the blood of Jesus, by a new and living way which He
consecrated for us, through the veil, that is, His flesh.*

HEBREWS 10:19–20

Our generation lacks a sense of wonder and reverence toward God. We want to bring God down to our level, to the commonplace. He is God! Though we have direct access to Him as His children, we ought never to forget that this access was purchased with the precious blood of His only Son. No one who truly understands this ever enters God's presence without a sense of holy awe. No one who comprehends the incredible price paid at Calvary ever takes his relationship with God for granted.

We will never truly understand God and the way He relates to us unless we first comprehend a true sense of His holiness and His demand for holiness among His people. If we are in God's presence, we are on holy ground! We must never act as if it were God's purpose to make us successful. It would be preposterous for us to become impatient when God does not answer our prayers when and how we think He should! He is God; we are not!

As you meditate on the price Jesus paid to give you access to the Father, you will come to treasure your prayer times with Him. Worship will become a privilege you seize with gratitude. Scripture will be dear to you as you strive to be holy in all that you do (2 Cor. 7:1; 1 Pet. 1:15).

If you have lost your wonder at the incredible gift of salvation that has been given to you, you need to revisit the cross and witness your Savior suffering for you. How priceless God's gift of salvation is!

Testing Reveals Your Heart

And you shall remember that the Lord your God led you all the way these forty years in the wilderness, to humble you and test you, to know what was in your heart, whether you would keep His commandments or not. So He humbled you, allowed you to hunger, and fed you with manna which you did not know nor did your fathers know, that He might make you know that man shall not live by bread alone; but man lives by every word that proceeds from the mouth of the Lord.

DEUTERONOMY 8:2–3

God allows us to suffer difficulties and hardships for a purpose. God led the children of Israel to wander through the wilderness for forty years in order to humble them and test them. When they refused to obey Him and enter the Promised Land, the Israelites revealed that they did not really know Him. If they had, they would have had more faith. God spent the next forty years testing the hearts of His people to see if they were prepared for His next assignment.

Testing reveals what is in your heart and produces a robust faith (James 1:3, 12). God allowed His people to hunger so they could experience His provision and develop a deeper level of trust in Him. As the people walked with God they came to understand that their lives depended upon His Word. They learned that God's Word was the most important thing they had. After depending on God for forty years while living in the desert, the people listened when God spoke, and they believed. When they finally entered the Promised Land and waged war against their enemies, the Israelites knew that God's Word meant life and death. They were prepared to listen to Him, and as a result He led them to an astounding victory.

Is God presently testing you in some area of your life? What has His testing revealed? Have you become bitter toward God because of where He has led you? Or have you come to trust Him more as a result of what you have gone through?

Raising Our Expectations

*Call to Me, and I will answer you, and show you
great and mighty things, which you do not know.*

JEREMIAH 33:3

Too often we settle for much less than what God wants to do through us. We read in Jeremiah 32:27: "I am the Lord, the God of all flesh. Is anything too hard for Me?" and we answer, "No, Lord." Yet when we face difficult situations we begin to qualify our belief in God and lower our expectations of what God will do. It is one thing to believe God could perform a miracle in the Bible, or a thousand years ago, or even in the life of a friend; it is quite another matter to wholeheartedly believe God can do anything He chooses to do in our lives!

When almighty God speaks to us, what we do next proves what we believe about Him, regardless of what we say. God revealed to Moses His plan to orchestrate the greatest exodus in human history, and He wanted to use Moses to accomplish it. Moses responded by arguing with God! Moses was overwhelmed by what he heard and began to make excuses for why he could not participate in God's activity. Moses would have readily acknowledged his belief in God's power; he simply did not believe God could do His miraculous work through *his* life. Moses' argument with God limited his ministry for the rest of his life (Exod. 4:13–16).

Do you sense there may be far more that God wants to do through your life than what you have been experiencing? Ask God to show you what it is. Then be prepared to respond in faith and obedience to what He tells you.

God's Ways Are Not Our Ways

"For My thoughts are not your thoughts,
Nor are your ways My ways," says the Lord.
"For as the heavens are higher than the earth,
So are My ways higher than your ways,
And My thoughts than your thoughts."

ISAIAH 55:8–9

Rarely does God do something exactly as we think He will. Our problem is that we try to second-guess God, saying, "Oh, now I know what God is planning to do!" Moses experienced this as he learned how God was going to deliver the Hebrews out of Egypt. God told him He would harden Pharaoh's heart. Yet, the result was not what Moses anticipated. Rather than allowing the Hebrews to leave, Pharaoh increased their hardship. Rather than becoming a hero among the Hebrews, Moses was despised by them for bringing greater suffering. Moses returned to the Lord and asked, "Lord, why have You brought trouble on this people? Why is it You have sent me?" (Exod. 5:22). Much of the frustration we experience as Christians has nothing to do with what God does or doesn't do. It has everything to do, rather, with the false assumptions we make about how we think God will and should act.

Have you ever done the will of God and then things seemed to become worse? Moses completely misunderstood what the results of His obedience to God would be. When things did not turn out as he anticipated, Moses became discouraged. God had told Moses what to do, but He had not told Moses what the consequences would be.

It is foolish to attempt to do God's work using your own "common sense." God does not eliminate your common sense; He consecrates it. He gives you His wisdom so you can understand His ways.

As you look back on God's activity in your life, you will recognize the supreme wisdom in how He has led you. As you look forward to what God may do, be careful you do not try to predict what He will do next. You may find yourself completely off the mark.

Christ Must Reorient You

When He had gone a little farther from there, He saw James
the son of Zebedee, and John his brother, who also were in the
boat mending their nets. And immediately He called them,
and they left their father Zebedee in the boat with the
hired servants, and went after Him.

MARK 1:19–20

We have a natural tendency to find our "comfort zone" and then position ourselves firmly in place. If you are in a situation or lifestyle where you are perfectly capable of handling everything, you have stopped growing in your understanding of God. God's desire is to take you from where you are to where He wants you to be. You will always be one step of obedience away from the next truth God wants you to learn about Him. You may experience a restlessness whereby you sense that there is far more you should be learning and experiencing about the Father. At times, this will mean that you should move to a new location or take a new job. It could indicate that you need a deeper dimension added to your prayer life. Perhaps you need to trust God to a degree you never have before.

The fishermen could not remain in their fishing boats and become apostles of Jesus Christ. Abraham was seventy-five years old when God gave him his major life assignment. These men had to disrupt their comfortable routine in order to reach new heights in their relationship with their Lord. Likewise, in order to experience God to the degree He wants you to, there will be adjustments He will ask of you. Are you prepared for Christ to reveal Himself to you in dimensions that will change your life? Are you willing to abandon that which makes you comfortable?

73

Truth Is to Be Experienced

When He had stopped speaking, He said to Simon,
"Launch out into the deep and let down your nets for a catch."

LUKE 5:4

When Christ teaches you something about Himself, He implements it into your life through experience. As the crowds gathered around, Jesus chose to board Peter's boat and teach the people from there. All day long Peter sat in the boat listening to Jesus teach the multitudes. At the close of His discourse, Jesus allowed Peter to experience the reality of what He had just been teaching the crowd. The crowd had *heard* the truth, but Peter was to *experience* it.

Jesus put His teaching into language a fisherman could understand. He told Peter to put out his nets into the deep water. Peter hesitated, "Master, we have toiled all night and caught nothing." Peter had been fishing all night, had washed and repaired his nets in the morning, and then listened to Jesus teach. He was tired. He probably was not expecting a dramatic encounter with God at a time like that. Yet, as Peter obeyed Jesus, he pulled in such a miraculous catch of fish that his boat almost sank! Peter was filled with amazement and recognized that he had just experienced the power of God (Luke 5:4–11).

Peter learned that with a command from Jesus, he could do anything. Thus, Jesus was able to reorder Peter's priorities from catching fish to catching men (Luke 4:10). Peter's obedience led to a dramatic new insight into the person of Jesus. This was an invitation to walk with Jesus in an even more intimate and powerful way.

God does not want you to merely gain intellectual knowledge of truth. He wants you to *experience* His truth. There are things about Jesus you will learn only as you obey Him. Your obedience will then lead to greater revelation and opportunities for service.

No Exceptions to Holiness

*And it came to pass on the way, at the encampment,
that the Lord met him and sought to kill him.*

EXODUS 4:24

oses had just received one of the greatest commissions in history. He was to be God's instrument to deliver the nation of Israel and to guide it to the Promised Land. He was to lead them to become a kingdom of priests and a holy nation (Exod. 19:6). Yet Moses had not obeyed all of God's commands himself, for he had never had his son circumcised. This was a long-standing command from God that Moses had ignored. God's response was to prepare to kill Moses. Here was one of history's greatest men about to be put to death before ever performing the task God had set before him. Moses could not expect to blatantly ignore a command of God and still be used mightily in His divine work. Had not Moses quickly responded in obedience, he would surely have lost his life.

Moses learned that God makes no exceptions for holiness. When God sets forth a requirement of His people, He most certainly demands it of the leaders. God wanted to make Moses' life a highway of holiness through which He could bring redemption to millions of people. God had to make some significant adjustments in the life of Moses before He would use him to lead His people.

Are you trying to serve God and yet ignore something He has told you to do? Are you living your life as if God does not notice your disobedience? Do you apply God's standards to yourself as rigorously as you apply them to others?

Stand Your Watch!

I will stand my watch
And set myself on the rampart,
And watch to see what He will say to me,
And what I will answer when I am corrected.

HABAKKUK 2:1

The watchman's job was vital. An approaching army left residents of an ancient city precious little time to flee or to prepare for battle. Everyone's life depended on the alert watchman as he peered into the horizon for the earliest glimpse of an approaching threat. It was critical that the people be alerted as soon as possible to what was coming.

As a Christian, God places you as a watchman for yourself, your friends, your family, and your church family. It is essential that you be attentive to what God is saying. It may be that a friend is in crisis and needs God's Word. As you study your Bible, God may choose to give you words of encouragement to share with your friend. It may be that as your children face difficult challenges, God will speak to you as you pray and reveal how you can help them. If you are spiritually alert, you may receive a warning from God that addresses specific dangers that those around you are facing.

If you are careless, on the other hand, your family may be struggling, but the answers God has for them will go unheard. If you are oblivious to God's message, those around you may miss the encouraging promise from God that He wanted to share through you. God holds His watchmen accountable for their diligence (Ezek. 33:6). Strive to be attentive to every word that comes to you from God. Your diligence will benefit you and those around you as you heed God's warnings and follow His commands.

God's Measure for Forgiveness

*"For if you forgive men their trespasses, your heavenly Father
will also forgive you. But if you do not forgive men their
trespasses, neither will your Father forgive your trespasses."*

MATTHEW 6:14–15

Perhaps you consider yourself a forgiving person, but you
are now facing someone whom you cannot forgive.
Whenever you struggle to forgive, you need to revisit what you
were like when God first forgave you. Ephesians 2 indicates you
were a "foreigner" and a "child of wrath." Yet God forgave your
most grievous sin and rebellion against Him. While you were still
rejecting God, Christ died for you (Rom. 5:8). This being so,
how can you refuse to forgive those who sin against you?
Forgiveness is not a spiritual gift, a skill, or an inherited trait.
Forgiveness is a choice. Jesus looked down on those who had
ruthlessly and mockingly nailed Him to a cross, yet He cried
out: "Father, forgive them, for they do not know what they do"
(Luke 23:34). How, then, can we refuse to forgive those who
have committed offenses against us?

Jesus said that the measure in which we are forgiving is the
same standard God will use in forgiving us. God's ways are very
different from ours. God's forgiveness is not based on standards
we determine, but on the standards He established in His Word.
God allows for no exceptions when it comes to forgiveness.

As we truly understand God's gracious forgiveness in our lives,
we will naturally want to express this same forgiveness to others
(Eph. 4:32; Col. 3:13). Before you ask God for His forgiveness,
take a moment to examine the condition of your relationships.
Would you want God to forgive you in the same way you are
presently forgiving others?

God's Provision Brings Glory

*Call upon Me in the day of trouble; I will deliver you,
and you shall glorify Me.*

PSALM 50:15

Did you know that you bring glory to God by calling upon Him when you are in distress? God promised He would deliver you if you turned to Him. You deny the Lord honor that is rightfully His every time you find yourself in difficulty and you fail to call upon Him for help! There may be times when God allows you to reach a point of need so that you can call upon Him, and thus let Him demonstrate to a watching world the difference He makes in the lives of His children. If God never allowed you to experience need, people around you might never have the opportunity to witness God's provision in the life of a Christian. If you never faced a shortfall, you might be tempted to feel self-sufficient and without any need of God in your daily life.

Pride will tempt you to think that you do not need to seek God's assistance. Self-regard will seek to convince you that you can handle your dilemma through your own wisdom, resources, and hard work. Pride will also rob glory from God and seek to give it to you. Don't allow your pride to take what rightfully belongs to the Lord. Call upon your Lord and wait exclusively upon Him to rescue you. Then give Him the glory that He deserves.

Self-sufficiency can greatly hinder your ability to experience God and bring Him honor. The next time you are in distress, turn to Him!

God's Abundance in Your Life

And God is able to make all grace abound toward you,
that you, always having all sufficiency in all things,
may have an abundance for every good work.

2 CORINTHIANS 9:8

When you relate to God you always deal with abundance, for God does nothing in half measures! This is true regarding His grace. The Lord is not miserly when it comes to providing grace to His servants. When you seek to perform a good work that God has asked you to do, you will always find an ample supply of God's grace to sustain you. If you begin to lose heart in the work you are doing, God's grace upholds you and gives you the love for God and His people you require in order to continue. When you face criticism and are misunderstood, God's grace enables you to forgive your accusers and to sense God's pleasure even when others do not understand what you are doing. When you make mistakes in the work God has appointed you to do, God's grace forgives you, sets you back on your feet, and gives you strength to continue the work. When you complete the task God gave you and no one expresses thanks for what you have done, the Father's grace surrounds you, and He reminds you that you have a heavenly reward where everything you have done in the Lord's service will be remembered.

God does not promise to provide all you need for your dreams and projects. He does assure you that, for every good work you attempt, you will never face a shortfall of His grace in order to successfully complete the task God has given you.

Why Do You Doubt?

Then His disciples came to Him and awoke Him, saying,
"Lord, save us! We are perishing!" But He said to them,
"Why are you fearful, O you of little faith?" Then He arose
and rebuked the winds and the sea, and there was a great calm.

MATTHEW 8:25–26

It is by faith that God's mighty power is released into the life of a Christian (Heb. 11:33–35). The fact that you have doubts indicates that you do not know God as you should. If your prayer life is infiltrated with doubts, you have denied yourself the greatest single avenue of power that God has made available to you. Without faith it is impossible to please God (Heb. 11:6). God never comforts you in your doubt. Jesus consistently rebuked those who would not believe Him. He had revealed enough of Himself for His disciples to have believed Him in their time of need.

God wants to build your understanding of Him until your faith is sufficient to trust and obey Him in each situation (Mark 9:23–25). The moment you turn to Him with a genuine commitment to rid yourself of doubt, God will match your doubt with a revelation of Himself that can convince you of His faithfulness. When Thomas doubted, Jesus revealed Himself to him in such a way that every doubt vanished (John 20:27). You can only resolve your lack of faith in God's presence. He must reveal Himself in such a way that any doubt you might have is removed. Jesus did this with His disciples. He involved them in a consistent, growing relationship with Himself. Jesus took them through teaching, to small miracles, to large miracles, and to the resurrection. Jesus knew that the redemption of the world rested on His disciples' believing Him. What does God want to do in the lives of those around you that waits upon your trust in Him and the removal of your doubts?

When Christ Gives a Command

*And He sent out two of His disciples and said to them,
"Go into the city . . ."*

MARK 14:13

The two disciples were given very detailed instructions to go to a certain town and look for a particular man performing a specific task. He would have a large room, furnished and ready to observe the Passover. These instructions might have seemed unusual had it not been their Lord speaking, but the two disciples obeyed and found everything just as Jesus had said. Jesus knew exactly what they would find, and so He guided them specifically. One of the most memorable and precious times the disciples would spend with their Teacher hinged on the obedience of these two.

Obedience to Christ's commands always brings fulfillment. When the Lord gives you instructions, obey immediately. Don't wait until you have figured it all out and everything makes perfect sense to you. Sometimes God will lead you to do things that you will not fully understand until after you have done them. He does not usually reveal all the details of His will when He first speaks to you. Instead, He tells you enough so you can implement what He has said, but He withholds enough information so that you must continue to rely upon His guidance. Your response will affect what God does next in your life. Your obedience may affect how others around you experience Christ as well. If there is any directive God has given you that you have not obeyed, obey that word immediately and watch God's perfect plan unfold in your life.

The Unthinkable

Now as they sat and ate, Jesus said, "Assuredly, I say to you,
one of you who eats with Me will betray Me."

MARK 14:18

Surely I would never betray the Lord! Each disciple earnestly pled his loyalty to Christ. As they reclined together in the comfort and security of the upper room, in the presence of their Lord, the disciples could not imagine themselves ever wavering in their loyalty to Christ. Yet Jesus looked at them and said, "One of you who eats with Me will betray Me!" How was it possible to share such an intimate and profound moment with the Savior and then rush so quickly toward betrayal and spiritual failure?

During the intense pressures of Gethsemane and the cross, the disciples did things they never thought they would do. They had no idea how cruel and hateful the world around them would be to their Lord. Jesus had cautioned them that the world would hate *them* because it hated *Him* (John 15:18–21; 16:33). But only Jesus knew the full extent of the temptation they would face. In the pressure of the moment the heart does surprising things. Scripture had predicted Judas would betray Jesus, despite having walked with Him for over three years. But Peter, too, would deny Him, and all would forsake Him.

How quickly the surroundings of your life can shift from the security and tranquility of an upper room to the harsh reality of Gethsemane and the cross. Guard your heart. Listen now to the Lord's gentle warning: the failure that was possible with His first disciples is also possible with you. You, too, are capable of forsaking Jesus, just as the first disciples did. If Jesus is warning you of an area in your life in which you could fail Him, heed His words today!

A Soul Distressed

He began to be troubled and deeply distressed.
Then He said to them, "My soul is exceedingly sorrowful,
even to death. Stay here and watch!"

MARK 14:33b–34

Who can know the depth and intensity of the heart of God? No one could measure His sorrow over an unrepentant sinner or His joy over a spiritual rebel who relinquishes everything to Him. We can begin to understand what is on the heart of God only when He shares His heart with us (Amos 3:7).

Are you aware of the fervent emotions in the soul of your Lord, as He carries the weight of the world? The disciples were unaware of the deep anguish in the heart of Jesus. Yet, He willingly shared His heart with them. The disciples often seemed disoriented to what Jesus was feeling. When He took delight in young children, His disciples attempted to chase them away (Luke 18:15–16). When Jesus had compassion for a woman living in sin, they acted confused (John 4:27). While Jesus wept at the hopelessness of those facing death, His closest friends grieved as if Jesus had no power to raise the dead (John 11:1–44).

You can choose to be alert to the heart of God. As you seek to understand what God is feeling, He may share with you the intensity of His heart. When you are around other people, God may sensitize you to the love He feels for them. When you see others suffering, you may feel the compassion Jesus feels. When sinners return to God in repentance, you may share the Father's joy. You will react to evil the way Jesus reacts. If you will remain alert in prayer, Jesus will share His heart with you.

Going Farther with God

*He went a little farther, and fell on the ground,
and prayed.*

MARK 14:35

S ome Christians are satisfied to have only a surface relationship with Christ. Others desire to share the holiest
moments with Him. On the night Jesus spent in sacred prayer in
the Garden of Gethsemane, the people responded to Him in various ways. There were those who were so indifferent to Jesus that
they were unaware He was even in the garden. Then there was
Judas, who knew where Jesus was but was too busy with his own
schemes to join Him. The rest of the disciples joined Jesus in the
garden, but they were distracted by sleep. Jesus told them the
urgency of the hour, but they did not comprehend it. There was
the inner circle of disciples, Peter, James, and John. They initial-
ly prayed with Jesus, yet even they could not grasp the significance of the moment. Ultimately, Jesus prayed alone. He went
farther than His disciples and prayed longer. At the greatest
moment of intercession in human history, there was no one willing to go with Jesus and watch with Him.

Throughout history God has looked for those willing to yield
everything to Him and His desire to redeem a world. At times
God has marveled that no one was willing to go with Him
(Isa. 63:5; 59:16). The prophets seemed to grasp more than the
common people, for while society carried on as though nothing
were wrong, the prophets agonized and wept over what they
knew God was preparing to do.

God is calling you to go deeper in your prayer life with Him.
If you are willing to be the person Jesus can take with Him into
the most sacred moments, you will experience things only the
angels shared with Jesus in the garden that night.

A Fatal Moment

"Watch and pray, lest you enter into temptation.
The spirit indeed is willing, but the flesh is weak."

MARK 14:38

At times your spirit must demand supremacy over your flesh. Your spirit will know what your Lord wants you to do, but your flesh will cry out for its own fulfillment. There are times when sleep must be denied, even when you are exhausted, because it would be disastrous for you to rest at such a time. When the Lord commands you to "watch and pray," it is crucial that you obey.

As Jesus prayed in the Garden of Gethsemane, He knew that the pinnacle of His ministry was quickly approaching. He was aware that the legions of hell were marshaling their forces to defeat Him. If there were ever a critical time for His closest friends to be undergirding Him in prayer, this was it. Jesus told them that He was deeply distressed, even to the point of death. Surely they could have sensed the intensity in His voice and the urgency of His demeanor, and surely they could have found the strength to obey His request. Yet He found them asleep. No excuses. They had fallen asleep at the most pivotal moment in human history, not once but three times!

Jesus asks you to join Him in what He is doing. He may ask you to watch and pray for an hour. You may have to deny your physical needs and desires in order to pray with Him. You may have to leave the comfort of your bed or your home. You may even have to sacrifice your safety in order to be where Jesus is. Seek to bring every physical desire under the control of the Holy Spirit so that nothing will impede your accomplishing what Jesus asks of you.

Facing Failure

Jesus said to them, "All of you will be made to stumble because of Me this night, for it is written . . ."

MARK 14:27

As you follow Jesus you will face moments of great distress. At times it will seem that events conspire to cause you to stumble in your relationship with Him. You do not initiate them, but they arise from opposition or the intensity of your circumstances. Nevertheless, failure is the end result. The disciples faced such fierce opposition to their Lord that they all failed Him on the night Jesus was crucified.

Peter boasted that he was incapable of forsaking Jesus (Mark 14:29–31). Yet Jesus assured the disciples even before their failure that it was inevitable. The Scriptures had prophesied it. God always knew the disciples would fail His Son; He wasn't caught by surprise. He had made provision for their shortcomings, knowing He would eventually develop them into apostles who would fearlessly preach the gospel, perform miracles, and teach others. Later, when the risen Christ encountered Peter on the seashore, He did not ask Peter for a confession of his sin, but a confession of his love (John 21:15–17).

You may fear that your failure has caught God by surprise. Perhaps you promised, like Peter, to stand with the Lord, but you failed. God was just as aware that you would fail Him as He was with the original disciples. He has made provision to respond every time you stumble. Don't think that somehow your failures are bigger or more complex than any God has dealt with. If you are facing challenges that seem overwhelming, don't be discouraged. God has already foreseen them and prepared for them (1 Cor. 10:13).

Too Late!

*Then He came the third time and said to them,
"Are you still sleeping and resting? It is enough!"*

MARK 14:41a

"It is enough!" How these words from the Master stung the disciples! They were given the opportunity to share a sacred moment with Jesus. They failed Him. This time, not even Peter had an answer for Jesus.

Jesus forgave them, and they went on to experience God working powerfully through their lives, but that unique moment with their Lord was lost. The angels had comforted the Savior on that lonely night as He prepared for the cross, not the disciples. Scripture indicates that the disciples later became diligent in prayer, but the memory of that night would remain with them for the rest of their lives.

Like the disciples, you receive unique opportunities to serve your Lord. There are times when Jesus will ask you to join Him as He is at work in the life of your friend, family, or coworker. If you are preoccupied with your own needs, you will miss the blessing of sharing in His divine activity.

God is gracious; He forgives, and He provides other opportunities. He will even use our failings to bring about good, but it is critical that we respond in obedience to every prompting from God. God does not need our obedience; He has legions of angels prepared to do His bidding when we fail Him. The loss is ours as we miss what God wants to do in our lives.

Respond immediately when God speaks to you. His will for you is perfect, and it leads to abundant life.

Oriented by the Scriptures

"But the Scriptures must be fulfilled."
Then they all forsook Him and fled.

MARK 14:49b-50

There are times when, in the darkest moments of your life, the only comfort left for you is a word from God. Jesus faced the cruel injustice of a hostile world, but perhaps His deepest pain came when His closest friends deserted and betrayed Him. What could possibly sustain Him at such a dark moment? Jesus found His comfort in the Scriptures (Matt. 26:20–25, 31). The Scriptures kept everything in perspective for the Savior, holding Him steadfast in the knowledge that everything He was experiencing was according to His Father's plan. Jesus could proceed with confidence because the Scriptures assured Him that the Father was in control.

The Word of God will guide you in the same way. There will be times when events around you will confuse you. Those in whom you've placed your trust will fail you. Others will abandon you. You will be misunderstood and criticized. In these times of distress, when your devotion and obedience are put to the greatest test, you must let Scripture guide and comfort you. Never let the faithlessness of others determine what you do. Turn to the scriptures and allow them to reorient you to God and His activity.

Even as a young boy, Jesus was already well acquainted with the Scriptures. He was never surprised by events; He lived with confidence because the Scriptures had prepared Him for everything that He would face.

If you will immerse yourself daily in the Word of God, you will not be caught off guard when crises come. Your focus will already be on God, and He will safely guide you through your difficult moments.

Tested Yet Secure

And the Lord said, "Simon, Simon! Indeed, Satan has asked for you, that he may sift you as wheat. But I have prayed for you, that your faith should not fail; and when you have returned to Me, strengthen your brethren."

LUKE 22:31–32

Jesus dearly loved Peter. Jesus spoke to him specifically and said, "Simon! Simon! Satan has made a request to sift *all of you* (plural) as wheat. But I have prayed for *you* (singular), that *your* faith will not fail. And when *you* (singular) have returned to Me, strengthen your brothers." Even as Jesus faced His imminent arrest and crucifixion, He took time to strengthen Peter for what was to come! He assured him that God had set limits on Satan's influence. He expressed His confidence that even though Peter's faith would falter, he would overcome, to the point of strengthening others. Since Jesus Himself was interceding for Peter, Peter might fail for a moment, but his life would ultimately be victorious.

Jesus is fully aware of every temptation and test you will encounter, and He stands ready to deliver you (1 Cor. 10:13). He intercedes for you just as He did for Peter (Rom. 8:34; Heb. 7:25). Temptation might catch you by surprise, but Jesus is already interceding with the Father on your behalf. Remember that temptation is not a sin. When you are tempted, turn immediately to Jesus. He will take you to the Father, and you will overcome the temptation, for Jesus has overcome everything you can face in the world (1 John 4:4). When you are tested and are secure in the intercession of Jesus, you, too, will be able to strengthen others.

If you are grappling with temptation, Jesus is interced ing for you with the Father even now. Be steadfast and encouraged!

Praise before Victory

And when they had sung a hymn,
they went out to the Mount of Olives.

MARK 14:26

Praise is greatly honoring to God! In the Old Testament account of King Jehoshaphat, God's people faced a seemingly insurmountable enemy who was determined to destroy them. Yet God assured them that they would "stand still and see the salvation of the Lord" (2 Chron. 20:17). The people of Judah believed God. Their army was led by singers, offering praises to the Lord for their promised victory, and the victory came. When King David led the procession bringing the ark of the covenant into Jerusalem, he praised God with all of his strength (2 Sam. 6:12–23). David's praise was pleasing to God, and God's powerful presence remained in David's kingdom to give him victory against every enemy.

Jesus was about to go to Gethsemane and to the cross, where God's greatest victory would be accomplished. He led His disciples to sing a hymn. The disciples were all about to fail Him, and Jesus was about to be cruelly executed, yet Jesus insisted that they praise God. Their praise looked beyond the cross to God's ultimate victory. Praise is rooted not in circumstances of the moment but in the nature and trustworthiness of God.

You ought to rejoice when God asks you to proceed in the work of His kingdom because you know the victory is already secured. Don't focus on the problems and failures of others. Focus on God's assurance of victory. If you have trouble praising God with a song in your heart as you serve Him, it may be that your focus is not on God, but on your circumstances.

Your Lord Precedes You

*"But after I have been raised,
I will go before you to Galilee."*

MARK 14:28

G od never sends you into a situation alone. He always goes before His children, as He did with the children of Israel when He led them with a cloud by day and a pillar of fire by night. You do not serve as His advance troops in a foreign and hostile situation. *He* always precedes *you* in any situation you encounter. God is never caught by surprise by your experience; He has already been there. He is prepared to meet every need because He has gone before you and knows exactly what you will need for your pilgrimage (Deut. 31:8).

Not only does God go *before* you, but He also stands *beside* you and *behind* you, to provide protection and comfort (Ps. 139:7–12). Jesus knew His disciples would be totally bewildered by His crucifixion, so He assured them in advance that no matter what happened, no matter where they went, they could go in confidence that He had already gone before them. Paul, too, experienced this assurance (Acts 18:9; 23:11). In the most bewildering circumstances, his Lord was there!

If you are going through a difficult or confusing time, know that your Lord has gone before you and He is present with you. He is fully aware of what you are facing, and He is actively responding to your need. There is nowhere you can go that you will not find Christ waiting for you to join Him. Even when you face death, you can be assured that He has gone before you in triumph. As a child of God, rest in the knowledge that your Savior preceded you, and He will walk with you through each experience of your life.

This Is Your Wisdom

*Therefore be careful to observe them; for this is your wisdom
and your understanding in the sight of the peoples who will
hear all these statutes, and say, "Surely this great nation
is a wise and understanding people."*

DEUTERONOMY 4:6

Wisdom is not what you know about the world but how well you know God. Human reasoning will not make you wise. It may even lead you to reject the ways of God (1 Cor. 1:18–25). God's purpose in creating a nation for Himself was to demonstrate His wisdom to the world through the obedience of His people (Zech. 8:23). As the Israelites followed God, He would bless them, and the wisdom of obeying God would be evident to all.

God gives you the same opportunity to base your life on His wisdom. When unbelievers make important decisions, they must rely on their own knowledge and understanding. You, as a Christian, have access to God's wisdom. God's Spirit is within you to guide you (John 16:13). The Holy Spirit will open your eyes to the truth of the Scriptures so that you can see things from God's perspective. Only God sees the future, so only He can accurately lead you to make correct decisions today.

As you allow God to direct your life, those around you will see true wisdom, wisdom not of the world but of God. Others will be confused about what to do in our complicated world, but God will guide you safely to the correct choices for you. Your family will be blessed because you make wise decisions. Your friends will have a wise counselor to come to for help. Your obedient life will demonstrate the wisdom of allowing the Holy Spirit to be your Guide.

Death Brings Much Fruit

*Most assuredly, I say to you, unless a grain of wheat
falls into the ground and dies, it remains alone;
but if it dies, it produces much grain.*

JOHN 12:24

Some things must die in order to be productive. Certain seeds will not germinate into a plant unless they freeze during the winter. Jesus knew that His death would bring salvation to the world.

The moment you became a Christian, your sinful nature died (Rom. 6:6), but there remained sinful aspects of your character that had not gone to their graves willingly. Before you became a Christian, were you self-centered? You may discover selfishness lingering in your life when you ought to be freely sharing what you have in the name of Christ (Matt. 10:8). Did you have a volatile temper? Now as a believer, you experience moments when anger wells up within you. Were you driven by ambition? You may still find yourself with the same motivation as you strive for recognition and position in the kingdom of God.

If these sinful attitudes are allowed to remain alive, they will stifle the fruits of the Spirit. Your temper may prevent some from coming to Jesus. Your selfishness will hinder you from being a blessing to those around you. Your ambition could cause you to use others to meet your goals. Your family may be suffering because of some areas of your life that you have never allowed Jesus to put to death. It is futile to say, "But that's just the way I am!" That is the way you were. But that person died with Christ; you are a new creation (2 Cor. 5:17). Allow God to complete His work in you and see what fruit your life produces.

The Risen Lord

His head and hair were white like wool, as white as snow, and His eyes were like a flame of fire; His feet were like fine brass, as if refined in a furnace, and His voice as the sound of many waters.

REVELATION 1:14–15

At times it is tempting to conclude: "If only I could have walked with Jesus, as the twelve disciples did, it would be so much easier to live the Christian life!" This thought reveals that we do not comprehend the greatness of the risen Christ we serve today. The Jesus of the Gospels is often portrayed as One who walked along the seashore, loving children and gently forgiving sinners. Yet the image of Jesus that we see at the close of the New Testament is far more dramatic! He stands in awesome power as He rules all creation. His appearance is so magnificent that when John, His beloved disciple, sees Him, he falls to the ground as though he were dead (Rev. 1:17).

We grossly underestimate the God we serve! To ignore God's Word or to disobey a direct command from Him is to ignore the magnificent nature of Christ. Our fear of other people proves that we do not understand the awesome Lord who walks with us. The Christ we serve today is the Lord of all creation. He is vastly more awesome and powerful than the gentle rabbi we often imagine.

If you struggle with your obedience to Christ, take a closer look at how He is portrayed in the Book of Revelation. If you are succumbing to temptation, call upon the powerful One who dwells in you. If you have forgotten how great and mighty the Lord is, meet Him through the vision of the beloved disciple. The encounter will dramatically affect the way you live!

Fresh Encounters
with Christ

*That which we have seen and heard we declare to you, that
you also may have fellowship with us; and truly our fellowship
is with the Father and with His Son Jesus Christ. And these
things we write to you that your joy may be full.*

1 JOHN 1:3-4

J ohn the apostle never ceased to marvel at the life-changing relationship he enjoyed with his Lord. It overwhelmed him to know that, at a particular time in history, the God of the universe chose to have fellowship with him, a simple fisherman. John was so overjoyed that he earnestly wanted to share his joy with others so they, too, might experience the same joy. A special fellowship or "bonding" developed between those who had personally encountered Christ as they rejoiced together at God's goodness to them.

Those around you desperately need to be encouraged by your latest encounter with Christ. Some have lost hope that they can experience the reality of God's presence in their lives. They don't need your philosophies or theological speculations. They don't need to hear your opinions on what they should do. They need to hear from someone who has just come from a personal, life-changing encounter with the living Christ. When you have had such an experience you will be like the apostle John, hardly able to contain yourself as you rush out to tell others of your amazing encounter with God. Your responsibility will not be to convince others of the reality of God, but simply to bear witness to what your Lord has said and done for you. The change in your life will be your greatest testimony of your relationship to Christ. There is nothing more appealing or convincing to a watching world than to hear the testimony of someone who has just been with Jesus.

He Spared Not
His Own Son

*He who did not spare His own Son, but delivered Him
up for us all, how shall He not with Him
also freely give us all things?*

ROMANS 8:32

If you ever feel that you are so insignificant that God does
not care about you or that He does not want to listen to
your prayers, you will be encouraged by Romans 8:32. There,
you are assured that your heavenly Father loves you unconditionally. There was nothing so precious to Him that He would
not give it up in order to provide for your salvation. When the
Father gave His precious Son to save you, He proved once for all
that His love is boundless.

The apostle Paul concluded that if God would not spare His
own Son in order to provide for our salvation, how would He not
willingly give anything else at His disposal in order to care for us?
He sacrificed so much to give us eternal life that we can rest
secure in the knowledge that He also wants to give us abundant
life (John 10:10).

In light of what God did for us at the cross, should we not
approach the throne of grace with confidence? God's response to
our prayers is not based upon our worthiness but upon His love
and grace. Our confidence in prayer comes not from who we are
but from who He is. Nothing we could ask of Him could ever
compare with the price He paid for us at the cross.

How wonderful to know that God loves us so much! We can
live with confidence and anticipation knowing that almighty God
is willing not only to give us eternal life, but also to help us experience it fully!

He Made Him to Be Sin

For He made Him who knew no sin to be sin for us,
that we might become the righteousness of God in Him.

2 CORINTHIANS 5:21

This verse should startle us and cause us to tremble. It is not a verse to be read quickly and passed over. As Christians we are grateful to be forgiven of our sins. We are thankful we have been adopted as God's children. Yet we will never comprehend the awesome price that Jesus paid to cleanse us of our sin and to give us His righteousness. How abhorrent was it for the sinless Son of God to have every sin of humanity placed upon Him? What love was required for the Father to watch His only Son bear the excruciating pain of our sin upon the cross?

The prophet Isaiah summarized the human condition: "We are all like an unclean thing, / And all our righteousnesses are like filthy rags" (Isa. 64:6). Even the high priest, Joshua, in his exalted position among God's people, was clothed in filthy rags before God (Zech. 3:3). The apostle Paul, who labored arduously to be righteous before God, realized that his most strenuous efforts to please God were no more valuable than rubbish (Phil. 3:4–10). The plight of humanity is that nothing we could ever do could satisfy God's desire for righteousness. But the miracle of God's mercy is that God exchanges our "filthy rags" for "rich robes" of righteousness (Zech. 3:4).

In this awesome exchange, God placed the sin of humanity upon His righteous Son. Jesus became so identified with our sin that Scripture says God made Him to be sin on our behalf. The holy Son of God could not possibly do more for us than this! Experiencing the Father's wrath upon the sin He carried would have been more painful to endure than any human rejection or physical suffering.

Never take the righteousness God has given you for granted. Never take the forgiveness of your sin lightly. It cost God a terrible price in order to forgive you and make you righteous. Walk in a manner worthy of the righteousness He has given you.

Changed through Meditation

But his delight is in the law of the Lord,
And in His law he meditates day and night.

PSALM 1:2

Meditation means "to think deeply and continuously about something." For a Christian, this means remaining in the presence of God and pondering each truth He reveals about Himself until it becomes real and personal in your life. This takes time. In His Sermon on the Mount, Jesus accused certain would-be followers of calling Him "Lord" and yet never doing what He told them (Luke 6:46). They had the correct truth in their heads, but it had never translated into obedience. When you meditate on Scriptures, the truth moves from your head to your heart and results in obedience. As the psalmist said: "Your word have I hidden in my heart, / That I might not sin against You" (Ps. 119:11).

When you know God's Word in your mind but not in your heart, it means that you have learned the principles and concepts and doctrines of God, but you have not come to know Jesus personally. You can reject a doctrine, or ignore a concept, or challenge a principle, but it is much more difficult to ignore a Person. You can have Scripture in your mind and still sin against God. There are those who can recite long passages of Scripture and yet live ungodly lives. However, you cannot have Scripture fill your heart and continue to sin against God. When God's truth is allowed to touch the deepest corner of your soul, the Holy Spirit will transform you into the image of Jesus Christ. Don't just read your Bible; *meditate* on God's Word and ask Him to change your heart.

98

Infinite Treasure

But we have this treasure in earthen vessels, that the
excellence of the power may be of God and not of us.

2 CORINTHIANS 4:7

Knowing God and having Him reside within you is a treasure of infinite value. Jesus likened this value to that of a
perfect pearl. The collector would readily sell everything he had
in order to possess this one matchless pearl (Matt. 13:45–46).
Your relationship with God places an immeasurable value on your
life. The treasures of God's wisdom and knowledge are available
to you through Christ (Col. 2:2–3). His love now fills you. His
incomprehensible peace surrounds your heart and mind (Phil. 4:7).
When Jesus dwells in your life, everything available to Christ
dwells within you (Eph. 3:19).

Paul was comparing our lives with the clay pots commonly
used in his day. The contents of the earthen vessels, not the con-
tainers themselves, were of great value. The jars would become
chipped and broken and would deteriorate over time, but
nobody thought of the jar—they were interested in its contents.
Paul noted that our great possession is that which God has placed
within us. When people focus on us they see a frail, imperfect,
and deteriorating vessel. Nothing that comes from our flesh is
worthy of praise. Our bodies are aging and losing strength
(2 Cor. 4:16). Only as we allow God to fill us and renew our
inner self will people see a treasure of immeasurable worth.

Don't focus on outward appearances and physical strength, for
these deteriorate. Rather, allow the Holy Spirit to convince you of
the infinite treasure that is within you because of God's presence.

Faithful in a Little

*"He who is faithful in what is least is faithful also in much;
and he who is unjust in what is least is unjust also in much."*

LUKE 16:10

God rewards those who are faithful. Throughout your life God will seek to grow you in your faith. He will continually bring you to times when you must trust Him. He will lead you into situations that require a "little" faith, and if you are faithful, He will then take you into situations that require even greater trust in Him. Each time you are able to trust God at a higher level, God will reveal more of Himself to you. Your faith and experiencing God are directly linked.

The best way to tell if you are prepared for a greater revelation of God is to see how faithful you have been with what God has given you. This is a foundational principle in God's relationships with us: If you have been faithful with the little He has given you, you are ready to be entrusted with more. If you failed to trust God with the little He gave you, He will not trust you with more. God will not lead you beyond your present level of trust and obedience to Him. He will return you to your area of unfaithfulness until you are prepared to trust Him. The children of Israel were unwilling to trust God to lead them into the Promised Land, and their generation never again was able to move forward with Him.

You stand at an exciting new door of opportunity to know God more intimately every time you believe Him. Every step of faith leads you to a deeper relationship of faith with Him. It is an open invitation to know God more intimately.

Where Is Death's Sting?

O Death, where is your sting?
O Hades, where is your victory?

1 CORINTHIANS 15:55

O ver the centuries, death has been our relentless and unyielding enemy. No one, regardless of worldly rank, strength, or wealth has been able to escape death. As soon as we are born, death becomes our destiny. Many have tried, but no one has developed an antidote for death.

The reality of the resurrection is that death has been defeated! It is no longer the impregnable enemy, for Christ marched through the gates of Hades and claimed decisive victory over death. He conquered death completely; now He assures His followers that we, too, will share in His victory. Christians need not fear death. Christ has gone before us and will take us to join Him in heaven. Death frees us to experience the glorious, heavenly presence of God. No illness can defeat us. No disaster can rob us of eternal life. Death can temporarily remove us from those we love, but it transfers us into the presence of the One who loves us most. God's glory is His presence. Death, our greatest enemy, is nothing more than the vehicle that enables believers to experience God's glory!

Do not allow a fear of death to prevent you from experiencing a full and abundant life. Death cannot rob you of the eternal life that is your inheritance as a child of God. Jesus has prepared a place for you in heaven that surpasses your imagination (John 14:1–4). Death will one day be the door by which you gain access to all that is yours in heaven.

Choices

*But when the young man heard that saying
he went away sorrowful, for he had great possessions.*

MATTHEW 19:22

Your life is the sum of the responses you have made toward God. Once God makes Himself known to you, what you do next is your decision. Your reaction reflects what you believe about Him. The rich, young ruler lived a moral life. He was well versed in Scripture and the laws of God. But his response to Jesus' invitation clearly showed that, although he possessed a head knowledge of the teachings of God, he did not know God in an experiential way that could be demonstrated by a response of faith (Matt. 19:16–22).

Whenever the Lord speaks to you, it will require an adjustment in your life. This truth can dramatically affect your prayer life. Every time you pray you must be aware that if God answers your prayer and reveals His will to you, it will immediately require you to reorient your life. Each time you read your Bible, you must be prepared to obey what God tells you.

Why did God use Peter and James and John so significantly to turn their world upside down? And why were others, like the rich, young ruler, never heard from again? Choices! The disciples chose to believe, and their belief was proven by their obedience. The rich, young ruler could not bring himself to obey, and Scripture tells us that he "went away sorrowful." You are faced with the same question as the rich, young ruler. What adjustments are you willing to make in order to respond positively to Christ?

Truth Is a Person

And they came to Him and awoke Him, saying, "Master, Master, we are perishing!" Then He arose and rebuked the wind and the raging of the water. And they ceased, and there was a calm. But He said to them, "Where is your faith?"

LUKE 8:24–25

Truth is a Person, not a concept. Jesus said He was the Truth (John 14:6). That means that you can never know the truth of your circumstances unless you have first heard from Jesus. The disciples thought they were perishing in the storm. They were fishermen who knew the sea and knew what their condition was. They had allowed their circumstances to convince them that the "truth" was their imminent death. But they were wrong. Truth was asleep in the back of their boat!

Since some of the disciples were fishermen, they trusted in their own expertise and wisdom rather than recognizing that only Jesus knew the truth of their situation. At times, our human knowledge in certain areas of life can blind us to our desperate need to hear a word from Truth.

When Jesus spoke, the disciples saw the real truth of their situation. There was absolute calm. The disciples had seen Jesus perform other miracles, but they had not yet witnessed His power over nature in such a dimension. Often we are like the disciples. God may have recently demonstrated His power to us in a mighty way; we may have experienced many spiritual victories in the past. Yet, when a new and frightening situation comes upon us we, too, panic and say, "Lord save me. I'm perishing!" God will remind us of His provision, saying, "I can handle this situation, too, and you will know more of Me because of it."

Have you become fearful instead of faithful? If you have, prepare for the rebuke, for it will come.

God's Thinking Is Not Man's Thinking

Beware lest anyone cheat you through philosophy and empty deceit, according to the tradition of men, according to the basic principles of the world, and not according to Christ.

COLOSSIANS 2:8

There is a subtle temptation that encourages Christians to be "practical." That is, they try to do God's work in man's way. "Getting results" becomes the primary focus. It almost seems that we believe that the end justifies the means. Don't be led away by the world's reasoning. An examination of God's Word shows that the means are sometimes even more important than the results. The world tries to convince you that as long as you can accomplish something for the kingdom of God, that's all that matters. For example, Ananias and Sapphira gave an offering to their church, which was a good thing, but they did it deceitfully. God judged them immediately, not for what they did, but for how they did it (Acts 5:1–11).

Satan tried to trap Jesus with this same temptation. Satan did not question the worthiness of Jesus' task, but simply offered "practical" solutions to accomplish Jesus' goal more quickly and at lesser cost. God's ways are not like man's ways. "Efficiency" from man's perspective is not prized by God. It did not seem efficient to have the children of Israel march around Jericho thirteen times and then blow their trumpets, but it brought the walls down (Josh. 6). It did not appear wise to select the youngest of Jesse's sons to become the next king, but God saw a man after His own heart (1 Sam. 16:11). At first glance, it does not seem logical for Jesus to have picked the twelve disciples He did, yet through them God dramatically affected their world.

It is never wise to attempt to do God's work in man's way. It is an age-old temptation that seems to make sense on the surface but often is at variance with the purposes of God.

Calling Down Fire

*And when His disciples James and John saw this, they said,
"Lord, do You want us to command fire to come down from
heaven and consume them, just as Elijah did?"*

LUKE 9:54

ames and John were called the "Sons of Thunder." When they discovered a Samaritan village that would not receive Jesus, they were fully prepared to call down fire to consume the entire community! Perhaps they felt that through such a show of power, their gospel message might be enhanced. The two brothers were willing to sacrifice the lives of the villagers in order to further the cause of the gospel. Jesus rebuked them.

Later, the apostles heard that Samaria had responded to the gospel (Acts 8:14). Who was commissioned to go and help them receive the Holy Spirit but Peter and John! God's purpose had not been to destroy those people but to save them. God chose not to rain down fire on the village, but to shower it with His Holy Spirit. What must have gone through John's mind as he saw those same people, whom he had been ready to destroy, now rejoicing in their salvation? How grateful he must have been that Jesus had prevented him from carrying out his plans!

What an enormous contrast between man's thinking and God's! Man's thinking would have resulted in the destruction of an entire village. God's plan brought salvation to it. People will benefit far more from what God wants to give them than from your best plans. Have you been shortchanging the people around you by merely giving them your plans instead of God's?

Why Are You Weeping?

Then they said to her,
"Woman, why are you weeping?"
JOHN 20:13

Mary Magdalene could vividly remember the day Jesus delivered her from her demonic bondage. She became His devoted follower that day (Luke 8:2). She watched Him heal the sick and teach people about God's love. Her life was transformed as she experienced the joy of being with Jesus.

Then her world seemed to fall apart! Her Lord was arrested and brutally murdered. The crowds that had shouted "Hosanna!" at the beginning of the week cried "Crucify him!" by week's end. A final blow came when she went to anoint Jesus' body at the tomb. She saw that His tomb was empty. Someone had apparently stolen His body. As she sobbed in despair, angels asked the poignant question, "Why are you weeping?" She was standing before an empty tomb! Jesus had risen, just as He had promised! Knowing that Jesus was alive put everything back into perspective, and Mary joyfully raced to share the good news with others.

The Christian life is not always easy. There are joyful moments of walking with Jesus, but there are also times when nothing makes sense and when your world seems to be crumbling. The world will mock your Lord, and you may grow discouraged. At those times, you need to peer into the empty tomb. It is the abandoned tomb that gives you hope, for it symbolizes the life that is yours from your risen Lord. The empty tomb promises that nothing, not even death itself, can defeat the purposes of your Lord. Are you weeping beside an empty tomb?

Help My Unbelief!

*Immediately the father of the child cried out and
said with tears, "Lord, I believe; help my unbelief!"*

MARK 9:24

Faith does not come from ignorance. Faith is based on what we know.

Before we will trust others with something precious to us, we first try to find out if they are trustworthy. This father was asking that he might come to know God in such a dimension that he could trust Him to cure his son.

His son had been possessed by an evil spirit since early childhood. The father did not know Jesus well, but he had heard and seen enough to convince him that if there was any hope for his son, it lay with Jesus. In desperation he cried out to Jesus for help. Jesus' response was to heal his son. The desperate father had correctly gone to Jesus with his problem even though he was struggling with his faith.

When you are struggling to believe, that is not the time to avoid Christ or to be ashamed of your struggle. You will never increase your faith by not going to Jesus! Rather, Jesus wants to help you with your belief. He can not only meet your need, but He will also give you faith to trust Him to provide for you.

If you are struggling to believe that God can take care of your need, it is because you don't know Him as He wants you to. Go to Him and allow Him to convince you of His ability to meet every need you will ever face.

No One Can Prevent You

But Joshua the son of Nun and Caleb the son of Jephunneh remained alive, of the men who went to spy out the land.

NUMBERS 14:38

The decisions and disobedience of others will not cancel God's will for you. Other people's actions will affect you, but no one can prevent what God wants to do in and through you. Joshua and Caleb trusted God and yet were forced to wander in a wilderness for forty years because of the fear and disbelief of others.

Have you ever felt that someone was thwarting God's will for you? Perhaps someone kept you from getting a job or earning a promotion. Perhaps the government would not approve your application or a committee disagreed with your recommendation. Do you believe that mere man can stop God from accomplishing His purposes in your life?

God did everything He intended to do in the lives of Joshua and Caleb. His primary assignment for them had not been to enter the Promised Land but rather to serve as godly leaders for their people. Joshua and Caleb could not lead the people if they were in the Promised Land by themselves while the people were still wandering in the wilderness! God kept these leaders in a position where they could exert a godly influence upon their nation, and, as a result, they became models of spiritual leadership for generations to come. Even so, God ultimately brought Caleb and Joshua into the Promised Land just as He had said. They had been delayed but not thwarted. Be assured of this: No one can hinder God from carrying out His plans for your life. Once God sets something in motion, no one can stop it (Isa. 46:11).

Acts 5: 39

The God of Second Chances

But go, tell His disciples—and Peter—that He
is going before you into Galilee; there you will see Him,
as He said to you.

MARK 16:7

oes God give second chances to those who have failed Him? He certainly did so for Peter. Peter had proudly announced that he was Jesus' most reliable disciple (Matt. 26:33). Yet Peter not only fled with the other disciples in the moment of crisis, but also blatantly denied he even knew Jesus (Matt. 26:69–75). Peter failed so miserably that he went out into the night and wept bitterly (Luke 22:62).

How compassionate the risen Christ was to Peter! The angel gave the women at the tomb special instructions to let Peter know that He was risen. Jesus took Peter aside to allow him the opportunity to reaffirm his love and commitment (John 21:15–17). The risen Lord also chose Peter as His primary spokesman on the day of Pentecost, when three thousand people were added to the church.

God's desire is to take you from where you are and bring you to where He wants you to be. When He found His defeated followers hiding together in an upper room, Jesus' first word was "peace" (John 20:19). Jesus' first words to you after you fail may also be "peace." Jesus will find you in despair and bring you peace. Then, He will reorient you to Himself so that you can believe Him and follow Him. Don't give up if you have failed your Lord. Remember what happened to Peter. God has not yet finished developing you as a disciple.

Knowing Christ

"You search the Scriptures, for in them you think you have
eternal life; and these are they which testify of Me. But you
are not willing to come to Me that you may have life."

JOHN 5:39–40

B ible study will not give you eternal life. You could memorize the entire Bible and be able to discuss minute issues
of biblical scholarship and yet fail to experience the truths found
in its pages. It is a subtle temptation to prefer the book to the
Author. A book will not confront you about your sin; the Author
will. Books can be ignored; it is much harder to avoid the Author
when He is seeking a relationship with you.

The Pharisees in Jesus' day thought God would be pleased
with their knowledge of His Word. They could quote long, complicated passages of Scripture. They loved to recite and study
God's Law for hours on end. Yet Jesus condemned them because,
although they knew the Scriptures, they did not know God. They
were proud of their Bible knowledge, but they rejected the invitation to know God's Son.

Can you imagine yourself knowing all that God has promised
to do in your life but then turning to something else instead? You
may be tempted to turn to substitutes. These substitutes aren't
necessarily bad things. They might include serving in the church,
doing good deeds, or reading Christian books. No amount of
Christian activity will ever replace your relationship with Jesus.
The apostle Paul considered every "good" thing he had ever
done to be "rubbish" when compared to the surpassing value of
knowing Christ (Phil. 3:8). Never become satisfied with religious
activity rather than a personal, vibrant, and growing relationship
with Jesus Christ.

Anointing Jesus' Feet

Then Mary took a pound of very costly oil of spikenard,
anointed the feet of Jesus, and wiped His feet with her hair.
And the house was filled with the fragrance of the oil.

JOHN 12:3

M ary seemed drawn to the feet of Jesus. It is not surprising that of all those who followed Jesus, Mary was the one to anoint His feet. The disciples would have their opportunity to show the same love, but pride would prevent them (John 13:12–13). Martha, too, was prone toward acts of service, but she had developed a different kind of relationship with Jesus than Mary had. While Martha had labored on Jesus' behalf in the kitchen, Mary had joyfully sat at Jesus' feet and listened to Him teach (Luke 10:38–42). Because Mary had come to know and love Jesus in this way, she was ready to humble herself and offer this poignant expression of love to Him. Such depth and sincerity of love comes only through spending time in close fellowship with Jesus.

The way we express our love for Jesus depends on the kind of relationship we have developed with Him. Our love for Him will not grow unless we spend time with Him, listen to His voice, and experience His love for us. If we find that our love for Jesus has waned or that we struggle to serve Him, it is a clear sign that we must take time to sit at His feet. We may have been involved in Christian activity on His behalf and yet neglected our relationship with Him. After we have spent time in intimate fellowship with our Lord, and after we have heard His voice and received His love, we will be prepared to serve Him, even laying down our life for Him if that is what He asks.

Beware of the Amalekites!

For he said, "Because the Lord has sworn: the Lord will have war with Amalek from generation to generation."

EXODUS 17:16

The Amalekites were the persistent and relentless enemies of the Israelites. When the Israelites sought to enter the Promised Land, the Amalekites stood in their way (Exod. 17:8–16). Once the Israelites were in the Promised Land and seeking to enjoy what God had given them, the Amalekites joined the Midianites to torment the Hebrews in the days of Gideon (Judg. 6:3). It was an Amalekite that caused the downfall of King Saul (1 Sam. 15:9, 28). The Amalekites continually sought to hinder the progress of God's people and to rob them of God's blessing. Thus God swore His enmity against them for eternity.

As you move forward in your pilgrimage with the Lord, there will be "Amalekites" that will seek to distract and defeat you. God is determined to remove anything that keeps you from experiencing Him to the fullest. If your commitment to your job is keeping you from obedience to Him, God will declare war against it. If a relationship, materialism, or a destructive activity is keeping you from obeying God's will, He will wage relentless war against it. There is nothing so precious to you that God will not be its avowed enemy if it keeps you from His will for your life. King Saul mistakenly thought he could associate with Amalekites and still fulfill the will of the Lord (1 Sam. 15:8–9). You may also be hesitant to rid yourself of that which causes you to compromise your obedience to God. Don't make the same mistake as King Saul. He did not take the Amalekites seriously enough, and it cost him dearly.

Spiritual Persistence

Then Elijah said to Ahab, "Go up, eat and drink;
for there is the sound of abundance of rain."

1 KINGS 18:41

uccess can distract you as you seek to follow God's will. Elijah's primary assignment was to announce when a drought would begin and end (1 Kings 17:1). God had told him to proclaim to king Ahab that the drought was an act of judgment upon a people who worshiped idols rather than God. In the middle of Elijah's assignment, a spectacular thing happened. Elijah confronted the prophets of Baal and called fire down from heaven, putting hundreds of priests of Baal to death. This was one of the most awesome displays of God's power recorded in Scripture. Elijah could easily have focused strictly on that event. Fire falling from heaven is much more spectacular than a rainstorm!

When something spectacular happens, we can easily be sidetracked. If Elijah lived today, he might have begun a "Calling Down Fire from Heaven" ministry! The dramatic is far more appealing to us than obedience to the mundane. Destroying hundreds of Baal's prophets would appear to be a climactic victory for any prophet of God. Yet Elijah persisted in his assignment. He announced the coming rain. This had been his primary message, and he delivered it.

If you aren't careful, you may become so distracted by the successes you experience that you never complete what God originally assigned you to do. Will your success today cause you to disobey tomorrow?

Living Water

For My people have committed two evils:
They have forsaken Me, the fountain of living waters,
And hewn themselves cisterns—broken cisterns that can hold no water.

JEREMIAH 2:13

There should never be "dry spells" in the Christian life. God said that He would be like an artesian well in the life of a believer. Artesian wells bubbled forth with a cold, fresh, never-ending supply of water from the depths of the earth, quenching any thirst and always satisfying. This is the picture of the spiritual refreshment that belongs to the person in whom the Holy Spirit resides.

Have you ever heard people say they are experiencing a dry spell in their Christian life? What are they saying? Are they saying that the Lord ran out of water? It should never cross your mind that the fountain of living waters residing within you should ever be reduced to a trickle. You don't need to run all over the country trying to find sources of spiritual refreshment. Conferences, retreats, and books can all bring encouragement; but if you are a Christian, the source of living water already resides within you.

Have you exchanged the living fountain for man-made cisterns that cannot hold water? Why would you exchange an artesian well for a broken water tank? Artesian wells do not dry up. Broken cisterns do. If you are experiencing spiritual dryness right now, is it because you have been attempting to find your source of spiritual refreshment from man-made sources, which will fail you every time? Jesus extended an invitation to you when He said: "If anyone thirsts, let him come to Me and drink" (John 7:37). Have you been refreshed by the living water only Jesus can provide?

Spiritual Bread

*And Jesus said to them, "I am the bread of life.
He who comes to Me shall never hunger,
and he who believes in Me shall never thirst."*

JOHN 6:35

We know how to use physical bread. Whenever we are hungry we simply go and eat. Do we do that spiritually? Jesus said if we believe in Him, we will never be spiritually hungry or malnourished, for He is the "bread of life." Every time we face a spiritual need, it is a simple matter of going to Christ and allowing Him to provide us with what we need.

Our problem is that sometimes we interpret Scripture based on our own experience. We say, "Yes, but I remember a time when I was spiritually hungry." If that is true, then either God did not tell the truth, or we misinterpreted our experience. Could it be that we tried to satisfy our spiritual hunger with human resources? Could it be that we relied so heavily upon friends and the experiences of others that we have never learned how to go to Christ for our own spiritual food? Could it be that we had a great spiritual feast several years ago, and we were so "full" of Christ that we thought we would never have to eat again? We grew lean and hungry because we were still operating on an encounter with God we had years ago. If you are lacking something spiritually, it is not because God does not have an abundance of resources prepared and available for you. It is that you have not come to Him in faith as He invites (John 10:10).

When God gave manna in the wilderness, the children of Israel had to go out each day to receive God's daily provision. Jesus taught His disciples to pray, "Give us this day our daily bread." Spiritual nourishment is something you must seek daily. Have you found spiritual food from Christ today?

Abide in the Vine

*"I am the vine, you are the branches. He who abides in Me,
and I in him, bears much fruit;
for apart from Me you can do nothing."*

JOHN 15:5

There are those who feel that they must be constantly laboring for the Lord in order to meet God's high standards. Jesus gave a clear picture of what our relationship to Him ought to be like. He is the vine, the source of our life. We are the branches, the place where fruit is produced. As we receive life from Christ, the natural, inevitable result is that fruit is produced in our lives.

In our zeal to produce "results" for our Lord, we sometimes become so intent on fruit production that we neglect abiding in Christ. We may feel that "abiding" is not as productive or that it takes too much time away from our fruit production. Yet Jesus said that it is not our *activity* that produces fruit, it is our *relationship* with Him.

Jesus gave an important warning to His disciples. He cautioned that if they ever attempted to live their Christian life apart from an intimate relationship with Him, they would discover that they ceased to produce any significant results. They might exert great effort for the kingdom of God, yet when they stopped to account for their lives, they would find only barrenness. One of the most dramatic acts Jesus ever performed was cursing a fig tree that had failed to produce fruit (Mark 11:14). Are you comfortable in abiding, or are you impatient to be engaged in activity? If you will remain steadfastly in fellowship with Jesus, a great harvest will be the natural by-product.

Contentment

*Not that I speak from want; for I have learned
to be content in whatever circumstances I am.*

PHILIPPIANS 4:11 (NASB)

Our world promotes dissatisfaction with our lives. We are constantly bombarded with newer and better things that will make our lives more complete if only we would obtain them! If we listen to the world, we will always be comparing the lifestyles and possessions of others with our own, and we will always be dissatisfied. If our contentment comes from possessions, activities, or other people, these can be altered or removed. If our contentment comes from our relationship with Christ, there is absolutely nothing that can take that away.

Paul had enjoyed power and status among his people. He had also been imprisoned and bound in stocks in the depths of a jail cell. He had stood before a king and been stoned almost to death by an angry mob. Paul had enjoyed the benefits and pleasures of life, yet he could give them all up and still be filled with the joy of the Lord. His contentment did not depend on his environment but on his relationship with Christ.

Contentment frees you to enjoy every good thing God has given you. Contentment demonstrates your belief that God loves you and has your best interest in mind. Discontent stems from the sin of ingratitude and a lack of faith that God loves you enough to provide for all that you need. Strive to be grateful for all that God has given you. A grateful heart has no room for envy.

The Way

*Jesus said to him, "I am the way, the truth, and the life.
No one comes to the Father except through Me."*

JOHN 14:6

If you are walking daily with the Lord, you will not have to find God's will—you will already be in it. If you are walking with Him in obedience day by day, you will always be in the will of God. The Holy Spirit's role is to guide you step by step to do God's will. Walking closely with God each day guarantees that you will be exactly where He wants you to be. You would have to reject all of the Holy Spirit's activity in your life in order to get out of the will of God.

The disciples never had to ask Jesus where they should go next. They simply looked to see where Jesus was going and stayed close to Him! Jesus was their "way." They didn't need a map as long as they had Jesus. Too often, we would prefer a road map of our future rather than a relationship with the Way. It often seems easier to follow a plan than to cultivate a relationship. We can become more concerned with our future than we are with walking intimately with God today.

Jesus will never give you a substitute for Himself. He is the only way to the Father. That's why it is critical that you clearly know when God is speaking to you (Isa. 30:21). If you are disoriented to how God speaks, you will not understand when He is giving you a new revelation about what He is doing. If you want to know God's will, take time to cultivate your relationship with Jesus and learn to identify His voice. He is more than willing to show you the way.

Jesus Is Your Door

"I am the door. If anyone enters by Me, he will be saved,
and will go in and out and find pasture."

JOHN 10:9

A s Christians, we talk about God "opening doors" to us as a means of His revealing His will. What we are asking God to do is engineer our circumstances to match what we think would be best. The problem is that we misunderstand what the door is. Jesus said *He* is the door. Circumstances are irrelevant, for *no one* can shut the door that Jesus opens (Rev. 3:8). If you have substituted activity for your relationship with Christ, then circumstances can disrupt your activity. When the activity is hindered, you may assume the door has been closed. Yet, if Christ is the door in your life, He will guide you into every experience of Him that He wants, and there will be nothing that people can do to stop Him.

When Paul and Silas were thrown into prison at Philippi, it appeared that the door to their ministry in Greece had been violently and firmly closed (Acts 16:22–24). The reality of their situation, however, was that their Lord had opened a door of ministry to a previously unreached group of men in prison. The Philippian jailer and his household would become a significant nucleus of the new church in Philippi. From a human perspective, a door had been closed; from God's perspective, Paul and Silas continued to minister exactly where God wanted them to.

When people oppose us, we can become discouraged or worry about what others are doing to us. We may even try to take matters into our own hands to accomplish what we think God wants. This reveals that we do not really believe Jesus is the door for our lives. If we did, we would be assured that through Christ we have access to everything He wants to do in and through us.

Christian Discipleship

Him we preach, warning every man and teaching every man in all wisdom, that we may present every man perfect in Christ Jesus.

COLOSSIANS 1:28

Discipleship is personally transferring the full dimensions of your relationship with Christ to the person you are walking with. It is not the imparting of spiritual disciplines as much as it is acquainting another with a Person you love. Paul said that he would teach and urge with all his strength that every person God placed in his life would come to a complete experience of the person of Christ (Col. 1:29). He was not satisfied with people becoming partially like Christ. He would not rest until those around him were perfect, or complete, in Christ. That is, that the fruits of the Spirit were being fully expressed through each life and the character of Christ was reflected in each person (Gal. 5:22).

We can mistake Christian activity with becoming like Christ. Christian activity and Christlikeness are not the same things. We must not assume that because our friend attends church and reads her Bible, she is growing as a Christian.

Christian activities are an important express of your relationship with Christ. They can lead you to a relationship, but the danger is assuming that your religious activity is the relationship. If you are only encouraging those around you to attend Christian activities, then you have not "discipled" them the way Paul did. You do your fellow Christians an injustice by teaching them that Christian activity is equal to Christian maturity. Do not rest until those around you have become "perfect" in Christ. If God has put new Christians under your care, you have an obligation to "stay with them" until they have reached Christian maturity.

Suffering for Others

*I now rejoice in my sufferings for you, and fill up
in my flesh what is lacking in the afflictions of Christ,
for the sake of His body, which is the church.*

COLOSSIANS 1:24

Ministry is costly. When the heavenly Father wanted to save His creation from sin, He could find no other way except the sacrifice of His Son (Rom. 5:8). Scripture gives a stark picture of the price our Savior paid to obtain our salvation: "He is despised and rejected by men, / A Man of sorrows and acquainted with grief" (Isa. 53:3). If Christ is your model for ministry, you cannot avoid going to the cross for the sake of others. Salvation comes with a great price, and if we are going to "take up our cross" and follow Jesus, then we must be prepared to go with Him to the place of suffering if that's what it takes to bring salvation to those around us.

If our goal is to bring others to Christ we must be willing, as He was, to r.   jection. People may disappoint us, misunderstand our motives, even despise and persecute us. Our Savior did not let suffering prevent Him from being used by God to bring salvation to those He loved. Love for His Father provided all the motivation that was necessary. Are you presently experiencing hardship because of the ministry to which God has called you? Have you begun to wonder if the price you are paying is too great? Take a moment to reflect on the price God was willing to pay in order to bring salvation to you. Are you glad He was willing to do what was necessary? Will you no.   Him in whatever is necessary to bring salvation to those around you?

For the Lord, Not Men

And whatever you do, do it heartily,
as to the Lord and not to men.

COLOSSIANS 3:23

There is an important difference between doing something for people and doing something for God. God always deserves our best effort. People will disappoint us, betray us, neglect us, and mistreat us. Some will constantly ask for what we can give while offering nothing in return. From our human perspective, these people deserve our minimal effort at best. What then should motivate us to serve people, except our love for God? God deserves our love, and He demands that we love others in the same way He does. We are to love our spouses, not as they deserve, but as God commands (Eph. 5:22–33). We are to treat our friends, not as they treat us, but as Christ loves us (John 13:14). We are to labor at our jobs, not in proportion to the way our employer treats us, but according to the way God treats us. God is the One we serve (Eph. 6:5).

Mediocrity and laziness have no place in the Christian's life. Christians must maintain integrity at home and in the workplace. Working for God, as opposed to working for other people, changes our perspective as we view our endeavors in light of what He has done for us. Our toil then becomes an offering to God. We not only worship God at church on Sunday, but our labor throughout the week is an offering of worship and thanksgiving to the One who has given us everything we have. When people do not measure up to our expectations and we feel our efforts are being wasted, we must keep in mind that we are toiling for holy God. He is worthy of our best effort.

God's Complete Protection

"While I was with them in the world, I kept them in Your name. Those whom You gave Me I have kept; and none of them is lost except the son of perdition, that the Scripture might be fulfilled."

JOHN 17:12

Nothing that Satan can do to you should cause you to fear (2 Tim. 1:7). Jesus chose the twelve disciples the Father had given Him and then jealously guarded them from the evil one. Jesus sent His disciples into the world where they experienced difficult and dangerous circumstances, but He interceded on their behalf with His Father that they would have His strong protection from the evil one (John 17:15).

In the same way, Jesus said that we, as His sheep, are held securely in the Father's strong hand (John 10:28). There is no better place to be than safely in the hand of almighty God. Do you believe this, or are you fearful of what Satan or people can do to you? The apostle John encourages us that we do not need to fear: "He who is in you is greater than he who is in the world" (1 John 4:4). This is not merely a theological concept but a profound reality in which you can have absolute confidence. It is not just a truth for meditation in the security of your home; it is a promise you can cling to in the midst of a hostile and menacing world.

What you do reveals what you believe. If you are living a fearful, anxiety-filled life, you are proving your lack of confidence in God's protection, regardless of what you may say. Live your life with confidence that Jesus is continually interceding with the Father on your behalf. If you trust Him completely, you will have nothing to fear.

The Joy of Christ

"But now I come to You, and these things I speak in the world, that they may have My joy fulfilled in themselves."

JOHN 17:13

If there is anything that ought to characterize the life of a Christian, it is joy! Jesus spoke many times to His disciples about His joy being complete and full in them. His disciples were filled with joy as they realized who they were: children of God and joint heirs with Christ (Rom. 8:16–17). They had been dead in their sins but were now made alive in Christ (Rom. 6:4). They had once been helpless victims of death, but now death had no hold over them (1 Cor. 15:55–58). With such a marvelous salvation experience with Christ, how could the disciples be anything less than joyful?

Don't deny yourself that which is your birthright as a child of God. Don't be satisfied with a joyless life. There ought to be in every Christian a deep, settled fullness of the joy of Christ that no circumstance of life can dispel. This comes as you allow the Holy Spirit to express Himself in your life. One of the fruits of the Spirit is joy (Gal. 5:22). This joy is unlike any happiness that is produced by the world. It fills you and permeates everything you do.

Jesus did not pray that you would merely be happy or even that you would escape grief. He prayed that you would have the same joy that the Father had given Him: a divine joy, a joy that comes from a deep and unwavering relationship with the Father. It is a joy that is grounded so firmly in a relationship with God that no change in circumstances could ever shake it. This is the kind of joy that Christ is praying will be in you.

God Brings You to Himself

You have seen what I did to the Egyptians, and how I bore
you on eagles' wings and brought you to Myself.

EXODUS 19:4

God did not deliver the children of Israel out of Egypt so that they could enjoy the Promised Land. He freed them from their bondage so they could come to know and worship Him. Three months after they left Egypt, God reminded His people why He had delivered them "on eagles' wings." It was to bring the people to *Himself*. That is, God saved them so that they could enjoy intimate fellowship with Him. The Israelites had been slaves with no freedom to worship God. Now, with their own land, they could come to know and serve God freely. God's call was not to destroy the idolatrous nations in Canaan, not to settle the lands they conquered, and not to establish a new nation, although all of these would be accomplished. Rather, God called them primarily to be a people who loved and worshiped Him. Through God's act of deliverance they came to know Him as an almighty and compassionate God, and they were now free to respond to Him.

We are so activity oriented that we assume we were saved for a task we are to perform rather than for a relationship to enjoy. God uses our activities and circumstances to bring us to Himself. When He gives us a God-sized assignment, its sheer impossibility brings us back to Him for His enabling. When God allows us to go through crises, it brings us closer to Him.

If we are not careful, we can inadvertently bypass the relationship in order to get on with the activity. When you are busy in your activity for God, remember that God leads you to the experiences in order to bring you to Himself.

I AM

And God said to Moses, "I AM WHO I AM." And He said, "Thus you shall say to the children of Israel, 'I AM has sent me to you.'"

EXODUS 3:14

hen Moses encountered God in the burning bush, he still had much to learn about his Lord. Moses was impressed with the miracle before him (Exod. 3:3). However, it would take much more than a burning bush to lead Israel out of captivity from the most powerful nation of Moses' day. Would the same God who could cause a bush to burn without being consumed also be able to do what was necessary to deliver a multitude?

God's answer was, "I AM!" That is, "Moses, I'll be whatever you need Me to be as you carry out my assignment. If you need miraculous signs in order to convince Pharaoh, then that is how I will express Myself. If you need Me to interrupt nature and part the waters of the Red Sea, then I will demonstrate Myself in that way. If you require food and water, then I will be your provider. If you are afraid, I'll be your strength."

At the beginning of Moses' walk with the Lord, Moses had no idea all that he would need God to do for him. Yet each time Moses faced a need, He learned something new about God. Moses came to realize that there was much more to God than a burning bush. What if Moses was so enamored with his experience at the bush that he built a tabernacle on the spot and established "The Church of the Burning Bush"? He would have missed out on so much more that God wanted to reveal to him!

Think back to your understanding of God when you first began walking with Him. How have your experiences expanded your knowledge of Him?

Comfortable in Our Bondage

And they said to them, "Let the Lord look on you and judge,
because you have made us abhorrent in the sight of Pharaoh
and in the sight of his servants, to put a
sword in their hand to kill us."

EXODUS 5:21

It is possible for people to become so accustomed to their bondage that they resist efforts to free them. The Hebrews had been slaves in Egypt for four hundred years. Slavery meant that they were not free to do God's will or to go where they wanted. Moses had come to tell the Israelites how they could experience freedom, yet they were more concerned about the reaction of their taskmasters than they were about pleasing God. For them to be free would mean that the pharaoh they were serving would be angry! It would mean that the Egyptians they had served all their lives might attack them. Freedom from their slavery did not seem to be worth the hardships they would inevitably endure.

When God sets out to free us, there will often be a price we will have to pay. Grief can be a terrible form of bondage, yet we can become comfortable with it. We can grow so comfortable with fear that we don't know how to live without it. As destructive as our sinful habits and lifestyle might be, we may prefer living with the familiar, rather than being freed to experience the unknown. We may recognize the harmful influence of a friend but choose to reject God's will rather than offend our friend.

As incredible as it seems, the Israelites were angry at Moses for disrupting the life of slavery to which they had grown accustomed. Have you been lulled into a comfortable relationship with your bondage? Do you fear change more than you fear God? Are you willing to allow God to do what is necessary in order to free you?

Go up and Possess It

*Look, the Lord your God has set the land before you; go up
and possess it, as the Lord God of your fathers has
spoken to you; do not fear or be discouraged.*

DEUTERONOMY 1:21

One of the paradoxes of the Christian life is that God's gifts often require labor on our part. God brought the Israelites to the Promised Land and told them He was going to "give" it to them (Num. 13:2). The gift of the Promised Land sounded great to the Israelites until they realized that, with the gift, came battles against giants and fortified cities! Perhaps they assumed God was going to obliterate the inhabitants of the land before they entered. Ideally for the Israelites, they could then have entered a vacant land with houses and cities already built and ready to inhabit.

Instead, God said they would have to fight for it. They would not have to fight in their own strength, however; God would be present to fight for them. God would bring down the walls of cities, give them strategies to defeat their enemies, and empower their warriors to fight. The Israelites would have a divine advantage over anyone they fought, but they would still have to fight.

It would be wonderful if, when we become Christians, God would fill our minds with a complete knowledge of the Bible and with Bible verses already memorized. It would be easy if God would instill in us a delight in spending hours in prayer each day and a fearless desire to share our faith with others. But God doesn't relate to us that way. Instead, He gives us the free gift of His salvation and then tells us to "work out" our salvation in fear and trembling (Phil. 2:12b). Are you discouraged because the Christian life is more difficult and challenging than you expected? Don't be. God's gifts to you are perfect because, through them, God makes you perfect as well (Matt. 5:48; James 1:17).

That You May Marvel

"The Son can do nothing of Himself, but what He sees the Father do; for whatever He does, the Son also does in like manner. For the Father loves the Son, and shows Him all things that He Himself does; and He will show Him greater works than these, that you may marvel."

JOHN 5:19–20

Jesus, realizing that His role was that of a servant, never sought to initiate activity for the Father (Matt. 20:28). The servant never sets the agenda—the master does. The servant must be so alert to what the master is doing that whenever the master begins to move in a direction, the servant quickly joins him. Even the Son of God did not assume He knew the best thing to do in a situation. Instead, He looked to see the Father's activity and then joined Him. Jesus knew His Father so well that He was keenly sensitive to divine activity around Him, immediately recognizing His Father at work.

It is possible for us to be so busy trying to bring God into our activity that we don't even notice Him at work around us. He seeks to redirect our attention so that we might join *Him,* but we tend to be self-centered, evaluating everything by how it affects *us.* We must learn to view events around us from God's perspective. Then we will see our world very differently. When God brings someone across our path, we will look to see if God is convicting that person of his need for salvation. Perhaps God is comforting someone in her sorrow. God might be encouraging your friend as she faces a challenge. We will then adjust our lives to join God as He works in that person's life. We ought to live each day with tremendous anticipation as we look to see where God is working around us. As our eyes are opened to His activity, we will marvel at His great works.

Putting Your Brother First

Let no one seek his own, but each one the other's well-being.

1 CORINTHIANS 10:24

As a Christian you are obliged to view your actions in light of how they will affect other Christians. You will discover God's will for your life when you consider His activity in the lives of others. This goes contrary to worldly thinking. The world encourages you to live your own life, taking care of your own needs and wants first. Sin promotes independence. It isolates you from others and separates you from those you could help or who could encourage you. God designed you for interdependence.

Whenever you meet another Christian, you come face to face with Christ (John 13:20). There ought to be a deep respect within you as you encounter other lives guided by the Holy Spirit. Do not live as if you have no responsibility toward your Christian brothers or sisters. God holds you accountable for how you relate to them. Don't revel in your "freedom in Christ" to the point that you neglect your responsibility toward others (Rom. 14:15). Paul celebrated his freedom in Christ, but he was keenly sensitive to what might cause other Christians harm (1 Cor. 8:13). He was aware that his sin could not take place in isolation but could bring pain to many others (1 Cor. 5:6).

You have a responsibility to live in such a way that you do not hurt others. You must deny yourself and allow the Holy Spirit to put to death your natural inclination to be self-centered. As long as you focus on yourself, you will be oblivious to the needs of others. Ask God to free you from selfishness so that your life is free to bless others.

Success without God

*Then he said to Him, "If Your Presence does not go with us,
do not bring us up from here."*

EXODUS 33:15

I t is possible to experience success and yet be void of
God's presence. If success is what is important to you,
you may be tempted to choose accomplishments over your relationship with God. God offered to send an angel with the
Israelites as they entered the Promised Land to ensure their success in every venture. No army could withstand them. No city
wall could stop them. The wealth of the land lay before them.
Everything they had ever dreamed of appeared to be theirs for
the taking. The only thing missing would be the presence of
God. God said they were an obstinate people, and He would not
go with them when their hearts were far from Him.

The Israelites' experience reveals that victory and great accomplishments are not necessarily a sign of God's presence. Do not
assume that your good health, your profitable business, or the
growth of your ministry is due to the presence of God. It may be
that you have inadvertently chosen success over your walk with
the Lord.

Moses wisely concluded that success, no matter how great, is
not a substitute for fellowship with God. Moses knew how quickly worldly achievements could disappear. His security came from
his relationship with God. Success in the world's eyes is not a sign
of God's blessing. It may, in fact, indicate that you have chosen a
substitute for intimate fellowship with God. Would you be satisfied to have success, power, and wealth, but not a relationship
with God? Do you value God's presence in your life more
than the greatest achievements you could experience in
the world?

131

Fix Your Eyes on God

And Moses and Aaron gathered the assembly together before
the rock; and he said to them, "Hear now, you rebels!
Must we bring water for you out of this rock?"

NUMBERS 20:10

It is easy to see why Moses became frustrated with the Hebrew people. They were so hard-hearted and weak in their faith that Moses lost his patience and became angry with them. Yet every time Moses shifted his focus away from God, it cost him. When he sought to help his people by taking matters into his own hands, he spent the next forty years herding sheep in the wilderness (Exod. 2:11–15). This time his impetuous behavior cost him the opportunity to enter the Promised Land (Num. 20:12). In his frustration at the peoples' irreverence, Moses committed the very same sin, blatantly disobeying God's instructions. How did this happen? Moses allowed his attention to shift to the behavior of others rather than focusing on the activity of God.

This could happen to you as well. God has put people around you who need your ministry to them. You will never be able to properly help them, however, unless your primary focus is on God. If you concentrate on people, their weaknesses, their disobedience, their lack of faith, and their stubbornness will quickly frustrate you. You may, like Moses, commit the very sins you are condemning. If, however, your eyes are fixed on holy God, you will become more like Him—gracious, forgiving, long-suffering, and righteous. When a friend's behavior disappoints you, go immediately to the Lord. Seek to discern what God is wanting to do in your friend's life rather than concentrating on your friend's sin. Then you will have the strength, wisdom, and patience you need to help your friend in the way God desires.

Faithful Wounds

Faithful are the wounds of a friend,
But the kisses of an enemy are deceitful.

PROVERBS 27:6

Jesus never gave relief to people who were under conviction. When Zaccheus, in remorse for his sin, shared his generous plans for restitution, Jesus did not say, "Now Zaccheus, the important thing is that you feel sorry for what you did." Jesus brought no comfort to him as he dealt with his sin (Luke 19:1–10). Neither did Jesus excuse disbelief. We never find Jesus saying, "Well, that's all right. I know I'm asking you to believe a lot, and that's not easy." On the contrary, Jesus was quick to chastise His disciples when they failed to believe Him. Jesus loved His friends too much to condone or comfort them in their sin.

It is possible to be too gentle with your friends. When a friend is under deep conviction by the Holy Spirit, do you try to give comfort? Don't ever try to ease the discomfort of someone whom the Holy Spirit is making uncomfortable! Be careful not to communicate to your friends that you find their lack of faith acceptable. You are not acting in true friendship if you condone disobedience or even if you look the other way. Kisses are far more pleasant than wounds, yet they can be even more devastating if they lull your friend into being comfortable with sin.

In our attempt to appease our friends and our reluctance to share a word from God, we can actually cause great harm. If we see our friends in danger and do not warn them, God will hold us accountable for our silence (Ezek. 33:6). Are you a friend of such integrity that you would risk wounding your friends in order to deter them from their sin?

Praying after the High Points

And when He had sent them away,
He departed to the mountain to pray.

MARK 6:46

What do you do after a spiritual victory? Where do you go after reaching a high point in your Christian life? Jesus went to pray. Jesus had just fed a multitude with only five loaves of bread and two fish (Mark 6:34–44). If there were ever a time to relax and bask in the glow of God's power, it should have been then. Instead, Jesus climbed a mountain to pray. When Jesus prayed, the Father clearly revealed His will and His ways to His Son. It eventually dawned on Jesus' disciples that Jesus prepared for every major decision and difficult challenge with a time of prayer (Luke 11:1).

As Jesus prayed on the mountain that day, the Father knew His Son was about to face a fierce storm (Mark 6:48). The disciples raced headlong into the tempest unprepared, but Jesus entered the storm after communing with His Father in prayer. The Father had prepared Jesus for what was coming, and Jesus met the crisis with all the power of God.

It is tempting to relax after a spiritual victory, but a crisis could follow at any time. You must stand guard over your high points. It is at these times when you experience God mightily that you should immediately get alone to pray. Then you will not be caught unprepared when trials come. Have you experienced a spiritual victory? Follow your Lord's example and go immediately to a place of prayer so the Father can prepare you for what is coming.

Servants of Christ

*"So likewise you, when you have done all those things
which you are commanded, say, 'We are unprofitable servants.
We have done what was our duty to do.'"*

LUKE 17:10

The servant carries out the master's will. The servant doesn't
tell the master what to do. The servant does not choose
which tasks to perform for the master, nor does the servant sug-
gest days or times when it would be convenient to serve the master. The servant's function is to follow instructions. The master,
on the other hand, gives directions. The master does not tell the
servant to develop a vision that will guide the master. The master
is the one with the vision; the servant's task is to help fulfill the
master's purposes.

We are the servants; God is the Master. We tend to try to
reverse this! God's revelation of Himself, His purposes, and His
ways depends directly upon our obedience. He may not reveal
today His intentions for the next five years, but He will tell us
what our next step should be. As we respond to God's revelation,
He will accomplish what He desires, and He will be the One who
receives the glory.

Our fulfillment comes from serving our Master.

The world will encourage you to strive for positions of authority and power. God wants you to take the role of a servant. As
God's servant you should have no other agenda than to be obedient to whatever He tells you. God does not need you to dream
great dreams for your life, your family, your business, or your
church. He simply asks for obedience. He has plans that would
dwarf yours in comparison (Eph. 3:20).

Iron Sharpens Iron

As iron sharpens iron,
So a man sharpens the countenance of his friend.

PROVERBS 27:17

The Christian life is a pilgrimage. At times the road is difficult, and we get lonely. Sometimes we may become discouraged and consider abandoning the journey. It is at such times that God will place a friend alongside us. One of God's most precious gifts to us is friends who encourage us and lovingly challenge us to "keep going."

According to Scripture, a friend is one who challenges you to become all that God intends. Jonathan could have succeeded his father to become the next king of Israel. But he loved his friend David, and he encouraged him to follow God's will, even though it meant Jonathan would forfeit his own claim to the throne (1 Sam. 19:1–7).

The mark of biblical friends is that their friendship draws you closer to Christ. They "sharpen" you and motivate you to do what is right. True friends tell you the truth and even risk hurting your feelings because they love you and have your best interests at heart (Prov. 27:6).

Be careful in your choice of friends! Jesus chose His closest friends wisely. He did not look for perfect friends, but friends whose hearts were set to follow God. It is equally important to examine the kind of friend you are to others. As a friend, it is your duty to put the needs of others first (Prov. 17:17). Strive to find godly friends who will challenge you to become the person God desires. When you have found them, be receptive to the way God uses them to help you become spiritually mature. Strive also to *be* the kind of friend that helps others become more like Christ.

Faithful with the Impossible

Then the Lord turned to him and said, "Go in this might of yours, and you shall save Israel from the hand of the Midianites. Have I not sent you?"

JUDGES 6:14

In Gideon's mind, victory over the Midianites was an impossibility, and he was absolutely right! The Midianites, along with their allies, overwhelmed the feeble Hebrews. Yet the moment God told Gideon to fight them, victory was no longer an impossibility!

When Jesus commanded His small group of followers to make disciples of all nations, was that possible (Matt. 28:19)? Certainly, if Jesus said it was! When Jesus told His disciples to love their enemies, was He being realistic? Of course, because He was the One who would achieve reconciliation through them (2 Cor. 5:19–20).

Do you treat commands like these as implausible? Do you modify God's Word to find an interpretation that seems reasonable to you? Don't discount what is possible with God (Phil. 4:13). When God gives an assignment, it is no longer an impossibility, but rather it is an absolute certainty. When God gives you a seemingly impossible task, the only thing preventing it from coming to pass is your disobedience. When God speaks, it can scare you to death! He will lead you to do things that are absolutely impossible in your own strength. But God will grant you victory, step by step, as you obey Him. How do you respond to assignments that seem impossible? Do you write them off as unattainable? Or do you immediately adjust your life to God's revelation, watching with anticipation to see how He will accomplish His purposes through your obedience? God wants to do the impossible through your life. All He requires is your obedience.

Speaking with Authority

*And they were astonished at His teaching, for He taught
them as one having authority, and not as the scribes.*

MARK 1:22

Jesus was not the first person to teach the Scriptures to a
group of disciples. The people in Jesus' day had heard
other teachers of the Scriptures. What set Jesus apart was that He
taught with authority. To many of the scribes, the Scriptures were
meaningless, dry collections of theological speculation, but Jesus
taught them as the living words of God. John the Baptist claimed
that a man could only receive that which had been given to him
by God (John 3:27). When the religious leaders searched the
Scriptures, they came away empty-handed. When Jesus read the
same Scriptures, the Father gave Him a full measure of His wisdom and His authority.

There is a radical difference between practicing religion and
sharing a word directly from the Lord. There is a significant difference between worldly reasoning and counsel that comes straight
from the living Word of God. Is it possible to teach a message from
the Bible but not from the Lord? Yes! The scribes and Pharisees did
this regularly and left their listeners spiritually destitute. Is it possible to counsel someone with advice that seems appropriate and reasonable and yet is contrary to God's Word? Of course!

Whenever you teach, counsel, or share a word of encouragement, be very careful that the words you share are indeed from
the Lord and are not just your own thinking. Otherwise, you
could become a false prophet (Deut. 18:20–22). God promises
to stand by every word He has ever spoken (Isa. 55:10–11).
When you share a word that has come from God, you can do so
with utmost confidence!

The Cost to Others

Now there stood by the cross of Jesus His mother,
and His mother's sister, Mary the wife of Clopas,
and Mary Magdalene.

JOHN 19:25

There is no Christianity without a cross, for you cannot be a disciple of Jesus without taking up your cross. Crosses are painful; they forever change your life. But sometimes the greatest cost will not be to you but to those you love. You may be prepared to obey the Lord's commands, whatever they are, because you've walked with Him and know that His way is best. Yet there will be those close to you who have not related to Jesus in the same way and have not heard His voice as clearly.

Jesus understood that His Father's will for Him led to a cross. The cross would mean a painful death for Jesus, and it would also bring suffering to those closest to Him. Because of the cross, Jesus' mother would watch in agony as her son was publicly humiliated, tortured, and murdered. Jesus' aunt and close friends would witness His excruciating death. His disciples would be scattered in terror and confusion in what would be the longest, darkest night of their lives. Because of Jesus' obedience, there would also be a cross for each of His disciples.

Obedience to your Lord's commands will affect others (Luke 14:26). Don't refuse to obey what you know God is asking because you fear the cost to your family will be too great. Beware lest you seek to prevent those you love from taking up the cross God has for them. Don't ever try to protect those you love by disobeying God. The cost of disobedience is always far greater. Rather, look to Jesus, your model, and see what it cost those around Him for Him to be obedient to His Father.

Making Necessary Adjustments

Oh that my head were waters, And my eyes a fountain of tears,
That I might weep day and night
For the slain of the daughter of my people!

JEREMIAH 9:1

eremiah was invited by God to be a weeping prophet. His call came during turbulent, agonizing times as his society suffered from pervasive moral and spiritual decay. The nation of Judah had turned so far from God that it was soon to face His fierce judgment. This was not a time for merrymaking but for weeping. God looked for someone He could mold into the kind of prophet needed for such a bleak time. He found Jeremiah. The cost to Jeremiah was intense; he sacrificed much of the freedom of his youth in order to be God's messenger. He forfeited family and reputation. He endured misunderstanding, ridicule, and persecution. He was imprisoned and mocked by those to whom he had come to warn of God's impending judgment.

Satan will try to convince you that obedience carries much too high a price, but he will never tell you the cost of not obeying God. If you are to be used in God's service, you must expect to make adjustments in your life. Can you measure the distance between the throne room of heaven and a cattle shed in Bethlehem? How far is it from the Lordship of the universe to the cross? Don't be deceived into thinking there is no cost involved in obedience.

What adjustments is God asking you to make? Will you face the hardships and opposition that will come when you align your life with God's will? Jeremiah had the deep satisfaction of knowing he was a faithful and beloved servant of God. Your reward will be the same when you choose to fully obey Christ, regardless of the cost.

Obedience Step by Step

*Now it came to pass after these things that God tested
Abraham, and said to him, "Abraham!" And he said,
"Here I am." Then He said, "Take now your son, your only
son Isaac, whom you love, and go to the land of Moriah,
and offer him there as a burnt offering on one
of the mountains of which I shall tell you."*

GENESIS 22:1–2

Our difficulty is not that we *don't* know God's will. Our discomfort comes from the fact that we do know His will, but we do not want to do it!

When God first spoke to Abraham, His commands were straightforward. "Go to a land I will show you" (Gen. 12:1). Then God led Abraham through a number of tests over the years. Abraham learned patience as he waited on God's promise of a son, which took twenty-five years to be fulfilled. Abraham learned to trust God through battles with kings and through the destruction of Sodom and Gomorrah. The pinnacle of Abraham's walk of faith was when God asked him to sacrifice the one thing that meant more to him than anything else. Abraham's previous obedience indicated that he would have quickly and decisively sacrificed anything else God asked of him, but was he prepared for this? God did not ask Abraham to make such a significant sacrifice at the beginning of their relationship. This came more than thirty years after Abraham began walking with God.

As the Father progressively reveals His ways to you in your Christian pilgrimage, you, like Abraham, will develop a deeper level of trust in Him. When you first became a Christian, your Master's instructions were probably fundamental, such as being baptized or changing your lifestyle. But as you learn to trust Him more deeply, He will develop your character to match bigger tests, and with the greater test will come a greater love for God and knowledge of His ways. Are you ready for God's next revelation?

A Noticeable Difference

Now when they saw the boldness of Peter and John, and perceived that they were uneducated and untrained men, they marveled. And they realized that they had been with Jesus.

ACTS 4:13

There is no mistaking a life transformed by God! The disciples had been vain and fearful when Jesus enlisted them. James and John sought to outmaneuver their fellow disciples in order to gain the places of greatest honor next to Jesus (Mark 10:37). Over and over the disciples' actions showed that they did not truly understand who Jesus was (John 6:7–9; Mark 6:49). Even after three years with Jesus, Peter was afraid to confess Christ before a young servant girl (Matt. 26:69–75). Anyone who knew these men would realize they were not the kind of people on which you build a worldwide kingdom. Yet something happened to them as they were with Jesus. The Holy Spirit transformed them, giving them new boldness and wisdom. Now they could perform miracles and preach fearlessly and persuasively to multitudes. Even their enemies noticed in their changed lives the same power they had witnessed in Jesus.

Sometimes we desperately want others to believe that we have changed, that we are more godly, more devoted, more Spirit-controlled. It is not necessary, however, for those who have been truly transformed by Christ to convince others of the difference; the change will be obvious.

Don't become too introspective, always focusing on yourself and the small changes you see happening over time. As you walk with Jesus daily, let the witness of the changes taking place in you come from others and not from you. If you have to prove to someone that God has really changed you, He has not. Those around you will surely notice when your life has been transformed by your relationship with Jesus.

God's Manner of Forgiveness

Now therefore, the sword shall never depart from your house, because you have despised Me, and have taken the wife of Uriah the Hittite to be your wife.

2 SAMUEL 12:10

What is required for God to forgive sin? Repentance. But even repentance does not ensure the removal of the consequences of sin. The consequences often remain as a reminder of the terrible, destructive nature of sin.

David was forgiven for his grievous sins of lust, adultery, robbery, and murder. God forgave him absolutely and removed his sin from him completely (Ps. 103:12). God did not, however, remove the pain that David would endure as a result of his transgressions. The child born of David's adultery died (2 Sam. 12:14). David's son Amnon raped David's daughter Tamar (2 Sam. 13:14). David's son Absalom murdered Amnon (2 Sam. 13:28–29). Absalom brought the kingdom into rebellion (2 Sam. 15). For the rest of David's reign, violence filled his home and his kingdom. Although David knew he was forgiven, he bore the painful consequences of his sin for the rest of his life.

It is presumptuous to assume that God removes every consequence the moment you repent of your sin. Do not think that the instant you show remorse God will restore everything as it was. He may not. Some sins, such as adultery, come from a flawed character. God forgives sin immediately upon repentance, but it takes longer to build character. It is character, not forgiveness, that determines what God brings next to your life.

Because we know the devastating consequences of our disobedience, let us diligently avoid every sin and "run with endurance the race that is set before us" (Heb. 12:1b).

143

On Mission with God

*Then the Spirit said to Philip,
"Go near and overtake this chariot."*

ACTS 8:29

Missions is God finding those whose hearts are right with Him and placing them where they can make a difference for His kingdom. Some of the great missionaries in history did not live long lives, but their lives dramatically affected eternity.

God had access to Philip, and the Book of Acts gives the exciting account of how God used Philip's life to take the gospel to the ends of the earth. Philip was preaching powerfully in the city of Samaria (Acts 8:5). So mightily did God use him that the entire city was rejoicing at the miracles God was doing (Acts 8:6–8). This would be any evangelist's fondest desire, to see an entire city responding to the gospel through his preaching. Yet Philip was not activity-centered in his Christian life. He was God-centered. Philip was not preoccupied with expanding his reputation as a great preacher or miracle worker, he was concerned that his life remain in the center of God's activity. When he was instructed to leave his fruitful ministry, he did not hesitate (Acts 8:27).

God continues to seek those as responsive as Philip to go on mission with Him. The reason God has not brought great revival to more places is not that He is unable or that He is unwilling. He first looks for those willing to have their lives radically adjusted away from their self-centered activities and placed into the center of God's activity around the world. Have you seen the activity of God around you? What is God presently inviting you to do? How are you responding?

Memorials of Faithfulness

"Assuredly, I say to you, wherever this gospel is preached in the whole world, what this woman has done will also be told as a memorial to her."

MARK 14:9

We may assume that our expressions of devotion to God are small and insignificant, but in God's eyes they may hold much meaning. Our love and dedication to Christ may even create memorials to God for future generations.

This woman performed a profound act of love for Jesus. She did not do it to impress His disciples or to gain public attention or to gain praise from Jesus. She simply sought to express her love for Jesus. She did nothing spectacular; she performed no miracles; she preached no sermons. Yet Jesus was so moved by her selfless loyalty that He deemed it worthy of remembrance throughout the remainder of history.

We do not know all that God finds most pleasing, nor do we know what acts of our love He may choose to honor through our children and future generations. Abraham could not have known that the day he demonstrated his willingness to sacrifice his only son would be memorialized and would bless many generations who heard of his obedience. David could not have known that his walk with God would please Him so much that David's example would bless generations who followed him.

God can take your faithfulness and begin a spiritual legacy, making it a blessing to others for generations to come. You will never know until eternity all who received a blessing because of your righteous life. That is why it is so important that you daily express your love and devotion to Jesus.

The Agony of Prayer

And being in agony, He prayed more earnestly.
Then His sweat became like great drops of blood
falling down to the ground.

LUKE 22:44

Prayer is not difficult to understand. It is difficult to do. When was the last time your heart so grieved for those you were interceding for that your entire body agonized along with your mind and heart? (Heb. 5:7).

We are a generation that avoids pain at all costs. This is why there are so few intercessors. Most Christians operate on the shallowest levels of prayer, but God wants to take us into the deep levels of intercessory prayer that only a few ever experience. Deep, prolonged intercession is painful. It involves staying before God when everyone else has gone away or sleeps (Luke 22:45). It involves experiencing brokenness with the Father over those who continually rebel against Him. How many of us will experience this kind of fervent intercession?

We long for Pentecost in our lives and in our churches, but there is no Pentecost without Gethsemane and a cross. How do we become mature in our prayer life? By praying. When we do not feel like praying is precisely the time we *ought* to pray. There are no shortcuts to prayer. There are no books to read, seminars to attend, or inspirational mottoes to memorize that will transform us into intercessors. This comes only by committing ourselves to pray and then doing so.

Why not accept God's invitation to become an intercessor? Don't allow yourself to become satisfied with shallow, self-centered praying. Stay with God in prayer until He leads you to pray at the level He wants.

Whoever Is Least

"Assuredly, I say to you, among those born of women there has not risen one greater than John the Baptist; but he who is least in the kingdom of heaven is greater than he."

MATTHEW 11:11

John the Baptist's role was to decrease in prominence while Jesus' ministry increased (John 3:30). John allowed his disciples to leave him in order to follow Jesus. His ministry lasted only about six months before he was wrongfully imprisoned and executed on the whim of a cruel monarch. Yet Jesus said that no one who had come before John was any greater in the kingdom of heaven. Moses had parted the Red Sea; Elijah had raised the dead and brought down fire from heaven; Isaiah had written a revered book of Scripture; yet in the brief time of service granted to John, he had matched them all for greatness in the kingdom of heaven!

Incredibly, Jesus said that we have the opportunity to be even greater in the kingdom of heaven than John the Baptist. He announced the coming of Christ, but we, as Christians, have Christ living within us. We must remember that service to God is the greatest privilege we can receive in life. To serve God in even the most menial way is an honor far greater than we deserve. John was given less than a year to complete his assignment, and he did so with all that he had. We have the opportunity to allow Jesus to carry out His work through our lives, so that greater things are done through us than were ever accomplished through John the Baptist. Our mandate is the same as John's: to lift up Jesus while denying ourselves. Oh, that we would do so with the same fervor as John the Baptist!

God's Ways

He made known His ways to Moses,
His acts to the children of Israel.

PSALM 103:7

Are you satisfied with merely knowing the *acts* of God, or do you also want to know His *ways?* There is a difference. This difference is illustrated in the lives of the children of Israel as compared to Moses. The Israelites witnessed the miracles God performed; they walked across the dry Red Sea just as Moses did. They ate the manna and quail from heaven even as Moses did. They were content to receive God's provision without ever knowing God Himself. Yet Moses saw beyond the *provision* of God to the *person* of God. Others, such as the Egyptian magicians, might perform miraculous acts, but no one else did things the *way* God did (Exod. 7:11–12). The way God acted provided a window into His nature. If Moses had been content with only God's power, he could have accepted the presence of an angel and been victorious in his efforts (Exod. 33:15). But Moses wanted to experience more. He wanted to experience God Himself, not just God's activity.

Some today, like the Israelites, are content to experience God's activity without ever coming to know God. They are the recipients of answered prayer, yet they never come to know the Provider. They are blessed by God's providential care over their families, their homes, and their jobs, yet they are satisfied not knowing the One from whom the blessings come. They benefit from God's protection, yet they never become acquainted with the Protector.

Have you come to know God more personally as a result of your experiences with Him? As you observe the acts of God, look beyond them to the revelation of His character (Gen. 22:14; John 6:35).

Rejoicing in God's Word

Your words were found, and I ate them,
And Your word was to me the joy and rejoicing of my heart.

JEREMIAH 15:16

If you were to receive a note from the leader of your country or someone famous, you would probably save it as a keepsake. How much more precious is a message from almighty God!

Sometimes we find ourselves in circumstances that are beyond our control. This was the case for Mary and Martha as they were grieving the death of their brother Lazarus. At these times a word from Jesus can bring much rejoicing (John 11:41–45). Other times when Jesus speaks, His words bring correction. "Get behind Me, Satan!" (Matt. 16:23) and "O you of little faith" (Matt. 14:31) do not seem to bring joy. Yet Jeremiah said that God's Word brought him joy.

It is overwhelming to consider that holy, almighty God would speak directly to us! What a privilege that He would care enough to challenge our destructive thoughts or practices. No matter whether His words are praising us or chastising us, we ought to consider it joy to receive life-changing words from our Master!

Every time we prepare to worship the Lord, we ought to do so with anticipation that almighty God may have something to say to us. Whenever we open our Bibles, we should expect that God has something to tell us in our time with Him. We ought to be far more concerned with what God will say to us during our prayer times than with what we intend to tell Him.

When you receive a word from your Lord, whether it be of praise or of correction, consider it joy that almighty God would speak to you.

Every Careless Word

*"But I say to you that for every idle word men may speak,
they will give account of it in the day of judgment."*

MATTHEW 12:36

J esus spoke plainly about our idle words, yet His warning often goes unheeded. Jesus said that for every idle word there will be a time of accounting in the day of judgment. We would expect Jesus to condemn profane and vile uses of the tongue, but idle words? Idle words are things we say carelessly, without concern for their impact on others. We too quickly assume that the sins of our tongue are minor sins, sins that God will overlook. Yet Jesus was fully aware of the devastating nature of our words, for the idle words that come from our mouths give a lucid picture of the condition of our heart (Matt. 15:17–20).

The Book of Proverbs encourages us to speak less rather than risk saying something offensive (Prov. 17:28). Often when we have nothing significant to say we are tempted to speak injurious, idle words. The more time we spend in idle chatter, the greater the likelihood that we will say things that are harmful. James cautioned believers to be "swift to hear, slow to speak, slow to wrath" (James 1:19). We are in much less danger of saying something offensive when we are listening than when we are speaking!

Think carefully about the words that come from your mouth. Christians should speak only words that uplift and bring grace to others (Eph. 4:29). Do you need to speak less? Do you need to be more careful about the kind of humor you use? Ask the Holy Spirit to help you evaluate whether your words build up others or whether they destroy and hurt others.

Faith That Doesn't Ask

"A wicked and adulterous generation seeks after a sign, and no
sign shall be given to it except the sign of the prophet Jonah."
And He left them and departed.

MATTHEW 16:4

Asking God for a miracle may indicate a lack of faith. Some feel that they demonstrate great faith by continually asking God for miracles. They assume that in every situation God wants to do the spectacular. They presume, for example, that God wants to heal anyone who is sick or provide a miraculous escape from every difficulty they face. Jesus condemned those who insisted that He perform miracles, because He knew their hearts. He recognized that they could not believe Him without constantly undergirding their faith with signs. Their faith was not strong enough to survive without a regular supply of the miraculous. Jesus condemned this lack of faith and left them.

There are times when we prefer the miracle over the miracle worker. God calls this idolatry, and He discouraged it by refusing to provide miracles on demand (Jer. 2:11–13). Sometimes the greatest act of faith is *not* to ask for a miracle. One of the most amazing statements of faith in the Old Testament came from Shadrach, Meshach, and Abednego as they faced the fiery furnace because of their obedience to God. They expressed true faith when they assured king Nebuchadnezzar: "Our God whom we serve is able to deliver us from the burning fiery furnace, and He will deliver us from your hand, O king. But if not, let it be known to you, O king, that we do not serve your gods, nor will we worship the gold image which you have set up" (Dan. 3:17–18). They were confident in God's ability to deliver them, but they trusted Him so completely that they did not ask to be spared.

Does your faith need miracles to sustain it? Or do you trust God so totally that you can say, "But if not, I will still trust the Lord!"?

Trusting God First

Thus says the Lord:
"Cursed is the man who trusts in man
And makes flesh his strength,
Whose heart departs from the Lord."

JEREMIAH 17:5

The Israelites of Jeremiah's day believed they could trust in their army, the diplomacy of their king, and their foreign alliances to protect them from the powerful Babylonian empire. They gave lip service to their trust in God, but their actions showed where their faith really was: in their military and financial might. God spoke through Jeremiah to warn them that He would not bless those who trusted in anyone or anything instead of Him.

Placing your ultimate trust in anything other than God is idolatry. How can you know if your faith is not truly in God? Ask yourself these questions: Where do I turn when I experience a crisis? When I am hurting or afraid, to whom do I go? When I have a financial problem, whom do I want to tell first? Where do I seek comfort when I am under stress or discouraged?

Could it be that you are saying you trust in God, but your actions indicate otherwise? God often uses other people as His method of providing for you. Be careful lest you inadvertently misdirect your faith toward His provision instead of toward the Provider. God may meet your need through your friends, but ultimately your trust must be in God.

The Israelites were so stubbornly committed to trusting in human strength instead of God that, even as the Babylonian army approached Jerusalem, they continued to desperately seek for a person, or a nation, or an army that could rescue them. They realized too late that they had neglected to trust in the only One who could deliver them.

Don't make the same mistake as the Israelites. Go straight to the Lord when you have a need. He is the only One who can provide for you.

Friends of God

"No longer do I call you servants, for a servant does not know what his master is doing; but I have called you friends, for all things that I have heard from My Father I have made known to you."

JOHN 15:15

You do not choose to be a friend of God. That is by invitation only. Only two people in the Old Testament were specifically described as "friends of God." Abraham walked with the Lord so closely that God referred to him as His friend (Isa. 41:8). Moses spoke to God face to face as a man speaks with his friend (Exod. 33:11).

By His very nature God is a friend to us. He loves us with a perfect love and reaches out to us with salvation when we can offer Him nothing in return. It is quite another thing when someone has a heart so devoted to Him that God initiates a special friendship. David's heart was totally devoted to God (1 Kings 11:4). Although David was not sinless, he loved God. David hated sin (Ps. 103:3); he loved to worship God (Ps. 122:1); he took genuine delight in God's presence (2 Sam. 6:14); he loved to speak about God (Ps. 34:1); he was keenly aware of his transgressions (Ps. 51:3–4); and he delighted in offering gifts of song, thanksgiving, and praise, asking for nothing in return (Ps. 100). So closely did David walk with God that his words were on Jesus' mind as He hung upon the cross (Matt. 27:46).

Jesus called His disciples friends. He said He would disclose to them things that the Father had shared with Him, because they were His friends. There developed such an intimate friendship between them that He would share what was on His heart with His friends.

If you cannot describe yourself as a friend of God, commit yourself to seek after God with all your heart.

The Terror of the Lord

Knowing, therefore, the terror of the Lord, we persuade men;
but we are well known to God, and I also trust
are well known in your consciences.

2 CORINTHIANS 5:11

The fear of God is the greatest deterrent for sin (Exod. 20:20; Prov. 16:6). Those who perceive God as a benevolent and gentle grandfather will treat their sin superficially. They will worship halfheartedly. They will live life on their own terms rather than God's. But a reverent fear of holy God will dramatically affect the way a person lives. Even though Paul was an apostle of Jesus Christ, he feared God and knew that one day he would stand in judgment to give an account for everything he had done (2 Cor. 5:10).

Our world does not applaud fearfulness. We teach our children to love God, but not to fear Him. We want to present a loving and nonthreatening image of God to nonbelievers in the hope that Christianity will be more appealing to them. One of the great condemnations of our day may be that we have lost the fear of God. We promote Him as a "best friend" who saves us and "lives in our hearts," but we do not fear Him. It is true that we are God's adopted children and that we are fellow heirs, even friends, with Jesus (Rom. 8:16–17; John 15:14–15), but we are not His equals. He has forgiven us, but we are still His creatures. He is God, and we are not!

If you find that you have become complacent with God's commands and have become comfortable in your sin, you are completely isolated from God's holiness. Take time to meditate upon the awesome holiness of God and allow the Holy Spirit to instill into your life a proper reverence for almighty God (Isa. 40:12–26). A deep sense of awe is essential to knowing God.

Repentance

Now after John was put in prison, Jesus came to Galilee,
preaching the gospel of the kingdom of God, and saying,
"The time is fulfilled, and the kingdom of God is at hand.
Repent, and believe in the gospel."

MARK 1:14–15

Repentance is one of the most positive of all words. John the Baptist centered his preaching on repentance (Matt. 3:2, Mark 1:4, Luke 3:3). Jesus also preached repentance, commanding His disciples to do likewise (Mark 1:14–15; Luke 24:47). The angel predicted that the Messiah would save His people from their sins (Matt. 1:21). The requirement for this salvation would be repentance.

To repent means to stop going one direction, to turn around completely, and to go the opposite way. Repentance involves a dramatic and decisive change of course. God urges us to repent when the path we are taking leads to destruction. Repentance will save us from disastrous consequences! What a wonderful word! How comforting that the Creator loves us enough to warn us of impending danger!

Our problem is that we think of repentance as something negative. When we recognize our sin, we prefer to "rededicate" our lives to God. We may even tell others we have resolved to be more faithful to God than we were before we failed Him. Yet the Bible does not speak of rededicating oneself. It speaks of repentance! Repentance indicates a decisive change, not merely a wishful resolution. We have not repented if we continue in our sin!

Repentance involves a radical change of heart and mind in which we agree with God's evaluation of our sin and then take specific action to align ourselves with His will. A desire to change is not repentance. Repentance is always an active response to God's Word. The evidence of repentance is not words of resolve, but a changed life.

The Condition of the Heart

*But the ones that fell on the good ground are those who,
having heard the word with a noble and good heart,
keep it and bear fruit with patience.*

LUKE 8:15

At any time, the receptiveness of your heart will determine your response to God's Word (Luke 8:5–18). If your heart is like the trampled ground, hardened by the sin of bitterness and unforgiveness, you will be unable to accept a message from God. Though you hear the words of the message, you will remain unchanged. If your heart is like the shallow soil on top of a rock, you will accept God's Word in your mind, but the truth will not penetrate your heart to make a difference in your actions. A heart like thorny soil is a life that is distracted by the cares of the world; the pursuit of earthly pleasures prevents God's Word from taking hold and producing righteousness. The heart that is like good soil receives a word from God, applies it, and brings forth fruit in due time. This is the heart that Jesus desires in us, for the fruit will be a Christlike life.

Any time you hear a word from God, whether through Bible reading, prayer, or worship, the way you respond will depend on how you have cultivated your heart (Hos. 10:12). How do you develop a heart that is like good soil? Repent of any bitterness, anger, or unforgiveness that is hardening your heart. Meditate on God's Word until it enters deep into your heart and not just your mind. When you read or hear a word from God, apply it to your life and let God bring His word into reality in your life (Gal. 6:9). Protect your lifestyle. See that you don't devote all of your energy to worldly concerns, rather than to pursuing your relationship with God. The condition of your heart will vary, depending on how you cultivate it. If it was receptive to a word from God yesterday, this does not guarantee it is receptive today. *Daily* prepare your heart for the word God has for you!

God Weighs
Your Motives

All a man's ways seem innocent to him,
But motives are weighed by the Lord.

PROVERBS 16:2 (NIV)

How quick we are to question the motives of others, yet we are so slow to question our own! When others harm us, we may assume the worst of intentions. When we are guilty, we often excuse our offenses, concluding that others are far too sensitive! Regardless of how we monitor our motives, God weighs them in His scales of righteousness. It is futile to try to deceive God with our pious justifications, for He sees our hearts.

Is it possible to do the right thing for the wrong reason? Of course! You can attend worship services with a heart that is far from worshipful (Isa. 1:10–17). Could you show concern for the poor and yet have a heart that is opposed to God? Judas did (John 12:4–8). Could you make bold statements of love for Christ and actually be aiding the work of Satan? Peter did (Matt. 16:21–23). Could you offer sacrifices to God and be in total disobedience to Him? King Saul did (1 Sam. 13:8–9). Could you pray with the wrong motives? James said you can (James 4:3).

Many things cause us to do what we do. We can be motivated by good things, such as love for God, compassion, generosity, and faith. Or our actions can come from unhealthy motives such as pride, insecurity, ambition, lust, greed, guilt, anger, fear, and hurt. It is even possible to do the best things based on the worst motives. When the Lord measures our motives He looks for one thing: love. All that we do should proceed from our love for God and for others (1 Cor. 13). Take time to look past your actions to what lies behind them. Ask God to show you what He sees when He examines your motives.

What Manner of Person
Ought You to Be?

Therefore, since all these things will be dissolved,
what manner of persons ought you to be
in holy conduct and godliness?

2 PETER 3:11

When God told Abraham He was going to destroy Sodom and Gomorrah, Abraham's life was immediately and radically affected. Noah could not carry on business as usual once he knew what God was planning for his generation. Knowing that God is preparing judgment brings a sobering reality to Christians, helping us recognize what is eternally significant and what is not.

Peter cautions us that a catastrophic time of judgment is coming. On the day of the Lord there will be a great noise, and the elements will melt with a fervent heat. On that day, he warns, the earth will be consumed. Peter assures us that this is not mere speculation; it is certain and imminent. He then asks the crucial question that applies to each generation: "What kind of persons ought you to be?" With judgment pending for us and countless millions of people facing destruction, how should we live our lives?

Many Christians attach great value to temporal things. Hobbies and possessions consume us, leaving little time or energy to invest in what is eternal. More than anyone else, Christians should be sensitive to the times in which we live. We should walk so closely with God that if He were preparing to bring judgment upon people, we could warn those in imminent peril. Since Christ has been long-suffering in His return so that no one might perish (2 Pet. 3:9), should we not invest our effort in building God's eternal kingdom? Should there not be an urgency about us to complete the tasks that God gives us?

Sow Generously

But this I say: He who sows sparingly will also reap sparingly,
and he who sows bountifully will also reap bountifully.

2 CORINTHIANS 9:6

You are called to be intentional about your Christianity. You must be determined to experience the fullness of God in every area of your Christian life and never to settle for a shallow, lackadaisical relationship with almighty God. God will bless you according to how you respond to His invitations. If He finds in you a generous heart that willingly and freely gives what it has to others, then God responds toward you in like manner.

When the apostle Paul encouraged the believers in Corinth to help the Christians in Jerusalem, he promised them that if they would sow generously, they would reap a generous return from God.

This truth holds life-changing potential for us. If we invest everything we have in our relationship with God, we will experience the full dimensions of being children of God. If our desire is to know God more intimately, and if we spend ample time studying His word, God will generously enrich our relationship with Him. If we discipline ourselves to remain in prayer even when praying is difficult, He will reward us with a deeper, more powerful prayer life. If we reconcile any broken relationships and prepare our hearts before worship, and if we participate fully and reverently in every part of worship, God promises that we will meet Him and our lives will be changed.

Why is it that some Christians grow rapidly in their Christian faith and others remain unchanged year after year? Our Christian maturity is deeply affected by what we sow. Let us choose to sow generously in everything we do in our Christian lives. The harvest we reap will be Christlikeness.

God Speaks in Many Times and Ways

*God, who at various times and in various ways spoke
in time past to the fathers by the prophets,
has in these last days spoken to us by His Son.*

HEBREWS 1:1

Our generation is preoccupied with methods. When we find a program that works in one business, we immediately want to package and distribute it so that it will work for others. This attitude carries over into the spiritual life as well. We spend much energy looking for spiritual disciplines, books, seminars, or conferences that "work" in order to feel satisfied with our Christian life. God does not want us to trust in methods. He wants us to trust in Him.

Trusting in methods rather than in a Person seriously limits the way we experience God. When we expect Him to speak to us only in predictable ways, we forget that God is much more complex than our perception of Him. In times past, God spoke in dreams and visions. He used nature; miraculous signs; prophets; a still, small voice; fire; trumpets; fleece; the casting of lots; and angels. He spoke in the middle of the night, during worship services, at mealtimes, during funerals, while people were walking along the road, through sermons, in the middle of a storm, and through His Son.

The important thing was not *how* God communicated, but *that* He spoke. If God always spoke to us through dreams, we would remain in our beds awaiting a divine revelation! The means God uses to communicate with us is irrelevant; the fact that He is communicating is what is critical.

Don't limit yourself to a method, expecting only to hear from your Father in predictable ways. Rather, open yourself up to other means by which God wants to commune with you. Allow the Holy Spirit to sensitize you to God's message at all times, in every location, under any circumstance. Then you will experience God in entirely new dimensions as you are receptive to His voice.

Tempted As We Are

For in that He Himself has suffered, being tempted,
He is able to aid those who are tempted.

HEBREWS 2:18

You will never face a temptation so strong that God has not made complete provision for you to overcome it. God, out of His love, has done everything necessary for you to be victorious whenever you face temptation. He has clearly revealed His will to you in Scripture so that you will not be confused about the right thing to do. He has placed the Holy Spirit within you to guide you in your decisions and to convict you when you make harmful choices. With every temptation God also provides a way of escape so that you never have to yield to it (1 Cor. 10:13). Everything is in place for you to experience victory over every temptation.

God in His infinite love, however, has done even more to safeguard you from temptation. He has allowed Himself to suffer the full brunt of temptation. The very Son of God humbled Himself, taking on all the limitations of frail human flesh, and was tempted in every way that we are. Jesus knew what it was like to grow tired, to be hungry, to experience the same limitations we have; yet He was without sin. It is to this One that we turn when we are facing temptation. Ours is not an unsympathetic God who is unconcerned with our struggle to live righteously, but we follow a God who knows how difficult it is to resist sin and withstand temptation. We can approach Christ with confidence, knowing that He understands our plight. He knows how to aid us when we are tempted.

As for Me
and My House

And if it seems evil to you to serve the Lord, choose for
yourselves this day whom you will serve, whether the gods
which your fathers served that were on the other side of the
River, or the gods of the Amorites, in whose land you dwell.
But as for me and my house, we will serve the Lord.

JOSHUA 24:15

Serving God was not Joshua's only option. He could have adopted the religious beliefs and practices of his family heritage in the pagan land of Egypt. He could have accepted the idolatrous religion of his neighbors in the region where he now lived. These options probably looked like easier choices than worshiping God. But Joshua had witnessed God's faithfulness (Josh. 23:14). He was convinced that his Lord was the only true God and that serving Him would bring victory and blessing.

Joshua decided to serve God alone. He was determined to teach his entire household to honor his Lord as well. He had trusted God for victory on the battlefield, and he knew that God could also give him spiritual victory in his home.

You, too, must decide whom you will serve. An assortment of popular religions clamors for your allegiance. If you come from a Christian heritage, you may choose to embrace the faith of your parents and grandparents. If you did not grow up in a Christian home, you can decide, as Joshua did, to reject your heritage of unbelief and begin a generation that serves the Lord.

If you set your mind wholeheartedly on serving God, your example will bring a tremendous blessing to your family. If you place your confidence in God, those around you will witness your faith, and they may decide to trust Him too. Choose, as Joshua did, to serve God unashamedly with all your heart, and then watch to see how God blesses your family.

The Fruit of the Spirit

*But the fruit of the Spirit is love, joy, peace, long-suffering,
kindness, goodness, faithfulness, gentleness, self-control.
Against such there is no law.*

GALATIANS 5:22-23

An examination of the fruits of the Spirit can be intimidating. Working all nine of these traits into your life seems impossible, and indeed it is. But the moment you became a Christian, the Holy Spirit began a divine work to produce Christ's character in you. Regardless of who you are, the Spirit works from the same model, Jesus Christ. The Spirit looks to Christ in order to find the blueprint for your character. The Spirit will immediately begin helping you experience and practice the same *love* that Jesus had when He laid down His life for His friends. The same *joy* He experienced will now fill you. The identical *peace* that guarded the heart of Jesus, even as He was being beaten and mocked, will be the peace that the Spirit works to instill in you. The *patience* Jesus had for His most unteachable disciple will be the patience that the Spirit now develops in you. The *kindness* Jesus showed toward children and sinners will soften your heart toward others. There will be a *goodness* about you that is only explainable by the presence of the Spirit of God. The Spirit will build the same *faithfulness* into you that led Jesus to be entirely obedient to His Father. The Spirit will teach you *self-control* so that you will have strength to do what is right and to resist temptation.

All of this is as natural as the growth of fruit on a tree. You do not have to orchestrate it on your own. It automatically begins the moment you become a believer. How quickly it happens depends upon how completely you yield yourself to the Holy Spirit's activity.

The Keys of the Kingdom

"I will give you the keys of the kingdom of heaven,
and whatever you bind on earth will be bound in heaven, and
whatever you loose on earth will be loosed in heaven."

MATTHEW 16:19

The keys of the kingdom represent the access you have to the Father through your relationship to Jesus Christ. With this relationship you have access to everything that is accessible to Christ. However, this access is not given indiscriminately; Jesus gave the keys to His disciples only after they recognized that He was the Christ. Once the disciples were convinced that Jesus was the Savior, they entered into a unique and personal relationship with Him. Their relationship to Jesus gave them direct access to their heavenly Father. Likewise, your relationship with Christ opens the door of heaven for you and gives you direct access to the Father.

Peter discovered that once he had keys to the kingdom, he could go to the Father in every situation. When he stood to preach before thousands on the day of Pentecost, this simple fisherman opened the door to the kingdom for three thousand people in one day (Acts 2:41). When he encountered a lame man, he used his access to God and His healing power, and the man was healed (Acts 3:6). When he was imprisoned, Peter discovered that the keys of the kingdom could open even the most secure prison door (Acts 12:6–10).

If you are a Christian you, too, have keys to the kingdom of heaven. You do not need an intermediary, for you have an unobstructed access to God. With that access come all the resources you need to face any circumstance. When you are afraid, you have access to God's peace that surpasses comprehension (Phil. 4:6). When you have a broken relationship, you have access to the God of reconciliation (2 Cor. 5:18–21). When you meet someone in need, you have access to God's provision for that person. What an incredible privilege to be entrusted with keys to the kingdom of heaven!

What Comes out of Your Mouth?

"But those things which proceed out of the mouth come from the heart, and they defile a man."

MATTHEW 15:18

The Bible stresses that what you say is an accurate indicator of what is in your heart. If your words bless and encourage others, they give evidence of a compassionate heart. If you often share the good news about Christ, you demonstrate a heart that is grateful for your own salvation. When others are in a crisis, do they know they will find peace and comfort in your words? Do you frequently and spontaneously offer prayers for others? Do your words and the manner in which you say them reveal a patient heart? All of these behaviors indicate a heart that is like the heart of the Father.

Or do you often regret your words? Are there people even now who are hurt or angry because of something you have said? Do you enjoy gossip? Do you tend to criticize others? Do you feel that you are not responsible for what comes out of your mouth when you are angry? Does your mouth spew grumbling and complaints? These behaviors come from a heart that is unlike God's heart.

You may say, "Oh, but that's just the way I am! I'm always saying the wrong thing!" Yet Scripture clearly states that an abusive tongue is not under the control of the Spirit (James 3:3–10). A sanctified mouth is a wonderful instrument for the Lord. A heart like the Father's heart will produce only pure and loving words. Without making any excuses for your words, ask the Holy Spirit to forgive you for any words that have brought harm. Then ask Him to discipline your mouth so that every word you speak is used by God to encourage and edify others.

Noah Walked with God

But Noah found grace in the eyes of the Lord. . . .
Noah was a just man, perfect in his generations.
Noah walked with God.

GENESIS 6:8–9

No matter how ungodly the environment you may be in, God will always find you and walk with you. Noah lived in perhaps the most wicked age in history. No one worshiped God. All the people worshiped idols and pursued their own sinful pleasures. Noah's neighbors were evil; every person he associated with in the marketplace, or along the street, or in public gatherings, ridiculed the very thought of being faithful to God. Every temptation imaginable was abundantly available to Noah. How oppressive such an environment would have been to a righteous person!

The people of Noah's day were so wicked that God planned the most complete and drastic act of judgment recorded in Scripture. Nevertheless, Noah was not lost to God in the crowd of sinners. God noticed every act of Noah's righteousness. Noah had chosen to live uprightly before God despite what everyone around him was doing, and God had observed him. There may have been times when Noah wondered if it mattered if he lived a righteous life, since no one else was. Yet he continued, and his persistence in righteousness saved his life and the lives of his family members.

Are you constantly surrounded by evil? Do you struggle at times to live a righteous life when those you associate with each day have no concern for God? Find assurance in the life of Noah. God watches you, even as He observed Noah. God will seek you out of the crowd every time, and He wants to bless you and your family just as He blessed Noah.

A Godly Influence

*Then the Lord said to Noah, "Come into the ark,
you and all your household, because I have seen that you
are righteous before Me in this generation."*

GENESIS 7:1

The children of Noah faced a significant decision. They lived in a world where everyone blatantly disregarded God. Wickedness was the norm. No one would have condemned Noah's sons for living evil lives like the rest of society—no one except their father. In a world rampant with ungodly attitudes and every form of wicked behavior, they were fortunate to be Noah's sons. When their father invited them to spend the next hundred years building an ark in obedience to a word from God, Noah's sons had to choose whether to believe those around them or to trust their father. They chose to join their father. What a wonderful testimony of Noah's godly influence in his home! How fortunate for Shem, Ham, and Japheth that their father refused to compromise his integrity, even though everyone else in his society had done so.

Your life has an influence on those around you as well. Your spouse and your children are profoundly affected by your choices. Your co-workers, your neighbors, and your friends will all be impacted by your life. As the world tries to persuade people to follow its standard, your life should stand in stark contrast as an example of a righteous person. Your life should convince those around you of the wisdom of following God. Do not underestimate the positive effect that your obedience will have upon those close to you.

The Spirit Bears Witness

The Spirit Himself bears witness with our spirit that we are children of God, and if children, then heirs—heirs of God and joint heirs with Christ, if indeed we suffer with Him that we may also be glorified together.

ROMANS 8:16–17

It is impossible to perceive all that became ours when we were born again. There is no way we can understand all that heaven is like. How could we ever comprehend all that is ours as fellow heirs with Christ? The knowledge that we will share Christ's inheritance with Him absolutely astounds us! Left to our own, we could not begin to understand all that we received once we became children of the King. The Holy Spirit convinces us that we are indeed children of God and helps us understand the riches of our inheritance.

Perhaps you did not have a loving father. The Spirit's role is to teach you how to respond to a Father who relates to you only in perfect love and how to live like a child of the King. Perhaps you grew up in poverty. The Spirit will show you the inexhaustible riches available to you as a child of God.

If you were simply declared an heir and then left on your own, you could not begin to use your inheritance. But the Father has given you His Spirit to serve as your Guide and Teacher. The Holy Spirit will lead you to the magnificent promises and resources that became available when God adopted you into His family. Take time to meditate on the wonderful promises of God that are available to you. Let the Holy Spirit convince you of the reality that you are, indeed, a child of God and a fellow heir of Christ.

Abba, Father

And because you are sons, God has sent forth the Spirit of His Son into your hearts, crying out, "Abba, Father!"

GALATIANS 4:6

The word *father* conjures up different images for everyone. To some it brings the picture of love, laughter, respect, and acceptance. Unfortunately, others associate the term *father* with fear, rejection, and disappointment. That is why it is so important not to take your understanding of your heavenly Father from your experience. Take it from Scripture. You undoubtedly had an imperfect earthly father, perhaps even one who brought you harm. But, as in all of your Christian life, the key is not to understand the Bible based on your experience, but to understand your experience in light of the Bible. God is your model of a father in the truest sense of the word.

Your heavenly Father was willing to pay any price in order to save you (Rom. 8:32). Your heavenly Father is always ready to meet your needs (Luke 11:11–13). Your heavenly Father loves you so much that He is willing to discipline you to bring you to Christian maturity (Prov. 3:11–12; Heb. 12:5–10). Even when you rebel against Him and reject His love, your Father continues to do what is best for you (Rom. 5:8). He does not make His love for you conditional upon your love for Him. He loves you even when you are not loving Him (1 John 4:19). He has made you His heirs and reserves a home for you in heaven (Rom. 8:15–17).

This is what a father is like biblically. If this has not been your experience, it can be now. There is One who has adopted you and who wants to love you in a way you have never experienced. Take comfort and strength from Him—your heavenly Father.

A Way That Seems Right

There is a way that seems right to a man,
But its end is the way of death.

PROVERBS 16:25

Things are not always what they seem. Proverbs warns that we can be deceived into believing we are going down the right path and yet be heading toward death, the opposite direction from God's will. People do not naturally seek God or pursue righteousness (Rom. 3:10–18). Only as the Spirit awakens our hearts to the Person of Christ are we able to desire God's will. If we make decisions apart from the guidance of the Spirit of God, we will be like a ship trying to sail without a compass. We will do what makes the most sense, based on our own wisdom. But what looks attractive may actually lead to sin, ultimately destroying what is precious to us, for our most profound human thinking is mere foolishness to God (1 Cor. 1:18–20). Only God knows the way that leads to life, and He wants to lead us to walk in it (Matt. 7:13–14).

Don't assume every opportunity that arises is from God. Satan will disguise himself as an "angel of light," and his invitations will seem to be in your best interest (2 Cor. 11:14). Yet his way leads only to death (John 8:44). The Word of God will be like a light to your path, guiding you in the ways of righteousness (Ps. 119:105).

It can be perilous to follow a path that seems right without first consulting the Holy Spirit for guidance (John 16:13). Take time to seek the Holy Spirit's direction when you face decisions. He knows the full ramifications of your choices. The Holy Spirit will assist you to understand truth and to experience abundant life. Trust Him as He leads you.

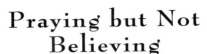
Praying but Not Believing

*When she recognized Peter's voice, because of her gladness
she did not open the gate, but ran in and announced that
Peter stood before the gate. But they said to her,
"You are beside yourself!" Yet she kept insisting
that it was so. So they said, "It is his angel."*

ACTS 12:14–15

You can say prayers in your mind but doubt in your heart. At times God will answer such prayers as He did when Peter was in prison, scheduled for execution. The believers in Jerusalem were powerless to free him, so they prayed. When God released Peter, their reaction revealed the doubt in their hearts. They argued that Peter could not possibly be free, even as he stood outside knocking on the door!

Is it possible to be a "person of prayer" and yet not have faith? Is it possible to fool yourself into believing that because you ask God for help, you have faith in His ability to meet your needs? Is your faith so weak that you are surprised when God answers your prayer? As a child of God, you ought to expect God to answer your prayers. Do you ask God to do something without adjusting your life to what you are praying? If you are praying for revival, how are you preparing for its coming? If you are praying for forgiveness, are you still living with guilt? If you have asked God to provide for your needs, do you remain worried and anxious?

Ask God to increase your faith, and then begin living a life that reflects absolute trust in Him. Out of His grace, God may choose to respond to your requests despite your lack of faith, but you will miss the joy of praying in faith.

When God Says No

Then he killed James the brother of John with the sword.
And because he saw that it pleased the Jews,
he proceeded further to seize Peter also.

ACTS 12:2–3a

Can you accept God's will when His answer is no? If you are praying in God's will, He will always answer you when you pray (Jer. 33:3). However, sometimes His answer will be no.

King Herod arrested Peter and prepared to have him executed. During the night, as his church prayed, Peter's life was spared when an angel freed him. God miraculously answered the prayers of His people that night. Yet not long before, James, too, had been arrested by Herod. James, however, was executed. Surely the church had prayed for James as fervently as they did for Peter, yet that time God's answer had been no.

Did God love Peter more than James? Of course not. James had been one of Jesus' closest friends. Yet God allowed James to die while He continued to use Peter in His service. The church in Jerusalem did not become bitter toward God. They accepted His answer because they trusted His love and wisdom.

There are times when God wants us to persist in our praying until He has completed His work in us (Luke 11:5–8; 18:1–6). However, when God's answer is no, it is futile to continue pleading for a yes. Some refuse to take no for an answer, insisting that if you pray long enough and hard enough, God will ultimately grant any request you make. It is an affront to your Lord to continue pleading with Him when He has clearly said no. The purpose of prayer is not to conform God to our will but to adjust our will to God. We must learn to trust God so that if He says no, we accept that His will is best.

Spiritual Famine

"Behold, the days are coming," says the Lord God,
"That I will send a famine on the land,
Not a famine of bread,
Nor a thirst for water,
But of hearing the words of the Lord."

AMOS 8:11

One way God communicates is through silence. The Israelites blatantly ignored and rejected God's Word to them, and God responded by sending a famine. This famine was far more severe than a shortage of food and water. Instead, they were deprived of His words of life.

God's silence may be hardly noticeable at first. You may still remember times when God spoke to you, but you gradually realize you've not heard His voice for a long time. If you realize you are in a "drought," immediately seek God and ask Him what adjustments your life requires so you can once again enjoy fellowship with Him. It may be that you disobeyed His last instructions to you and that He is waiting on your obedience before giving you a new direction. It may be that there is unconfessed sin in your life or that you have a damaged relationship (Isa. 1:15; 1 Pet. 3:7). It is possible that you have done too much talking in your prayer times and that He wants you to listen. God's silences can be powerful times for Him to communicate with you.

God is God! Because He is God, when He speaks He expects a listening ear and an eager response. He will not be mocked! (Gal. 6:7). When we ignore Him, He may withhold His voice until we repent and get right with Him. The prophet Isaiah assured King Asa, "The Lord is with you while you are with Him. If you seek Him, He will be found by you; but if you forsake Him, He will forsake you."

173

Spiritual Markers

And the children of Israel did so, just as Joshua commanded,
and took up twelve stones from the midst of the Jordan,
as the Lord had spoken to Joshua, according to the
number of the tribes of the children of Israel, and carried
them over with them to the place where they lodged.

JOSHUA 4:8

Spiritual memory is crucial in the Christian life. Do you vividly recall times when you know God spoke to you? It would be tragic if, in your haste to advance in your Christian faith, you neglected to leave spiritual markers at the key crossroads of your life. Without the help of these markers, you will lose your spiritual bearings.

The Israelites experienced a tumultuous pilgrimage. Their doubt that God was powerful enough to give them victory cost them forty years of wandering in the wilderness. Then God miraculously parted the waters of the Jordan River so they could pass over and continue their conquest. God knew that at times the Israelites would face intimidating enemies and would need a reminder that He was powerful enough to protect them. The Israelites might be tempted to think they made a mistake entering Canaan. For this reason God instructed them to build a monument on the banks of the Jordan River. Whenever they returned to this spot, they would see the monument and be reminded of God's awesome power. This marker would give them confidence to meet the new challenges they faced.

A spiritual marker identifies a time of decision when you clearly know that God guided you. Can you remember the moment you became a child of God? Were there specific times when He called you to His ways of living? Can you point to times when He clearly guided you in a decision? Were there times when He spoke powerfully to you about a commitment you should make? Keep track of these important moments! Regularly rehearse them and notice the steady progression in the way God has led you. This will help you understand God's activity in your life and give you a sense of direction as you face future decisions.

Kingdom Greatness

"For who is greater, he who sits at the table, or he who serves?
Is it not he who sits at the table?
Yet I am among you as One who serves."

LUKE 22:27

The measure of greatness in the kingdom of God differs vastly from that of the world. Our society idolizes the rich, the powerful, the beautiful, and the athletic. We even make celebrities out of those who brazenly flaunt their immorality. The world claims it is demeaning to serve others. However, God's kingdom completely rejects the world's measure for esteem, giving the greatest honor to the one who serves most. The person who serves selflessly, lovingly, without complaint, and without seeking recognition is highly regarded in the kingdom of God.

When Jesus and His disciples entered the upper room, the disciples looked for a prominent place to sit; Jesus looked for a place to serve. As they awkwardly waited to be served, Jesus took a towel and basin and washed their feet (John 13:1–15). We Christians like to refer to ourselves as servants, but we are seldom content to be treated as servants! We are tempted to adopt the world's evaluation of importance. But when we look to Jesus as our model, we see that it takes a far more noble character to serve than to be served.

The world will estimate your importance by the number of people serving you. God is more concerned with the number of people you are serving. If you struggle to be a servant, your heart may have shifted away from the heart of God. Ask Jesus to teach you selflessness and to give you the strength to follow His example. Watch for Jesus' invitation to join Him in serving others. It will come.

Be Merciful!

"Should you not also have had compassion on your
fellow servant, just as I had pity on you?"

MATTHEW 18:33

Mercy is a gift. It is undeserved. Punishment and consequences are sin's just reward, but the merciful person does not demand justice for the guilty person. If it were not for God's mercy, we all would have faced His terrible judgment long ago. If not for His mercy, He would have condemned us after our first offense. If not for His mercy, He would punish us each time we sin. But rather than letting us bear the full punishment for our sin, God demonstrated His mercy when He paid the penalty for our sin Himself.

Do you find it hard to show mercy? It may be that you do not comprehend the mercy that God has shown to you. Jesus commanded His disciples to extend the same mercy to others that they had received from God. When they considered the incredible, undeserved mercy they had been granted, how could they refuse to extend the same unconditional mercy to others?

Could anyone sin against us to the same degree that we have sinned against God? Could any offense committed against us be as undeserved as the abuse hurled against the sinless Son of God? How quickly we forget the mercy that God graciously bestowed on us, only to focus on the injustices we endure from others!

If you find it difficult to forgive others, you may need to meditate on the mercy of God that prevents you from experiencing God's justifiable wrath. Scripture describes God as "Ready to pardon, / Gracious and merciful, / Slow to anger, / Abundant in lovingkindness" (Neh. 9:17b).

Furthering the Gospel

*But I want you to know, brethren, that the things
which have happened to me have actually turned out
for the furtherance of the gospel.*

PHILIPPIANS 1:12

There are two ways to look at every situation: How it will affect you, and how it will affect God's kingdom. The apostle Paul was always concerned with how his circumstances might aid the spreading of the gospel. When he was unjustly imprisoned, he immediately looked to see how his imprisonment might provide God's salvation to others (Phil. 1:13; Acts 16:19–34). When he was assailed by an angry mob, he used the opportunity to preach the gospel (Acts 22:1–21). When Paul's criminal proceedings took him before the king, his thoughts were on sharing his faith with the king (Acts 26:1–32)! Even when Paul was shipwrecked on an island, he used that opportunity to share the gospel there. Regardless of his circumstance, Paul's concern was how he could use his current situation to tell others of God's good news of salvation.

Often when we encounter a new situation, our first thoughts are not about God's kingdom. When we face a crisis, we can become angry or fearful for our own well-being, rather than looking to see what God intends to do through our circumstances. If we remain self-centered we will miss so much of what God could do through our experiences, both for us and for those around us.

Ask God to make you aware of how He could use your present circumstances to bless others. Perhaps someone around you needs to see the difference Christ's presence makes in your life. Are you willing for God to use your circumstances to demonstrate His saving power to those around you?

Blameless

There was a man in the land of Uz, whose name was Job;
and that man was blameless and upright, and one who
feared God and shunned evil.

JOB 1:1

There is a tremendous sense of freedom in living a blameless life. Job was blameless. Neither Satan nor any person could accuse him of wrongdoing. Even through the most rigorous tests, Job remained above reproach.

The apostle Paul said he diligently sought to relate to others in such a way that he would never regret his actions (Acts 24:16). This desire should be ours as well. The Book of Revelation indicates that those in heaven will be blameless (Rev. 14:5). This condition does not mean they never sinned on earth, but that God forgave their sins and granted them His righteousness.

Blameless does not mean perfect. It means that in every situation you do the correct thing. If you sin against someone, you confess your sin and ask for forgiveness. If you sin against God, you repent and begin to obey Him (Prov. 28:13). Often the way you handle your sin is as important as the sin itself. When you become aware of your transgression, seek to be blameless in the way you deal with it. If you attempt to conceal your sin, deny it, justify it, or blame others for it, you make the original offense much worse.

Have you been blameless in your dealings with God and others? When you have failed to treat people as you should, have you responded with integrity as you reconciled with them? If you are to be blameless, you must do everything in your power to correct any wrongdoing and reconcile any broken relationship. There is a profound sense of peace for the one whose way is blameless!

Pride Brings You Down

A man's pride will bring him low,
But the humble in spirit will retain honor.

PROVERBS 29:23

Pride is the great enemy of the Christian. Pride is an overly high opinion of yourself. It motivates you to do things that you know are not Christlike, and it hinders you from doing what brings glory to God. Pride influenced Adam and Eve to try to become like God (Gen. 3:5). Pride motivated Cain to murder his brother (Gen. 4:5). Pride provoked Joseph's brothers to sell him into slavery (Gen. 37:8). Pride caused King Saul to resent David so deeply that he tried to murder him (1 Sam. 18:8). Pride led King Hezekiah to foolishly reveal his nation's wealth to his enemies (Isa. 39:2). Pride was at the root of the Pharisees' anger toward Jesus. Pride was the reason the disciples argued over rank in the kingdom (Luke 9:46).

Pride is your relentless enemy. If you succumb to its influence, there will be consequences. You may know that you have offended someone, but pride holds you back from asking forgiveness. You may realize you need to reconcile a broken relationship, but pride will lead you to deny that need. The Spirit may convict you that you are living a sinful lifestyle, but pride will discourage your admitting it. Pride will convince you that you deserve better treatment. Pride will impede your serving others. Instead, pride will have you striving for places of prominence. Pride will have you listen to flatterers and ignore honest counselors. Pride will lead you to isolate yourself so that you are not accountable to others.

Humility, on the other hand, is pleasing to God and places your life in a position where God will honor you. If pride has crept into some areas of your life, ask God to give you victory over it before it robs you of God's will for you.

Where Your Treasure Is

*For where your treasure is,
there your heart will be also.*

LUKE 12:34

What you value most is your treasure. Where you spend your time and your money is your treasure. Whatever dominates your conversation is what you treasure. What others know you for is a good indication of what your treasure is.

Most Christians are quick to claim that God is their first priority. Yet often their actions reveal that their treasure is not God but things of this world. Some Christians find it difficult to discuss their relationship with God, but they can chatter easily about their family, friends, or hobbies. Some find it impossible to rise early in order to spend time with God, but they willingly get up at dawn to pursue a hobby. Some find it difficult to give an offering to God but readily spend lavishly on recreation. Some boldly approach strangers to sell a product, yet they are painfully timid in telling others about their Savior. Some give hundreds of hours to serve in volunteer organizations but feel they have no time available to serve God.

If you are unsure of where your treasure is, examine where you spend your available time and money. Reflect on what it is you most enjoy thinking about and discussing. Ask your friends to tell you what they think is most important to you. Ask your children to list the things most valuable to you. It may surprise you to know what others consider to be your treasure.

Bearing One Another's Burdens

*Bear one another's burdens, and
so fulfill the law of Christ.*

GALATIANS 6:2

When God places people in your life who are in need, He is aware of what they lack, and He knows He has given you the resources to meet those needs. You know God does nothing by accident. When a need surfaces around you, immediately go to the Father and say, "You put me here for a reason. You knew this was going to happen. What did You intend to do through me that would help this person become closer to You?"

Recognizing a need in someone's life can be one of the greatest invitations from God you will ever experience. It's easy to become frustrated by the problems of others. They can overwhelm you as you become aware of need after need. Rather than looking at each new problem as one more drain on your time, energy, or finances, ask God why He placed you in this situation. Allow God to help you see beyond the obvious needs of others to the things He wants to accomplish in their lives. Don't miss God's activity because you're reluctant to carry the load of others.

Is God blessing you materially? It may be He is developing a "supply depot" in your life through which He can provide for others. Has God granted you a strong, healthy family life? It may be that He requires such a home to minister to the hurting families all around you. Has God released you from sinful habits? Has God's peace comforted you in a time of great sorrow? Has God miraculously provided for your needs? It may be that He has been purposefully building things into your life so that you can now be the kind of person who will carry the burdens of others.

Seeing the Multitudes

And seeing the multitudes, He went up on a mountain,
and when He was seated His disciples came to Him.
Then He opened His mouth and taught them.

MATTHEW 5:1–2

hrist sees people far differently than we do. Throughout the Gospels we see a pattern in the way Jesus taught His disciples. Whenever He saw the multitudes, Jesus would reveal to the disciples what was on His heart for the people. Jesus wanted His disciples to share His love for the people: The disciples did not always understand all He was telling them, but He assured them that later the Holy Spirit would reveal the significance of His words (John 14:25–26). When the multitudes began pressing in on Him, Jesus would get alone with His disciples and teach them about God's love for people.

You will experience this same pattern as you walk with Jesus. When God places you in a crowd, you may sense the Holy Spirit impressing upon you the heart and mind of God for those people. Perhaps your Lord will lead you to a solitary place where He shares with you His compassion for the people you have been with. He may reveal to you His will for the people and invite you to join Him in His redemptive activity. He may place a burden on your heart to pray for them. If you are among people and are unmoved by their spiritual condition, God may develop your love for them so that you are prepared to minister to them as He desires.

The next time you are in a crowd, listen to what the Holy Spirit is saying. You may discover that God has much on His heart for those people and that He is waiting for one of His disciples to respond to His prompting.

Slaves of Righteousness

*And having been set free from sin,
you became slaves of righteousness.*

ROMANS 6:18

Before you were a Christian you were a slave, in bondage to sin. Even when you did not want to sin, you were unable to do otherwise (Rom. 7:15–24). When God saved you, He freed you from sin, but you remained a slave. Now, rather than being bound to sin, you are bound to righteousness. In every area of your life you are obligated to do what honors God.

There are some who believe that when Christ sets them free, they are free to do whatever they want. That is not so. The apostle Paul realized that when he began following Christ he became a "bondservant" of Christ, and his life was no longer his own (Rom. 1:1). Now, rather than being enslaved to sin, he was enslaved to God and His righteousness. When people mistreated him, he had forfeited the right to respond from his natural feelings but was compelled to offer a righteous response. When he was tempted, he was no longer free to succumb to his feelings. Paul could not enter the workplace and act selfishly. He understood that, as a slave of righteousness, he was obligated to live a holy life, honoring his Master.

Righteous living is not an option for a Christian. Nor is it something we must try to do over time. It is an obligation, mandatory for every child of God. Our freedom in Christ is not freedom to do what we want. It is freedom to live righteously, something we could not do when we were in bondage to sin. Now that we are free to live righteously, we must allow the Holy Spirit to produce in us a holy, sanctified life (1 John 3:7).

Integrity Upheld

As for me, You uphold me in my integrity,
And set me before Your face forever.

PSALM 41:12

Joseph was a righteous man who had cultivated a reputation for godliness in his community. Then word spread across the community that Mary, the woman to whom he was engaged, was expecting a child. There would be many who would assume the worst of this apparently scandalous situation. Joseph probably experienced gossip from some, ostracism from others. Yet he was a man of integrity, aware that God knew the truth of his relationship with Mary.

At times, God will be the only witness to your righteous behavior. Sometimes God is the only one who will understand your motives. Sometimes you will do all you know God has asked you to do, only to face ridicule from others. At such times all you can do is maintain your integrity, trusting that God always keeps His eyes on you. God looks favorably upon those who walk with integrity, doing what they know is right, regardless of how others perceive their actions.

The most important thing is not that people know the truth. The most important thing is that you are a person of integrity before God. When no one seems to understand why you have done something or when others question whether you have done all you should have done, your confidence should not be in the hope of vindication in the eyes of others. It should be in the knowledge that God keeps you in His sight. If you have this confidence, it will be enough to sustain you.

Strongholds

*"And you shall make no covenant with the inhabitants of this
land; you shall tear down their altars." But you have not
obeyed My voice. Why have you done this? Therefore I also
said, "I will not drive them out before you; but they shall be
thorns in your side, and their gods shall be a snare to you."*

JUDGES 2:2–3

God gave the Israelites specific instructions: Drive the
Canaanites out of every corner of the land, and obliterate
any vestige of their abominable idol worship. This assignment was
challenging! Their enemies had formidable chariots. The
Canaanites had seemingly impregnable fortresses that were dangerous and difficult to overcome. The Israelites failed to drive all
the Canaanites from the land. Much about the Canaanite lifestyle
and religion appealed to the Israelites' sinful nature. Rather than
destroying them and their idolatry, Israel compromised. The
Canaanites would prove to be a troublesome distraction to the
Israelites. Their idol worship would present a constant temptation.

When you became a Christian, God declared war on sin's strongholds in your life. Sinful behaviors and attitudes were firmly
entrenched in your character, but God commanded you to tear
them down. The Holy Spirit pointed out areas of your life that were
resistant to God's will. Were you tempted to merely establish a truce
rather than obliterating every sin? Is anger one of sin's strongholds?
If so, it will rise up against you in moments of weakness. Is there a
stronghold of lust in your life? If so, you will succumb to it when
caught off guard. In careless moments, these strongholds will still
tempt you to continue your past sinful behaviors.

Do not underestimate the destructive power of sin. If there are
strongholds in your life that you have never defeated, the Holy
Spirit is still prepared to bring you complete victory.

What More Could Have Been Done?

*What more could have been done to My vineyard
That I have not done in it? Why then, when I expected it to
bring forth good grapes, Did it bring forth wild grapes?*

ISAIAH 5:4

The prophet Isaiah told the story of a man with a vineyard on a fertile hill. The man cultivated the ground and removed the stones so that nothing would hinder the vines' growth. He planted only the best quality vines. He built a tower in the middle of the vineyard so he could watch for wild animals and intruders. He constructed a wine vat so that he would be ready for the ripe grapes. Then he waited. Rather than producing good grapes, however, the vineyard produced worthless ones.

The story illustrates the relationship between God and His people. God has done everything necessary for us to produce an abundance of spiritual fruit in our lives. He saved us when we were without hope. He gave us His Holy Spirit to produce fruit in our lives (Gal. 5:22–23). He removed our sin so that we are free to serve Him. We have the Bible in numerous translations. We have access to more Christian books, music, videos, conferences, schools, radio and television stations, magazines, and seminars than ever before. There are churches of every kind and size. We have teachers and pastors to instruct us and encourage us. Most of all, we have direct access to God through prayer. Jesus said that to whom much is given, much is expected (Luke 12:48). One day God will hold us accountable for all that He has done for us. He will ask us to show Him the fruit of all of His bountiful provision for our lives. What will He find?

Choose to Rejoice

But at midnight Paul and Silas were praying and singing hymns to God, and the prisoners were listening to them.

ACTS 16:25

Your joy as a Christian should not depend on your circumstances. Joy comes from God, and therefore it cannot be affected by what is outside of you. Don't be fooled into letting the actions of others determine your joy. True joy comes from knowing that God Himself lives within you and has fellowship with you, regardless of your environment. Real joy lies in the knowledge that holy God has completely forgiven you of every sin, and even now, He has a home prepared in heaven where you can spend eternity with Him (John 14:3). The circumstances of your life cannot change these truths!

Paul and Silas faced some of the most difficult circumstances imaginable. They were falsely accused, arrested, and imprisoned. They were beaten and shackled in the darkest, coldest section of the prison. But they refused to allow their horrific situation to dampen their joy! They did not blame God for allowing these things to happen to them. Instead, they praised Him for His goodness! In the darkness of the night, they prayed and they sang. God brought a miracle that released them from their chains, but perhaps the greater miracle was that His Holy Spirit could so fill them that even in their painful imprisonment they could overflow with joy!

Do not allow difficult events to cancel the joy of knowing you are a child of God. Choose to allow God's Spirit to fill you with His unquenchable joy, and your life will be a miracle to those who watch you face the trials that come.

Return to God

Thus says the Lord of hosts: "Return to Me,"
says the Lord of hosts, "and I will return to you."

ZECHARIAH 1:3

God places much of the burden of what we will become on our response to Him. If we have drifted from God, His call is to return to Him. God promises that if we will return, He will immediately renew His relationship with us. James 4:8 promises that if we draw near to God, He will draw near to us. Matthew 7:7 guarantees that if we seek Christ, we will find Him. Much of the Christian life rests upon our response and our desire to experience God to the fullest.

Why is it that some Christians seem to go so much deeper in their walk with God than others? Why have some had such powerful intercessory prayer ministries that have changed the courses of nations? Why has God chosen to anoint the words of some so that, when they speak or pray or preach, it is obvious that their words are consecrated by God? It is because these individuals have committed themselves to pursue God until His presence is powerfully real in their lives. They have decided to settle for nothing less than a vibrant relationship with God, and He has honored their desire.

Have you become complacent in your relationship with God, or are you hungering for more? Don't become satisfied with a relationship with God that is broken by sin and void of the power of the Holy Spirit. You have just as much of God's powerful presence available to you as the greatest saint in Christian history! Return to God. There is so much more in store for you if you will return to Him. He awaits your response.

An Imperishable Crown

Do you not know that those who run in a race all run,
but one receives the prize? Run in such a way that you may
obtain it. And everyone who competes for the prize is
temperate in all things. Now they do it to obtain
a perishable crown, but we for an imperishable crown.

1 CORINTHIANS 9:24–25

Athletes are willing to push themselves harder and longer and farther than anyone else. They strive to bring their bodies and minds completely under control so that they excel and receive a prize. Others go home to relax, but athletes continue to train. While most people protect themselves from any form of discomfort, athletes push themselves to the limits of their endurance. While some remain satisfied with mediocre performance, athletes pay any price for excellence. Paul said that despite their most valiant efforts, the athletes' successes and prizes are eventually forgotten. Even the greatest athletic achievements have not affected eternity.

If an athlete can be motivated to make incredible sacrifices for a perishable reward, how much more ought Christians to strive for an imperishable one? If an athlete will labor day after day in order to receive glory from others, how much harder ought Christians to work for the "well done" of their Master? Are you striving to bring your body into subjection for the glory of God? Are you training your mind to think the thoughts of God rather than thoughts of the world? Are you disciplining your life in prayer? When others are sleeping, are you interceding? Have you studied God's Word so diligently that you are prepared to find answers to the challenges you face? Have you equipped yourself in evangelism so that you are ready to share your faith? Have you prepared yourself as a Christian in order to qualify for the imperishable crown that awaits you?

189

A Highway of Holiness

A highway shall be there, and a road,
And it shall be called the Highway of Holiness.
The unclean shall not pass over it,
But it shall be for others.
Whoever walks the road, although a fool,
Shall not go astray.

ISAIAH 35:8

The nation of Israel was designed to have a place where other nations of the world could come to worship the true God. The temple in Jerusalem was to be the center from which the good news of God's salvation would spread to every corner of the world. But those who were supposed to be God's people forsook Him and practiced every kind of sin. Rather than being ambassadors for God, they disgraced His holy name. Rather than attracting the nations of the earth to God, they became stumbling blocks to those who were seeking the true God. The Israelites fell so far from God's original intent that God judged them and sent them into exile. Yet God promised that one day His people would be an avenue by which others could find salvation.

It is God's desire that anywhere there is a Christian, God has a way for people to learn of His salvation (Rom. 10:14–15). Whenever an unbeliever meets a Christian, the unbeliever ought to be face to face with everything he needs to know in order to follow Christ.

Sadly, however, Christians can be like the Israelites of Isaiah's day. We can be so involved in our sin that we are completely disoriented to God, ill-equipped to direct others to Him. If our lives are filled with hypocrisy, we may turn people away from God, rather than helping them come to Him. If our lives are filled with doubt or anger, we will impede others from coming to Christ. Our lives ought to be a highway of holiness, providing easy access to God for anyone around us who seeks Him. Ask God to remove any obstacle in your life that hinders others from coming to know Jesus.

Effective, Fervent Prayer

*The effective, fervent prayer
of a righteous man avails much.*

JAMES 5:16b

God promises all believers that if we live righteously and pray fervently, our prayers will be effective and produce significant results. How do we treat a promise like this? We might argue, "But I *do* pray, and nothing happens!" Our problem is that we do not hold ourselves accountable to the Scripture. God's Word says that prayer ought to accomplish much. If our prayer life is not accomplishing much, what should we do? If we are praying but seeing no results, should we conclude that this promise is untrue? Should we excuse this Scripture as impractical and unrealistic? Or should we examine ourselves to see if we meet its conditions?

James says that *fervent* prayer avails much. Could it be that we are not as fervent in our praying as we should be? Fervent prayer means we do not quit easily. Fervent prayer means we purposefully spend sufficient time in intercession. Fervent prayer means we cry out to the Father, sometimes in tears, with our heart and soul. Fervent prayer comes as the Holy Spirit assists us in praying with groanings too deep for words (Rom. 8:26).

According to James, our righteousness will ensure effective prayer. God's standard of righteousness is different from ours, for He looks beyond our actions, even beyond our thoughts, directly to our hearts. How then should we hold ourselves accountable if our prayers are accomplishing little? If nothing happens when we pray, the problem is not with God. The problem is with us, for God's Word is absolutely reliable. If we adhere to what God requires, He will lead us to pray for things that align with His purposes, and God will answer our prayers in a mighty way.

Bitterness

Looking carefully lest anyone fall short of the grace of God;
lest any root of bitterness springing up cause trouble.

HEBREWS 12:15

itterness has a tenacious way of taking root deep within the soul and resisting all efforts to weed it out. Bitterness occurs for many reasons. It might come from deep hurts you received as a child, hurts you cannot forget. Time, rather than diminishing the hurt, only seems to sharpen the pain. Bitterness can result from the hurtful words of a friend or coworker. Often the person who hurt you is unaware of the extent of your bitterness. You find yourself rehearsing the offense over and over again, each time driving the root of bitterness deeper within your soul. Bitterness can derive from a sense of being unjustly treated.

Bitterness is easy to justify. You can get so used to a bitter heart that you are even comfortable with it, but it will destroy you. Only God is fully aware of its destructive potential. There is nothing so deeply imbedded in your heart that God's grace cannot reach down and remove it. No area in your life is so painful that God's grace cannot bring total healing. No offense committed against you is so heinous that God's love cannot enable you to forgive.

When you allow bitterness to grow in your life, you reject the grace of God that can free you. If you are honest before God, you will admit the bitterness and allow God to forgive you. Bitterness enslaves you, but God is prepared to remove your bitterness and replace it with His peace and joy.

Confident Hope

Let us hold fast the confession of our hope without wavering,
for He who promised is faithful.

HEBREWS 10:23

Hope in the Christian's life is not wishful thinking. It is confident expectation. Those without Christ may wish things were different and wish they knew someone who could change their situations. The Christian is personally related to the Lord of the universe, who is sovereign not only over all creation but also over every circumstance we experience. We can live with confidence because our hope is in One who is faithful.

When God speaks, He stands by His word to see that it comes to pass (Isa. 55:11). When God speaks a word to you, trust Him completely, for God never deceives His children. If God has indicated to you that He is going to do something, you can be absolutely confident that He will do it.

Do you wonder why unrighteous people seem to prosper while righteous people suffer? Jesus promised that each would eventually receive a just reward (Luke 16:19–31). Do you wonder if all the effort you have put into training your children in God's ways will bear fruit when they become adults? God promised it would (Prov. 22:6). Do you wonder if the things you renounced when you became a Christian will be replaced by God's blessings? Jesus assured us we would receive a hundred times as much (Mark 10:29–30). Do you doubt that Jesus will return and join us with those who have already died? Scripture indicates this certainty (1 Thess. 4:13–18).

Our hope is not mere speculation in what God *might* do. God has given His word on many areas of life regarding things He *will* do. We can have confident hope in everything that He has promised.

Wait on the Lord

Wait on the Lord; Be of good courage,
And He shall strengthen your heart;
Wait, I say, on the Lord!

PSALM 27:14

aiting is one of the hardest things to do. We want to be people of action. We feel better if we are doing something to address our need, but waiting forces us to rely on God. David learned what it meant to wait. He was chosen by God to be the next king of Israel, then spent years waiting for the day God's Word would come to pass in his life. As he waited, a paranoid, egocentric king occupied the throne that had been promised to him. David spent his time hiding in caves and living among his enemies. As he waited he saw good friends murdered and his family and possessions taken. He saw Israel's enemies wreak havoc on his nation. Perhaps no one ever faced greater adversity while waiting upon God's promise than David did. He certainly understood what it meant to become discouraged and fearful.

But David also enjoyed the reward for waiting upon the Lord. He became the greatest king in Israel's history, and, more importantly, through his trials he became a man after God's own heart. The psalms David wrote during his days as a fugitive have been cherished words of encouragement for millions of people through the ages. Through David's descendants came the Messiah. David's willingness to wait has blessed us all.

Times of waiting on the Lord can be some of the most precious moments in your life (John 11:1–6). If you are waiting on God for something, read Isaiah 40:31 and find encouragement as you wait for Him to fulfill His promises to you.

Godly Sorrow

*For godly sorrow produces repentance leading to salvation,
not to be regretted; but the sorrow of the world produces death.*

2 CORINTHIANS 7:10

There is a difference between worldly sorrow and godly sorrow, though both are deeply felt. You can feel genuine sorrow over something you have done. Your mind can become consumed with your failure and offense against God and others. Judas felt this kind of sorrow. He betrayed the Son of God for thirty pieces of silver, the standard price of a slave. Yet his sorrow did not lead him to repent and to seek restoration with his fellow disciples, but rather to a lonely field where, in his anguish, he took his own life (Matt. 27:3–5). Judas carried his sorrow to his grave.

How different Peter's sorrow was! Peter, too, failed Jesus on the night of His crucifixion. Peter also went out and wept bitterly (Luke 22:62). Yet Peter returned to Jesus and reaffirmed his love for Him (John 21:15–17). Peter was not only remorseful; he was also repentant. Peter's life changed. There is no record of Peter ever denying his Lord again, even when he was persecuted and threatened with death. Peter repented, turned his life around, and never committed that sin again.

Don't allow mere unhappiness over what you have done to rob you of genuine repentance. You can blame yourself and be angry with yourself for the sins you have committed, but that is not repentance. Allow the Holy Spirit to reveal to you the gravity of your sins. Ask the Spirit to clearly show you how God views your character. When you see your sin from God's perspective, you will experience godly sorrow.

God Will Not Forget

Can a woman forget her nursing child,
And not have compassion on the son of her womb?
Surely they may forget, Yet I will not forget you.

ISAIAH 49:15

G od never becomes preoccupied or neglectful toward one of His children. God said it would be more likely for a nursing mother to forget the infant at her breast than for Him to forget one of His children! The nursing mother has a keen sensitivity to her baby. Even if the infant is in another room the mother's senses are in tune with her child. The mother knows when it is time to feed and care for the child. The mother never becomes so preoccupied with other things that she neglects the needs of her child.

It is fitting that God chose this imagery to describe how He looks after His people, for He is more sensitive to the needs of His children than even the most loving mother. He anticipates every cry for help. Even before we can call out in need, God is responding with His answer (Isa. 65:24). This is one of the most comforting promises God has given to us: that He will never forget us.

Don't let the difficult circumstances you are facing convince you that God has forgotten you. Don't ever assume that God is more concerned with the needs of other, more significant, more spiritual people than He is with yours. Scripture teaches that God looks upon you with the same love, interest, and concern as a nursing mother would look upon her infant. It should reassure you to know that your Father loves you like that!

He Is at
Your Right Hand

I have set the Lord always before me;
Because He is at my right hand I shall not be moved.

PSALM 16:8

What does it mean to set the Lord always before you? It means that you choose to relate everything you encounter to your trust in God. What you choose to focus on becomes the dominant influence in your life. You may be a Christian, but if your focus is always on your problems, your problems will determine the direction of your life. If your focus is on people, then people will determine what you think and do. In biblical times, the right hand was the most distinguished position, reserved for one's chief adviser and supporter. When you choose to focus on Christ, you invite Him to take the most important position in your life as Counselor and Defender.

Every time you face a new experience, you should turn to Christ for His interpretation and strength. When people insult you and mistreat you, you should seek direction from your Counselor regarding the right response. When you face a crisis, you should receive strength from the One at your right hand. When you experience need, you should consult your Counselor before you react. When you face a fearful situation, you should take courage from the Advocate at your right hand. Everything you do is in the context of your relationship to Christ.

What an incredible act of God's grace that Christ should stand beside you to guide you and counsel you and defend you! How could you ever become dismayed over your situation with Christ at your right hand? What confidence this should give you!

God Honors Those
Who Honor Him

For those who honor Me I will honor, and those who despise Me shall be lightly esteemed.

1 SAMUEL 2:30

One of the many truths of the kingdom of God is that if we will honor God, He will honor us. If, however, we dare to treat Him disrespectfully, we will also be treated as least in His kingdom. The initiative rests with us. Our response to God determines His response to us.

Eli had been the priest of Israel for many years, and he knew the standards for righteous living that God required. Yet Eli faced a dilemma, for his sons were living in direct opposition to God. As their father, Eli had to decide whom he would honor. He could not defer to his immoral and ungodly sons and also exalt the God he served. By default, Eli chose to honor his sons, for he did not insist that their behavior conform to God's standards. Eli would have pleaded that he still loved God but that he simply could not bring honor to God with his family. Yet God viewed Eli's behavior differently (1 Sam. 3:13–14). Eli revealed his own heart when he failed to honor God before the people of Israel by the way he dealt with his sons. This is why God punished Eli and his sons severely (1 Sam. 4:17–18).

God is not pleased if you praise Him at church but not at your workplace. It is not acceptable for you to revere God when you are with other Christians but not in your school or neighborhood. He expects you to honor Him completely, with your words, with your actions, with your life. If you honor Him, He will honor you.

A Godly Person Set Apart

But know that the Lord has set apart for Himself him who is godly; The Lord will hear when I call to Him.

PSALM 4:3

No one is more precious in the Lord's sight than a godly person. God is pleased whenever He finds someone who strives to live a righteous life and bring glory to Him. God sets such people apart in a special place in His heart. They are always kept before Him, and He stands ready to respond to their faintest cries for help.

Sin separates us from God, causing Him to close His ears to our praying. It is futile for us to pray when we are knowingly practicing sin. But the opposite is also true. God chooses to honor us by listening to our every cry when we are living a godly life. An abiding security comes with living a blameless life. The righteous person never has to wonder whether God has listened to his prayer (1 John 5:14–15). The godly person has confidence that God has indeed heard her prayer and will immediately respond in all of His power.

It is exhilarating to be set apart by God, knowing that God observes your consecrated life and is pleased with what He sees. What a tremendous privilege to know that your life holds a special place in God's heart! The world may not accord any special status to you, but you will know that you are cherished by God. The world continues to find new ways to honor people, but even the world's most extravagant accolades are pitiful compared to the unfathomable blessing of holding a special place in the heart of God!

The Desires of
Your Heart

Delight yourself also in the Lord,
And He shall give you the desires of your heart.

PSALM 37:4

Your relationship with God ought to bring you more joy, satisfaction, and pleasure than any other relationship, activity, or material possession you have. Scripture exhorts you to delight yourself in the Lord, finding your greatest pleasure in God and the things dear to His heart.

How can you find pleasure in what God enjoys? Only as you spend time with Him will you begin to take delight in the things God loves. As you spend intimate time with God and allow Him to show you your situation from His perspective, you will begin to see things as God sees them. As you adjust yourself to God, your heart will begin to desire the same things God's heart desires. When you pray, you will find yourself asking for the very things God desires. Matters foremost on God's heart will be pre-eminent in yours. Your first request in prayer will not be for yourself, but for God's name to be exalted and His kingdom to be extended (Matt. 6:9–10).

Have you been asking God to give you the desires of your heart without first seeking to understand what is on His heart? God places this important requirement for those who pray: that we seek His priorities and make them our own. This great qualifier prevents us from asking out of selfishness. As we find joy in the Lord, we will see what is truly important, and we will long for these things as the Father does.

Knowing God

And God spoke to Moses and said to him, "I am the Lord.
I appeared to Abraham, to Isaac, and to Jacob, as God
Almighty, but by My name Lord I was not known to them."

EXODUS 6:2–3

As God has walked with His people through the generations, He has progressively revealed His nature according to His purposes and the needs of His people. Abraham, Isaac, and Jacob knew Him as God Almighty, because they needed His mighty power to protect them from their enemies. Moses and the Israelites learned that God was Lord, Master over every nation and every thing. God not only delivered them from the most powerful ruler in the world, but also brought them into the Promised Land. They came to experience Him as Lord, preeminently powerful over the pagan gods of their day.

God will continue to reveal His character to you according to your needs and according to His purposes. You will come to know more and more about Him as you obey Him. When you grieve, He will come to you as Comforter. When you are in need, He will demonstrate that He is the Provider. When you face a serious challenge, He will reveal that He is God Almighty.

Your understanding of God's character ought to be greater now than when you first became a Christian. You ought to know Him today better than you did five years ago. Sadly, some Christians continue to live year after year with the same basic knowledge of God that they had when they first began walking with Him. Whatever your present situation, view it in the light of what God is teaching you, through circumstances, about Himself and you will come to know God in dimensions you have never known Him before.

God's Initiatives

Now the Lord had said to Abram,
"Get out of your country, From your family
And from your father's house, To a land that I will show you."

GENESIS 12:1

The most dramatic changes in your life will come from God's initiative, not yours. The people God used mightily in Scripture were all ordinary people to whom He gave divine assignments that they never could have initiated. The Lord often took them by surprise, for they were not seeking significant mandates from God. Even so, He saw their hearts, and He knew they were trustworthy.

The Lord spoke to Abram when He was beginning to build a nation dedicated to His purposes. Through this nation would come the Savior. God appeared to Moses at the very time He had purposed to deliver Israel out of slavery in Egypt. God found in Jesse's youngest son David a godly man who could lead His people. God surprised Mary when He told her she would be the mother of the Messiah. God's Son selected the twelve disciples, all ordinary, uneducated men, when He was ready to take the good news of His salvation to the world. Through the ages God has taken the initiative in the everyday lives of people to accomplish things through them that they never could have imagined.

The Lord may be initiating some new things in your life. When He tells you what His plans are, trust Him and walk closely with Him. Don't let the busyness of your present activity keep you from experiencing all that God has in store for you. You will see Him accomplish things through your life that you never dreamed were possible (Eph. 3:20).

Born Again

*Jesus answered and said to him, "Most assuredly, I say to you,
unless one is born again, he cannot see the kingdom of God."*

JOHN 3:3

Entering a saving relationship with Christ is a life-changing experience! All things become new! Not *some* things, but *all* things (2 Cor. 5:17). For the first time in your life, Christ is Lord; God is Master. When you become a Christian, Christ's presence will affect every part of you. You will have new thoughts, new attitudes, new values, and new sensitivities. New priorities will dramatically affect your relationships. You will view everything in your life from a Christlike perspective. Christianity is not something you add to your life; it is life!

Nicodemus thought that salvation meant performing certain religious exercises and holding to particular religious teachings. He had no idea of the all-encompassing nature of salvation! When you become a Christian, God gives you a new heart so that *everything* becomes new! God gives you a new mind, like that of Christ, so you think differently. He gives you new emotions, so you feel deeply about completely different matters. You become sensitive to sin, so you are no longer comfortable with it. Your recreation will be affected as you are made aware of what is honoring to God and what is not. Your relationships will now be guided by the Holy Spirit. Destructive habits and attitudes, previously immune to change, will be transformed.

Have you noticed the changes God has brought to your life since you entered a vital relationship with Jesus Christ? These changes should be very noticeable as a testimony of the new life you received when you trusted Jesus as your Savior and Lord.

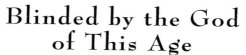

Blinded by the God of This Age

Whose minds the god of this age has blinded, who do not believe, lest the light of the gospel of the glory of Christ, who is the image of God, should shine on them.

2 CORINTHIANS 4:4

When you are blinded, you cannot see things as they really are, even though others around you see them clearly. You cannot experience the full reality of all that is around you. You may feel you are experiencing all that there is to life, yet you may be unaware that you are missing what God desires for you. You may even be in danger because of your blindness and not know it.

Paul warned that the "god of this age" can blind you to the reality of Jesus Christ. Christ's presence can make a significant difference in your life. However, if Satan convinces you to doubt that Christ can do what He promised, he will have blinded you to the reality of what your life is really like and to what it could become. Others may see what your unbelief causes you to miss, but you will be unaware of it. Your life may be steadily moving toward disaster, but you will be oblivious to it.

Christ comes to you as light (John 1:4, 5, 9). He illuminates your sin so that you see its ugliness and destructiveness. He reveals Himself so that you can appreciate the glory of His person and the marvelous riches He brings. His presence lights your path so that you can see impending danger. Don't let the god of this age distort your spiritual vision. Don't be fooled into thinking that everything is as it should be when, in fact, you are missing out on so much that God wants to do in your life. Ask Christ to illuminate your life and let you clearly see your spiritual condition.

Displaying God through Your Life

Work out your own salvation with fear and trembling;
for it is God who works in you both to will
and to do for His good pleasure.

PHILIPPIANS 2:12b–13

Salvation is not an event; it is a process. Salvation is God's gift, for there is nothing we can do to save ourselves (Eph. 2:8–9). Yet with salvation comes the responsibility to work out our salvation. Once we have been saved, we must claim all that has become ours.

Through salvation, God gave you victory over sin. That victory applies not only to past sins but also to every sin you will ever commit. When you became a Christian, God made you a new creation (2 Cor. 5:17). God wants to continually build new things into your life as you walk with Him. God gave you His joy when He saved you, and He wants to fill you with His joy daily. When you first repented of your sin, you relinquished your right to your life. God continues to ask you to yield your will to Him and to follow His leading rather than setting your own direction for your life. When you were converted, God made everything available to you; how you implement what He has given you is your choice (2 Pet. 1:3–9).

This is the great paradox of the Christian life. We are to work diligently on our faith, yet always with the awareness that only God can bring about lasting change in our lives. As we see God at work in us, we are motivated to work even more diligently. God will not force His changes upon us; neither can we bring about lasting change in our lives apart from the work of the Holy Spirit.

When you sense God developing an area of your life, join Him in His activity so that His salvation will be demonstrated fully.

The Difference Your Life Can Make

Brethren, if anyone among you wanders from the truth, and someone turns him back, let him know that he who turns a sinner from the error of his way will save a soul from death and cover a multitude of sins.

JAMES 5:19–20

One of the Christian's greatest deterrents from sin is the life of another Christian. Some Christians maintain that it is none of their business if another chooses to sin. They are convinced that they are being judgmental if they respond to someone in sin. The world persuades them not to get involved, but this inaction prevents them from being an effective intercessor.

As Christians we are aware that sin brings death (Rom. 6:23). Sin kills relationships, dismantles marriages, stifles joy, and destroys peace. When we see someone wander from the truth into error, how should we respond? When Jesus saw sin it broke His heart. He wept over entire cities as He saw them rejecting the truth (Matt. 23:37–39). He prayed fervently for His disciples to be strong when they were tempted (John 17). He warned those who were heading toward spiritual failure (Matt. 26:20–25, 34). Jesus was even willing to die to save people from their sins because He knew the devastation that sin causes. Jesus never stood idle as those around Him were led astray by their sin. He always took an active role in turning them back to God.

"Minding your own business" will save you some discomfort, but it will not help a brother or sister who needs to return to the Lord. If you are truly aware of the grave consequences for those who continue in sin, you will be moved to weep even as Jesus wept. Pray fervently for your friend. That will safeguard your motives and prepare you to minister to him. Be alert, in the event that God asks you to confront your friend. If you do so, be loving and gentle lest you, too, be tempted (Gal. 6:1).

Walking Worthy

Only let your conduct be worthy of the gospel of Christ.

PHILIPPIANS 1:27

Paul never lost his wonder at having been called by God. He understood that the way he lived ought to be worthy of the King who had chosen him. He knew that the mystery of the gospel had been hidden for generations and had only been revealed in his day through the life, death, and resurrection of Jesus Christ (Col. 1:26–27). Paul also understood that until people accept the gospel, they are spiritually dead and therefore without hope (Col. 2:13). As a result of God's plan of salvation, those who trust in Jesus are not only made alive in Christ but are also adopted as the Father's children (Rom. 8:16–17). Paul recognized that though the gospel sounds like foolishness to the world, it is the power of God that brings eternal life to those who accept it.

Because Paul's life had been radically transformed by the gospel, he was intent on living to honor the gospel that gave him life. It would have been tragic to receive the riches of the gospel and then to live as a spiritual pauper. It would have been disgraceful to be saved from death by the blood of Christ and then show no reverence for that sacrifice. It would have been foolish to accept such love from Christ and then to resent what He asked in return.

The way you live your life ought to be a tribute to the matchless grace that your Lord and Savior, Jesus Christ, has bestowed upon you.

Your Heavenly Father Knows You

*Therefore do not be like them. For your Father knows
the things you have need of before you ask Him.*

MATTHEW 6:8

Even before we call on Him, the Father has already begun to provide all that we need (Isa. 65:24). Jesus wanted His disciples to learn how intimately God knew and loved each of them. That is why He told them to pray. He assured them that even before they prayed, God knew all about their situation.

Prayer is not designed for us to inform God of our needs, for He already knows them. Why, then, should we pray? Prayer enables us to experience God more intimately. The more a child experiences the loving provision of a parent, the more convinced he becomes of his parent's unrelenting love. Often a parent will anticipate a child's need before the child recognizes it and be prepared in advance to provide for that need. Our heavenly Father knows exactly what we will face today and next week. He is eager for us to experience Him as He provides for us.

To our surprise, we often discover that God knows far better than we do what is best for us. At times we assume that we know what would benefit us. We can even be foolish enough to assume that we don't require anything of God. Yet God wants us to go to Him in our need (Matt. 7:7). He is ready to show His strength through our weakness. Our heavenly Father knows exactly what is best for us, and He is prepared to provide for every need, if we will but ask (Phil. 4:13).

Put Away Lying

Therefore, putting away lying, "Let each one of you speak truth with his neighbor," for we are members of one another.

EPHESIANS 4:25

Because you are a Christian, your life ought to be permeated with truth. When you were born again, God put the Spirit of truth in you (John 16:13). The Spirit's role is to guide you into all truth. The Spirit wants to fill your mind with whatever is true (Phil. 4:8). If you allow the Spirit to fill you with God's truth, you will be truthful in your actions and in your relationships. According to Jesus, this means that your yes will always mean yes, and your no will always mean no (Matt. 5:33–37).

The world considers truth optional. Deception permeates every corner of society because the prince of this world is the author and father of lies (John 8:44). From his first contact with people, Satan has been lying to them and persuading them to live in falsehood rather than in truth.

The world will tempt you to compromise the truth. You may be fooled into thinking that you can accomplish greater good by withholding the truth. That is a demonic deception. You cannot use deception to build the kingdom of God! God refuses to use sinful means to accomplish His holy purposes. You may be tempted to live a lie by projecting a false image of yourself. Jesus condemned this as hypocrisy (Luke 12:56). When you sin, you will be tempted to conceal the truth; yet only as you confess the truth will you be forgiven and set free (James 5:16).

What you say reflects what is in your heart (Matt. 12:34). If your heart is filled with deception, your mouth will speak falsehood. Ask God to permeate you with His truth so that you find falsehood, in any form, abhorrent.

Draw Near to God

Draw near to God and He will draw near to you.
Cleanse your hands, you sinners;
and purify your hearts, you double-minded.

JAMES 4:8

There may be times when God seems far away. You may feel as if your prayers go unheard. James said there is a simple reason for this and a solution. If you are far from God, it is because your sin has separated you from Him.

God is unchanging. His character stays absolutely holy. His faithfulness remains constant; it is we who change. We allow sin into our lives. We choose our own direction. We spend less and less time with Him in Bible study and prayer. Then one day we realize that we have gradually grown distant from God. The solution, according to James, is straightforward. We are to draw near to God. As we realize our need to be closer to the Father and we begin to return to Him, He meets us even as the father hurried to greet his prodigal son (Luke 15:20).

Drawing near to God requires you to take two actions. First, you must cleanse your hands (Isa. 1:15). You must cleanse your way of living. If you have been actively engaged in sin, you must renounce it. If you have done anything to offend or hurt someone, you must make it right. Second, you are to purify your heart (Ps. 51:10). You must make certain your attitudes, thoughts, and motives are right in God's eyes and are in harmony with God's Word. Jesus warned that you cannot serve two masters (Matt. 6:24). It is impossible to love anything else as much as you love God and still please Him.

If God seems distant, do what is necessary to cleanse your hands, purify your heart, and draw near to Him.

A Double Portion

*And so it was, when they had crossed over, that Elijah said
to Elisha, "Ask! What may I do for you, before I am taken
away from you?" Elisha said, "Please let a double portion
of your spirit be upon me."*

2 KINGS 2:9

There had never been a man like Elijah. Elijah had raised the dead, called down fire from heaven, and revealed God's plans for a devastating drought. The Israelites must have felt certain there would never be another prophet like Elijah, until Elisha came along. Moses was arguably the mightiest leader the Hebrews had ever followed, yet God prepared Joshua to accomplish what not even Moses had achieved. David's reign marked a high point for the nation of Israel, yet it was Solomon who carried out the task that was denied his father, by building the spectacular temple.

We can be tempted to put more trust in the leaders God gives us than in God Himself. History teaches that, as wonderful as these godly people are, God always has another Moses, Elijah, or David. Often the successor will come with a double portion of their predecessors' spirits.

God's purposes do not depend on us. He has limitless ways to accomplish His will. The same God who led Moses could also use Joshua. If no one were willing to serve Him, the Lord would accomplish His work by His own divine power. We are not irreplaceable to the Lord. He will achieve His purposes. The question is this: Will we be a part of God's activity, or will He find someone else? We deceive ourselves if we think we are indispensable to God. Service to the Lord is an honor God bestows on us, not a favor we do for God.

If you are mourning the loss of one of your leaders, do not despair. God has another leader, for He will see that His will is carried out. It may even be that He has been preparing you to be that leader.

Powerless

And she said, "The Philistines are upon you, Samson!"
So he awoke from his sleep, and said, "I will go out as before,
at other times, and shake myself free!" But he did not know
that the Lord had departed from him.

JUDGES 16:20

One of the signs of a heart that has shifted from God is the absence of spiritual power. If you are like Samson, you will not be immediately aware that God's power has left you. Only after he tried to defeat his enemies did Samson recognize that something was wrong. He went against the Philistines as before, expecting their swift defeat. But this time the Philistines easily prevailed over him.

If you allow sin to creep into your life, if you refuse to obey your Lord, if you do not reconcile with those who have hurt you, your spiritual vitality is waning. You may assume everything is fine, but when you pray, answers do not come as they once did. You once had a positive effect on those around you, but now your influence is negligible or even harmful. Your life once brought reconciliation, but now you experience problems in your relationships. Those around you who have relied upon your strength are discovering that you are not as helpful to them as you once were. Your lack of spiritual power is not crying out for attention; but you are seeing subtle changes in your spirit and in your relationship with God.

How can you stop this spiritual decline? You must regularly repent of any sin. You must invite God to search your life to see if there are attitudes, relationships, or activities that need to be removed. You must fervently obey His will. If you walk with God in this manner, you will grow in spiritual strength and be used mightily by Him.

God's Presence

*No man shall be able to stand before you all the days of your
life; as I was with Moses, so I will be with you.
I will not leave you nor forsake you.*

JOSHUA 1:5

God's assignment for Joshua might have caused him some
concern. Being the successor to Moses was no small task.
Through Moses, God had turned the waters in Egypt into blood,
parted the Red Sea, destroyed the Egyptian army, and miraculously fed the nation for forty years. God spoke to Moses on
Mount Sinai and gave him His law. Joshua must have wondered
how he could follow Moses.

To erase any doubt, God assured Joshua that Moses' accomplishments had all been due to God's presence. Joshua grew confident because the same God who walked with Moses now
walked with him (Josh. 1:6).

As you read the accounts of God's miraculous work through
men and women in the Bible, you may wonder if God still per-
forms such miracles today. Be assured that the same God who
walked with Moses, Joshua, Elijah, Peter, James, John, and Paul
now lives within you. No power can defeat the God who guides
you. The God who blessed them is just as capable of working out
His purposes through your life. The same God who gave them
victory over seemingly invincible enemies, who provided for
them when their own resources were insufficient, and who guided them in their decisions, is prepared to work as powerfully in
your life today. The heroes of the faith had one thing in common:
They were all ordinary people with no power of their own. The
difference is the mighty presence of God. Times may change, but
the effect of God's presence remains the same.

A Loyal Heart

*For the eyes of the Lord run to and fro throughout
the whole earth, to show Himself strong on behalf of those
whose heart is loyal to Him.*

2 CHRONICLES 16:9

If your heart is loyal to God, you do not have to look for Him; He is already looking for you! God told King Asa that He continuously watches for those who are steadfast in their commitment to Him. When He finds them, He makes His presence powerfully evident to them. King Asa had experienced God's awesome power when he faced a menacing army from Ethiopia (2 Chron. 14:9). God gave Asa victory, despite the overwhelming odds he faced. In spite of this miracle, the next time Asa faced an enemy he failed to trust God. Even though the army Asa faced was smaller than the one God had previously defeated, Asa's faith in God faltered. God encouraged Asa to take courage in knowing that God never rests or sleeps. He is never distracted, but diligently seeks individuals whose hearts are completely committed to Him.

Life's challenges sometimes seem impossible. Do you feel you are too weak to fight the battle? Don't give up! Keep your heart loyal to God, for He constantly watches over you, and He desires to demonstrate *His* strength in your life. God is willing and just as capable of giving you victory in your current challenge as He was with those in times past. The question is not whether God is looking for His people, but whether His people are seeking Him. Take comfort in God's promise that He watches over you and He wants to give you victory.

Delivered into Your Hand

And the Lord said to Joshua, "Do not fear them,
for I have delivered them into your hand;
not a man of them shall stand before you."

JOSHUA 10:8

No greater confidence will ever come to you or to any other Christian than the confidence of knowing you are doing God's will. God will not commission you to do anything without ensuring your success. God assured Joshua that there was no reason to fear as he prepared to battle the Canaanites. God would allow the Israelites to fight the battle, but the outcome was settled before they ever picked up their weapons. What confidence this gave them as they fought! Even though their enemies fought relentlessly, Joshua's army was certain of eventual victory.

God does not promise you victory in every task you devise, but He does promise that you will be successful whenever you follow *His* will (Deut. 28:7, 25).

Does it appear that people are keeping you from obeying God's will? Rest assured that God will not allow anyone or anything to prevent His children from accomplishing His purposes.

Be careful to evaluate success in the way that God does. Perhaps He is working to produce His peace in your heart as you face troubling times. Perhaps He is working to develop a forgiving spirit in you when others mistreat you. Perhaps He is working to eliminate a particular sin in your life. If you accept the world's understanding of victory, you may feel defeated. If you look to see what God is accomplishing through your situation, you will find that He is succeeding. When you face opposition but know you are doing what God has asked, have confidence that He will accomplish everything that He desires.

Asking for Mountains

"Now therefore, give me this mountain of which the Lord spoke in that day; for you heard in that day how the Anakim were there, and that the cities were great and fortified. It may be that the Lord will be with me, and I shall be able to drive them out as the Lord said."

JOSHUA 14:12

Caleb's faith in God never wavered, though everyone around him doubted. God convinced Caleb that the children of Israel should enter the Promised Land, but the people were intimidated by giants and fortified cities (Num. 13:28–33). Their disbelief forced Caleb to wait forty years in the wilderness before he finally entered the Promised Land. Even after all those years, Caleb was as confident as ever in God's power.

When God was dividing the land among the Israelites, the people were asking for the lush valleys and grassy plains. Caleb asked for a mountain. The Israelites had driven their enemies into the mountains, where they had built fortresses. This did not intimidate Caleb—he asked for a challenge! He did not trust in his own strength but in God's presence. Caleb longed to see God work in power, and he knew he would be less likely to rely on God if he dwelt in the easy places. He chose a situation in which he would have to trust in God. Caleb knew his inheritance from God was on the mountain. He refused to allow the difficulty of gaining it to stop him from enjoying all that God had promised him.

If you always choose the easy way, asking for the peaceful valleys, you will never see God's power displayed to enable you to take a mountain. Seek out the mountains, and you will witness God doing things through your life that can be explained only by His mighty presence.

Clean Hands; a Pure Heart

Who may ascend into the hill of the Lord?
Or who may stand in His holy place?
He who has clean hands and a pure heart.

PSALM 24:3–4a

God has rigid requirements for those who want to enjoy intimate fellowship with Him. There is no easy access to God for those with unclean hands or an impure heart. It is an affront to holy God to assume that we can indulge in our sin and blatantly disobey His word, then brazenly enter the holy of holies. In Old Testament times, one's hands represented one's activities. Clean hands symbolized pure activities. Priests washed their hands before serving in the temple to symbolize that only those who were cleansed could worship holy God.

There are levels of intimacy with God. The moment you become a Christian you begin a relationship with the Lord. However, if you persist in your sin, sin will separate you from God and keep you from enjoying close fellowship with Him. If you follow only God's basic commandments but resist every time God gives you specific, personal directions, you will never fully experience the depths of God's Person. If, however, you are like the psalmist and understand the holiness of God, you will adjust your life to His standards and respond to His prompting so that you may have deeper fellowship with Him.

The closer you get to holy God, the more obvious even your smallest sins become. The more you know of God's character, the more you will realize the need to wash your hands and purify your heart before you can get close to Him.

Are you willing for almighty God to make you absolutely pure before Him so that you can enjoy the maximum possible relationship with Him?

Not One Word
Has Failed

*And you know in all your hearts and in all your souls that not
one thing has failed of all the good things which the Lord your
God spoke concerning you. All have come to pass for you;
not one word of them has failed.*

JOSHUA 23:14

Near the end of his life, Joshua took time with the Israelites to review all that God had done for them since they first began following Him. God had given them an impossible assignment: to conquer a foreign and hostile land with fortified cities and armies more powerful than their own. The Israelites were to go forward with nothing more than God's promise that He would go with them and take care of them. Now Joshua looked back over their experience and reminded the Israelites that God had kept every promise. They had experienced numerous victories and had enjoyed God's provision for every need.

Sometimes hindsight gives us a clear picture of how faithful God has been. We are tempted during a crisis to wonder if God will be faithful to His promises. We focus on our problems, and our trust in God begins to waver. Twenty-four years after God promised Abraham and Sarah a son, they were still waiting on God to fulfill His promise. But in the twenty-fifth year, Abraham and Sarah could look back and see that God had been faithful. As David was fleeing for his life, he may have been uncertain how God would keep His promise to make him a king. But at the end of his long and prosperous reign, David could review how God had kept every promise.

You, too, can rely on God's faithfulness. Are you in a crisis? Hold to the promises of your Lord! He will not forget His promises to you. Look back over your Christian life and recount the many ways in which God has been faithful to His word.

A Jealous God

For the Lord your God is a consuming fire,
a jealous God.

DEUTERONOMY 4:24

Our God is a consuming fire. He is satisfied only when His love totally consumes us. We usually think of a jealous person as someone resentful and suspicious, but the Lord's jealousy on our behalf is something that should be precious to us! He has the complete right to our lives. He gave us life, and He wants to protect us from anything that could harm us. That is why He has commanded His children to worship no other gods, allowing nothing to distract us from His consuming love.

The Lord opposes anything that hinders our relationship with Him (Deut. 6:15). He knows the danger of other gods, how they will lure us away, deceive us, and leave us empty. He will tolerate nothing that takes precedence over our love for Him. Our faithfulness to God assures us of the abundant life He wants to give us. If we reject Him, He will pursue us until we return to Him.

We should not resent the fact that God wants to guard our relationship with Him. It should bring us comfort. Our relationship with God should be our top priority. It should dictate how we spend our time, our money, and our energy. If certain people or our possessions separate us from God, we must reexamine our hearts and give our devotion first to Him, as He commands. God wants each of us to love Him with all of our heart, mind, soul, and strength (Mark 12:30). Our love for God should extend to every corner of our lives. God loved us so much that He gave us His own Son. Let us respond by giving Him our highest devotion in return.

Now!

Then another of His disciples said to Him,
"Lord, let me first go and bury my father."

MATTHEW 8:21

Often our struggle as Christians is not in deciding whether we should obey Christ but in obeying *immediately*. We may acknowledge our need to follow Christ and commit ourselves to do what He has told us. Yet when God reveals His will to us, that is the time to obey! God's revelation of His will is His invitation to respond immediately.

Some would-be disciples pledged their willingness to follow Jesus, but they told Him they were not ready yet. In Jesus' day, a Jewish man was expected to care for his elderly parents until they died. One man wanted to wait until his father died before going with Jesus. This would be an honorable delay. The man had to choose between this important responsibility and heeding a call from the Lord. Yet God knew this man, and He knew the man's father. God would have taken care of the man's father, if he only would have followed Jesus. This was an opportunity to walk with the Son of God, yet the concerns of this life were competing for priority with obedience to God.

Timing our obedience is crucial. Invitations from God come with a limited opportunity to respond. Some opportunities to serve Him, if not accepted immediately, will be lost. Occasions to minister to others may pass us by. When God invites us to intercede for someone, it may be critical that we stop what we are doing and immediately adjust our lives to what God is doing. Missing opportunities to serve the Lord can be tragic. When an invitation comes from God, the time to respond is *now*.

Giving Your Best

You shall not sacrifice to the Lord your God a bull or sheep which has any blemish or defect, for that is an abomination to the Lord your God.

DEUTERONOMY 17:1

God's love moved Him to sacrifice that which meant the most to Him—His only Son. Our response, if we truly understand His love for us, is the desire to give back to God that which means the most to us.

The Old Testament reveals that God set forth high standards for the sacrifices He required of His people. A worthy sacrifice had to cost the people something. As their hearts shifted away from God, the people began struggling to give God costly offerings. They would bring blind, lame, and sick animals, assuming God could not tell the difference (Mal. 1:8). God saw what they were doing and declared their offerings to be in vain (Mal. 1:10). Throughout the Old Testament period, God was setting the stage for the ultimate, perfect, and sinless sacrifice of His Son for the sins of humanity.

The offerings we give back to God reveal our hearts' condition. A heart that overflows with gratitude for God's love will respond in selfless devotion. If we are unwilling to sacrifice our time, our possessions, our money, or our energy, we indicate that we do not love God as He desires. God takes delight in the person who gives to Him cheerfully out of a loving heart, a person who understands that God is the source of everything he has and who knows that God will more than compensate for whatever is sacrificed for Him (2 Cor. 9:8).

If you struggle in giving your best offerings to God, pause and reflect on what God sacrificed for you. Trust Him and give Him the best that you have because you love Him with all your heart.

Put Away Evil

So you shall put away the evil from among you.

DEUTERONOMY 22:21b

It is a dangerous and costly mistake not to take temptation seriously. The sad testimony of many who have succumbed to sin's enticements is that they thought they were strong enough to remain in the midst of temptation and resist it. God requires that His people remove evil from their midst (Deut. 21:21). One way to do this is to remove anything in your environment that may tempt you to sin. When wickedness surrounds you, you are in danger of becoming anesthetized to its destructive potential. Never assume that you are immune to temptation. Do not underestimate the craftiness of the evil one.

God does not tolerate evil, for evil cost the death of His Son. Sin causes untold pain and destruction to everyone it touches. Treating evil lightly shows foolish disregard for God's redemptive work. An honest evaluation of your life will reveal temptations that you should remove, such as some forms of entertainment or ungodly relationships. When God convicts you of evil in your midst, remove it immediately!

There are times, however, when you are powerless to remove ungodly influences, so you must remove yourself from the temptation. Paul urges us to avoid every kind of evil (1 Thess. 5:22). When Joseph was enticed to commit adultery by his master's wife, he fled immediately! (Gen. 39:12).

Do not lose your abhorrence of sin. Be diligent to keep any form of temptation out of your home, out of your relationships, out of your mind. You can do this only by maintaining your love relationship with God, recognizing that you are powerless to resist temptation in your own strength. You will not be able to walk closely with God unless you see sin as He sees it. Darkness and light cannot coexist. Run from the darkness to the light!

The Testimony of Others

"Here I am. Witness against me before the Lord and before His anointed: Whose ox have I taken, or whose donkey have I taken, or whom have I cheated? Whom have I oppressed, or from whose hand have I received any bribe with which to blind my eyes? I will restore it to you." And they said, "You have not cheated us or oppressed us, nor have you taken anything from any man's hand."

1 SAMUEL 12:3–4

There is a freedom that comes in having nothing to hide. Living a life of integrity allows you this freedom. Your integrity is measured not by what you say about yourself but by what God and people say about you. Samuel had lived all his life among the people of God. Leaders who preceded him were dishonest and corrupt; it would have been easy for Samuel to compromise in his dealings as well. Near the end of his life, however, Samuel could boldly stand before his nation and ask them to reveal any offense he had committed against any of them. They could not think of one.

In his position of leadership, Samuel could have taken advantage of people. Yet because he carefully guarded his motives and kept his relationships blameless, Samuel could fearlessly ask the people to report if he had mistreated them in any way. It takes courage to open your life up to the scrutiny of others, but Samuel did not fear what others would say about him. He did not have to avoid anyone whom he had offended. He had a confidence that comes from living a blameless life.

If you have mistreated others, you cannot change the past, but you can choose to live with absolute integrity from this day forward. Living righteously frees you to face any person unashamedly, knowing you have behaved in a Christlike manner. If your reputation is stained, seek forgiveness from those you have offended. Ask God to guide you daily in your relationships so that you have no regrets about your treatment of others.

Pleasing God, Pleasing Others

*For do I now persuade men, or God? Or do I seek to
please men? For if I still pleased men, I would not
be a bondservant of Christ.*

GALATIANS 1:10

At times you will have to make a choice between pleasing God and pleasing those around you, for God's ways are not man's ways (Isa. 55:8–9). As important as it is to strive for good relations with others, it is even more important to maintain a steadfast and obedient relationship with Christ. Disobeying God to keep peace with other people is never wise. Peace with God is always paramount.

Jesus warned that obeying Him might cause division in your relationships (Matt. 10:35–36). If Paul's primary goal had been to please others, he would never have become an apostle of Jesus Christ. Paul went completely against the wishes of his colleagues in order to obey Christ. At times, obedience to God sets family members at odds with each other (Matt. 10:35–36). When you follow Jesus' lordship, your family may misunderstand, or even oppose you, yet your obedience to God reflects your identity as His child. Jesus said that those who obey His will are His brothers and sisters (Luke 8:21). God does not intend to divide the home, but He places obedience before domestic harmony.

It is important to get alone in quietness with God so that you understand what pleases Him. The world's thinking will mislead you more easily when you are not clear about what God desires. It broke Peter's heart to know that the opinion of a servant girl had mattered more to him than the approval of his Lord! If the desire to appease others tempts you to compromise what you know God wants you to do, learn from Peter's mistake. Determine that you will please your Lord regardless of the opinions of others.

The Fragrance of His Knowledge

Now thanks be to God who always leads us in triumph in Christ, and through us diffuses the fragrance of His knowledge in every place. For we are to God the fragrance of Christ among those who are being saved and among those who are perishing.

2 CORINTHIANS 2:14–15

Whenever the Romans won a major military victory they would celebrate with a spectacular parade. The commanding general would lead the procession in a magnificent chariot, followed by his soldiers, musicians, and other officials. Then, soldiers would lead the defeated enemies through the city in bondage. As a part of the celebration, the Romans would burn fragrances on altars, filling the entire city with a pleasant aroma. Even those who could not witness the triumphal procession could hear the victory music and smell the pleasing incense. Everyone would know that their army had been victorious. The special fragrance came to symbolize victory to anyone who smelled it.

Paul used this vivid imagery to describe the effect that Christians should have in the world. According to Paul, God permeates our lives with the fragrance of the knowledge of Christ. Everywhere we go, our lives should demonstrate to others that Christ is victorious. As unbelievers observe our lives, they should become aware of the victorious power of Christ. As other Christians witness the victory Christ gives us over our sin, they can rejoice in the triumph of their Lord and gain confidence that Christ will bring victory in their lives as well.

The most compelling evidence that Christ is alive and triumphant is His activity in the lives of His people. It is a privilege to be the fragrance of Christ by which others learn of God's life-changing power over sin. Your life ought to be convincing proof that God continues to work powerfully in the lives of His people.

Showing Grace

*And be kind to one another, tenderhearted, forgiving one
another, even as God in Christ forgave you.*

EPHESIANS 4:32

The Book of Ephesians describes the behavior that ought
to characterize Christians as they relate to one another.
Our actions ought to be permeated with kindness. Kindness is
love expressed in practical ways; it is putting the needs of others
before our own. It is intentionally considering ways to meet other
people's needs.

Being tenderhearted means that we are keenly sensitive to the
feelings of others. When a fellow Christian experiences sorrow,
we grieve also (1 Cor. 12:26). When another believer is joyful,
we, too, rejoice. Being tenderhearted means showing compassion
toward those around us.

We show forgiveness because we, too, fall short of God's ideal.
Knowing that God has graciously saved us from destruction
motivates us to forgive others when they offend us. Often we are
less patient with our fellow Christians than we are with nonbelievers. We expect more of Christians, and we feel betrayed when
they fail us. When this happens, we need to look closely at the
cross and remember the forgiveness we received there. We must
set aside the self-centered attitude that leads to impatience and
criticism of others.

Jesus did not say that the world will know Him by our miracles, by our grand testimonies, or by our vast Bible knowledge.
The world will know Him by the love that Christians show to one
another (John 13:35). Are you constantly in conflict with others?
Ask God to give you kindness, a tender heart, and a forgiving
spirit. As you allow the Spirit to build these qualities into you,
your life will be a blessing to others around you.

Can We Continue in Sin?

*What shall we say then? Shall we continue in sin
that grace may abound? Certainly not!
How shall we who died to sin live any longer in it?*

ROMANS 6:1-2

A Christian has died to sin. Sin has no control over a corpse. Temptation can present itself enticingly and persistently, yet a corpse will not succumb! Before you were a Christian you were keenly susceptible to sin. Sin held you in its grip. When you became a Christian, your old self died (Gal. 2:20). Sin now has no more control over you than temptation has over a corpse. You have died to sin. You can still sin, but you are no longer in sin's power. If you choose to succumb to temptation, you are rejecting the freedom from sin that Christ gained for you by His death.

God's grace is a further motivation for us to resist sin. It was God's grace that enabled Jesus to endure mocking, beating, and crucifixion at the hands of those whom He had come to save. It was grace that led God to forgive our sin despite our rebellion against Him. It is this same grace that God expresses toward us each time we sin against Him. Knowing this grace, we cannot continue to practice sin (Rom. 6:1-2). We cannot presume upon God's forgiveness by committing further offenses.

You are no longer the helpless victim of your sin. The victory has already been won. God does not have to win a victory over your sin; He already has! You need only to apply His victory to each area of your life. If there is a sinful habit, an ungodly attitude, or an unrighteous relationship that you need to put to death, claim the victory of Christ's resurrection today. Then you will be free to experience the abundant life that God intends for you.

Victory over Sin

*For there is no difference; for all have sinned and fall short
of the glory of God, being justified freely by His grace through
the redemption that is in Christ Jesus, whom God set forth
as a propitiation by His blood, through faith, to demonstrate
His righteousness . . . that He might be just and the
justifier of the one who has faith in Jesus.*

ROMANS 3:22b–26

Because of sin, Adam and Eve fell short of the perfection God intended for them. Because of sin, the Israelites relinquished the glory they could have experienced as God's holy nation. Because of sin, Judas fell short of the opportunity to be an apostle of Jesus Christ. Sin will corrupt every area of your life that it touches. Sin will cause your marriage to fall short of the promise it held in the beginning. Sin will cause you to fall short as a parent, a church member, a worshiper, or a friend. Every area in your life is susceptible to sin's destruction.

The wonder of salvation is that God completely dealt with sin. He did what we could not do. Through Christ's sacrifice, God, by His grace, offered His salvation and canceled the penalty of our sin. By His grace, He takes a life that has fallen short of God's best and gives it meaning. He provides the opportunity to immediately confess our sin and to be cleansed from all unrighteousness (1 John 1:9). He mends a broken heart. His grace erases anger and bitterness. He restores severed relationships. He takes a life devastated by sin and makes it whole. He takes our failures and produces something good.

Only God can heal sin's devastation. Only He can bridge the gap between His glory and your sin (Rom. 3:23). You must trust Him to do so. If you will ask Him, He will free you from the bondage of your sin, reestablish your relationship with Him, and restore you to wholeness.

Hallowed Be Your Name

"Hallowed be Your name."

MATTHEW 6:9b

Our calling as Christians is to bring glory to the name of God. God's name represents His character. Taking the name of God in vain misrepresents God's character to others (Exod. 20:7). As Christians, we carry the name of our Savior. The way we live and relate to others is a direct reflection on the name of Christ.

Doing something "in Jesus' name" is to do something that is in accordance with His character (John 15:16). It means that Jesus would be pleased to join us in what we are doing. If, however, our actions detract from God's reputation, He will jealously guard His name. Sometimes we are too concerned with protecting the reputation of people but too little concerned with protecting the holy name of God. When the Israelites profaned God's name before the nations by the way they lived, God "hallowed" His name: He made His name holy by punishing them (Ezek. 36:22). When David sinned before his nation, God publicly disciplined him in order to protect the holiness of His name.

We can so tarnish the name *father* before our children that it hinders them from loving God as their heavenly Father. We can be such unforgiving Christians that our sinfulness discourages people from seeking forgiveness from our God. We can show such disrespect for God as we worship Him that those observing lose their reverence of Him as well.

Our supreme desire should be to glorify the name of God by the way we live.

We ought to pray daily, as Jesus taught us to, that God's name be treated as holy.

May God Rule in Our Midst

"Your kingdom come.
Your will be done
On earth as it is in heaven."
MATTHEW 6:10

In heaven, God's will is the only priority. A word from God brings angels to do His bidding, immediately and without question. Jesus instructed us to pray that God would accomplish His will in our world in the same way. This means that God's purposes would be preeminent in our homes, our businesses, our schools, our churches, and our governments.

Jesus taught His disciples to pray that God's purposes be carried out in the world around them. In modeling how they should pray, Jesus was teaching His disciples how to share God's heart. He demonstrated this again at Gethsemane when He prayed, "Nevertheless, not as I will, but as You will" (Matt. 26:39). It is as we seek God's kingdom on earth, and not our own purposes, that we gain the same mind as our heavenly Father. We become colaborers with God by praying faithfully in agreement with His desires.

As you seek the Lord's will, He will guide your praying. He will invite you not only to pray, but also to become involved in His activity as He answers your prayer. If He places a burden upon you to pray for an individual's salvation, that burden is also His invitation to join His activity in that person's life. Prayer will prepare you to be a servant through whom God can bring about His will on earth. Pray that the Lord's absolute rule on earth will begin in your life. Then watch to see how God uses you to extend His lordship to others.

Daily Bread

"Give us this day our daily bread."
MATTHEW 6:11

esus often reminded His followers not to worry. He told them not to be anxious about tomorrow's needs or potential problems (Matt. 6:25). Rather, Jesus stressed a *daily* reliance on the Father, who provides for His children day by day.

As the Israelites wandered in the desert, they had no way to get food. Miraculously, God provided manna that appeared on the ground each morning. God's provision was sufficient for one day at a time. Each day the children of Israel received fresh manna as a tangible reminder of God's love for them. If they attempted to store it for the days to come, they found that it had spoiled by the next day. It was impossible to stockpile God's provision because God wanted them to trust in Him, not in their pantry. God's grace was sufficient for each day.

God wants us to trust Him daily with our needs. This trust does not make us poor planners or careless with our futures, unprepared to face what may come. Rather, it keeps our relationship with the Lord in its proper perspective as He reminds us daily of our dependence upon Him. God is aware of what tomorrow will bring and how we should prepare for it. He knows the problems we will face, and He has already made provision for us to overcome them. He asks us to trust in Him daily. Our faith in Him today cannot substitute for our trust in Him tomorrow. If we walk with Him closely today, we will be in the center of His will tomorrow.

The Poor in Spirit

"Blessed are the poor in spirit,
For theirs is the kingdom of heaven."

MATTHEW 5:3

The Bible presents many paradoxes that challenge our human way of thinking. We think of the poor as possessing very little, yet Jesus said the riches of heaven belong to the poor in spirit. Self-reliance robs us of God's good gifts.

Jesus insisted that in order to follow Him, we must deny self. As long as we rely on our own resources, we will never place our trust in Him. As we acknowledge the poverty of our souls, we realize how desperately we need a Savior. Jesus declared: "Repent! For the kingdom of heaven is near" (Matt. 4:17). God has so much to give the one who recognizes his need and will call upon Jesus!

Jesus said it is easier for a camel to go through the eye of a needle than it is for a rich person to enter the kingdom of God. He had just encountered the rich ruler, who valued his possessions so much that he could not give them up to follow Jesus (Luke 18:18–24). Jesus later encountered Zaccheus, a wealthy, notorious sinner (Luke 19:1–10). Despite Zaccheus's material wealth, he recognized his spiritual poverty and found salvation. Jesus taught the disciples that true wealth is found in a relationship with God. Those who realize their inherent spiritual poverty apart from God will trust in Him, and He will enrich their lives immeasurably. Do not allow your resources, wisdom, talent, or abilities to prevent you from trusting the Person who can bring you abundant life.

Those Who Mourn

"Blessed are those who mourn,
For they shall be comforted."

MATTHEW 5:4

God wants us to experience His joy (John 15:11). Yet we cannot experience His joy until we have mourned over our sin. If we do not grieve over the weight of our sin, we have no concept of sin's devastating power. If we treat our sin lightly, we demonstrate that we have no sense of the enormity of our offense against almighty God. Our sin caused the death of God's Son. It causes us to fall short of what God intends (Rom. 3:23). It brings pain and sorrow to others, as well as to ourselves.

The Bible says that those who grieve over their sin will draw near to God (James 4:8–10). Those who mourn and weep over their sin are in a position to repent (Luke 4:18–19). There cannot be repentance without the realization of the gravity of sin. Regret for sin's consequences is not the same as sorrow for sinning against holy God. Confession of sin is not necessarily an indication of repentance. Repentance comes only when we acknowledge that our transgression has come from a heart that is far from God, and we are brokenhearted over our grievous offenses against holy God.

Jesus said that those who are heartbroken over their sin will find comfort. They will experience new dimensions of God's love and forgiveness. His infinite grace is sufficient for the most terrible sin. Do not try and skip the grieving process of repentance in order to move on to experience joy. God will not leave you to weep over your sin but will forgive you, comfort you, and fill you with His joy.

Hunger and Thirst

"Blessed are those who hunger and thirst for righteousness,
For they shall be filled."

MATTHEW 5:6

Hunger and thirst are the body's way of telling us that we are "empty." Our natural response to physical hunger and thirst is to seek food and water to satisfy our need. Each Christian has an inner longing that only Christ's righteousness can satisfy. But we cannot be filled with righteousness if we are filled with self. Throughout the Scriptures God emphasizes that the one who longs for Him with all his heart will find Him (Jer. 29:13). As we crave righteousness, we will repent of our sin, and God will remove it from us. Our selfishness will be replaced by the fruits of the Spirit: love, joy, peace, long-suffering, kindness, goodness, faithfulness, gentleness, and self-control (Gal. 5:22–23). The Spirit will make us to be like Christ.

Righteousness is not to be taken lightly, nor is it easily attained. Holy God does not give His righteousness to people indiscriminately. He gives it to those who know they cannot live without it. Our desire for personal righteousness must be powerful, all-consuming, dominating everything we do. Pursuing righteousness means that we value the opinion of God far more than we treasure the opinions of people.

Righteousness is not merely an absence of sin. It is allowing God to fill us with His holiness (Rom. 6:11). It is being like Christ. Jesus is our model of One who sought God's righteousness first, and then the Father glorified Him. We are not only to seek the kingdom of God, but we are also to pursue His righteousness (Matt. 6:33). If we will hunger and thirst for righteousness, we will be satisfied!

The Meek

"Blessed are the meek,
For they shall inherit the earth."

MATTHEW 5:5

In popular thinking the term *meek* implies weakness. The word Jesus used had a different meaning. His picture of meekness is that of a stallion that has been brought into subjection to its master. Whereas it once fought against any attempt to bring it under control, resisting direction with all its strength, now it yields its will to its master. The stallion has lost none of its strength or endurance; it has simply turned these over to the control of the master.

For the Christian, meekness requires submitting our will to the Master. Meekness is not submitting to everyone around us; it is taking our direction from God. Meekness means that we do not have to defend our rights, but we allow the Lord to defend us. Meekness means a life that is submissive to the Holy Spirit, giving Him the freedom to make any changes He knows are necessary. Meekness involves a self-control that comes from trusting God. Meekness demonstrates an attitude of long-suffering that allows God to deal with the injustices we face.

Jesus' life was the paragon of meekness. He could have called upon legions of angels to remove Him from the cross, yet He allowed sinners to torture and kill Him. Although Jesus was by no means powerless to defend Himself, He chose to yield His life to the Father's will. He did this because He trusted the Father completely. When we doubt the Father, we tend to act in our own strength, rather than relying on His power. Jesus said that in relinquishing control over our lives to God, we will gain life in abundance!

Victory One Step at a Time

And the Lord your God will drive out those nations before you little by little; you will be unable to destroy them at once, lest the beasts of the field become too numerous for you.

DEUTERONOMY 7:22

When God led His people into the Promised Land, He did so step by step. If He had allowed them to annihilate their enemies at once, the land would have been too difficult to manage. So He allowed some of the enemies to remain for a time in order to maintain the land and suppress the wildlife. In doing so, God taught His people to trust Him step by step. He gave them only as much responsibility as they could handle at one time.

As God leads you in your Christian growth, He will allow challenges that match your character and relationship to Him. God will not totally change your character at once when you become a Christian. Rather, He will lead you through a process to become more like His Son. He will keep working in an area in your life until it is controlled by the Holy Spirit. You may eagerly desire maturity in every area of your character, but steady, gradual growth is more lasting. God will not take shortcuts in His process of making you like Christ. He sees your life from eternity and will take as long as necessary to produce lasting spiritual growth in you.

Do not become impatient while God is producing Christlikeness in you. Do not seek more responsibilities than those He has given you. Obey all that you know He has asked, and He will lead you at a pace that fits your present character and His purposes for you.

The Spirit of Wisdom

The Spirit of the Lord shall rest upon Him,
The Spirit of wisdom and understanding,
The Spirit of counsel and might,
The Spirit of knowledge and of the fear of the Lord.

ISAIAH 11:2

Throughout His ministry, Jesus relied upon the Holy Spirit to direct Him as He made crucial decisions and faced relentless opposition (Mark 1:12). Centuries earlier, Isaiah had described what the Spirit's presence would mean for the Savior. The Spirit would give Jesus the knowledge of the will and ways of the Father. As a young boy, Jesus already possessed unusual knowledge of God's Word (Luke 2:47). The Spirit granted Him the wisdom to use this knowledge. The Spirit enabled Jesus to take the Word of God and apply it effectively to the specific needs of those He encountered.

If you are a Christian, the same Spirit abides in you. At times, you may pray and ask God to send His Spirit "in *power*." That is the only way the Spirit ever comes! More importantly, the Spirit will come in wisdom, bringing the understanding of God's ways.

You need God's wisdom for the decisions you face (Rom. 11:33). Perhaps God has placed you in a position of great responsibility, and you feel overwhelmed by the decisions you must make. It may be in your role as parent, or friend, or leader that you long for the wisdom of God. The same Spirit who enabled Jesus to see through the deceptions of Satan will also guide you through the temptations that confront you. Pray that God will fill you with His Spirit of wisdom so that through the decisions you make you can live your life effectively.

Abundant Life

"The thief does not come except to steal, and to kill, and to destroy. I have come that they may have life, and that they may have it more abundantly."

JOHN 10:10

Jesus warns us to be on guard for thieves who will try to rob us of what God has for us. Jesus wants us to enjoy abundant life (John 10:10). Since the time of Adam and Eve, people have had to choose whom to believe. Satan convinced Adam and Eve that forfeiting their obedience to God would gain them everything. Instead, their disobedience robbed them of all they had. For the rest of their lives they experienced only a fraction of the blessings God had intended. Scripture is replete with accounts of those who forfeited their inheritance as children of God in order to gain that which was transitory and empty.

The world seeks to convince you that you will find fulfillment if you adopt its standard of morality for your marriage, raising your children, advancing your career, or pursuing pleasure. If you believe this, you will never experience the blessings God intended for you. Sin brings death (Rom. 6:23). It is tragic to listen to the voices of the world instead of to the One who created life and who wants you to experience life to its fullest.

Jesus wants you to live your life with security, knowing that you are a beloved child of God. If you are not experiencing love, joy, and peace, you have settled for less than what God intends for you. If you have been making excuses for why you are not experiencing an abundant and joyful life, determine today to settle for nothing less than God's best for your life. Stop following the world's way of finding satisfaction. Instead, listen to the Savior's voice, and you will find true fulfillment.

Redeeming the Time

See then that you walk circumspectly, not as fools but as wise,
redeeming the time, because the days are evil.

EPHESIANS 5:15–16

These days we are bombarded with opportunities that entice us to invest our time and energy. Each day the voices of urgency cry out for every available moment. So many causes promise that time spent on them will reap great rewards; how can we recognize God's voice among so many competing voices?

A fool makes unwise choices with his time. With every new opportunity that comes along, the fool chases off in a different direction, not questioning whether that is the best choice. The loudest voice gains his attention. At some point the fool discovers to his dismay that he has squandered the investment of his time.

The days in which you live are evil. Marriages are under tremendous pressure; families are disintegrating. Multitudes are dying each year without hearing the gospel of Jesus Christ. Investing your life wisely is critical to you and to those around you. Foolishly spending your time in sinful or wasteful pursuits can cost you and others dearly.

Often, it is not evil pursuits that rob your time. Rather, the temptation is to sacrifice what is *best* for what is good. The enemy knows that blatantly tempting you with evil will be obvious, so he will lure you with distractions, leaving you no time to carry out God's will. He will tempt you to so fill your schedule with good things that you have no time for God's best. You may inadvertently substitute religious activity for God's will, pursuing your own goals for God's kingdom instead of waiting for His assignment. Time is a precious commodity. Be sure to invest it wisely.

Humble Yourself

"For whoever exalts himself will be humbled,
and he who humbles himself will be exalted."

LUKE 14:11

There are two ways to attain high esteem. One is the world's method: Take every opportunity to promote yourself before others; seize occasions for recognition and manipulate your way into the center of attention. The other way is God's way: Humble yourself. Rather than striving for recognition and influential positions, seek to put others first. Cultivate humility, for it does not come naturally. One of the many paradoxes of the Christian life is that when God sees your genuine humility, He exalts you.

Proverbs 16:18 warns that if we put our efforts into promoting ourselves, we will be brought down. Jesus told of a man who tried to enhance his own image (Luke 14:7–11). While attending a banquet, he immediately claimed the seat of honor. When the host saw this, he humiliated this man by asking him to move to the least honorable place to make room for a more distinguished guest. Jesus said the wise thing to do is to seek the lowest position and allow others to exalt you if they feel you are worthy.

There is an enormous difference between the way the world honors you and the way God does. Proverbs 25:27 indicates that glory is not legitimate if you seek it yourself. When the world exalts you, you are the one who receives the credit. When God exalts you, others will praise *Him* for what He has done in your life. If you honor God, He will honor you (1 Sam. 2:30). Strive to humble yourself and bring glory to God. Allow Him to be the One to honor you in the way that pleases Him!

Open Doors and Adversaries

For a great and effective door has opened to me,
and there are many adversaries.

1 CORINTHIANS 16:9

Open doors of service may also let in adversaries. Paul had many of both. As Paul wrote to the Corinthians from Ephesus, he was trying to determine where to go next. He chose to remain longer in Ephesus because of the open doors of service God granted him. Knowing that God had opened the doors of ministry, Paul was not going to leave, regardless of how many enemies he faced. We might assume that Paul would reach the opposite conclusion. In light of the opposition he faced, he could have concluded that it was best to serve in less hostile regions. Instead, Paul based his decisions on God's activity rather than on what *people* were doing.

As you respond to God's invitations, don't be caught by surprise when adversaries try to thwart what you are doing. If you concentrate on your opponents, you will be sidetracked from God's activity. Don't base your decisions on what people are doing. They cannot prevent you from carrying out God's will (Rom. 8:31). Many times the most rewarding spiritual work is done in the crucible of persecution and opposition. While Paul was in Ephesus, a riot broke out in reaction to his ministry. The city theater resounded with an angry mob who shouted for two hours in support of their god, "Great is Diana of the Ephesians!" (Acts 19:23–41). Despite this fierce rejection of the gospel, Ephesus became one of the chief cities from which the gospel spread throughout Asia.

It takes spiritual discernment to see beyond human activity to God's will. As you seek places of service, look beyond what people are saying to find what God is doing.

241

The Judgment Seat

For we must all appear before the judgment seat of Christ,
that each one may receive the things done in the body,
according to what he has done, whether good or bad.

2 CORINTHIANS 5:10

There are many motivations in the Christian's life. One is our awareness that one day we will give an account of our lives to Christ, as He sits in judgment upon humanity. It is much more comforting to believe that Christians will be ushered into heaven with no questions asked about our faithfulness upon earth, but that is not what Scripture says will happen.

Paul cautioned that in the final day of judgment, every Christian will give an account for his or her actions. This expectation terrified Paul and motivated him to strive to please God in everything he did (2 Cor. 5:9–11). Paul knew that although he might ignore the Spirit's quiet voice during His life on earth, a time of accounting would come when he would have to explain why he had rejected God's instructions. Paul never carelessly assumed that, because of all he had done for God's kingdom, God would overlook his sin. Instead, he understood that to whom much is given, much is required (Luke 12:48).

God does not force His will upon us. He *will* ask us to answer for the way we responded to Him. Christians have been pardoned by the sacrifice of Jesus. We are not condemned. But because God is absolutely just, we will be called on to give an account of our actions. The Christian life gives a tremendous freedom, but it also brings a pervasive sense of our accountability to God and to others. We can learn from Paul that accountability is healthy; it gives us a powerful motivation to please God.

A Ministry of Reconciliation

Now all things are of God, who has reconciled us
to Himself through Jesus Christ, and has given
us the ministry of reconciliation.

2 CORINTHIANS 5:18

The world abounds with people whose sin has alienated them from God. Christ's sacrificial work has restored Christians to a love relationship with the heavenly Father. As Christians, we are appointed as ministers of reconciliation. Once Christ dwells within us, we become His ambassadors, and we entreat others to be reconciled to Him (2 Cor. 5:20). We are God's messengers of peace, urging others to return to God (Matt. 5:9).

Sin breaks our relationship with God; it severs relationships with others as well. Broken relationships are the epidemic of our day. Sin alienates family members, separates friends, divides churches, and destroys marriages. Sin creates mistrust, jealousy, hatred, and greed, all of which devastate relationships. Only Christ has the remedy for the disastrous effect of sin on human relationships. As His ambassadors, we are to take the message of reconciliation to a broken, divided world. We urge reconciliation first with God, and then with each other.

How tragic when God's messengers of peace harbor enmity toward each other. It is a travesty to carry a message of love and yet be filled with hatred. If there is someone whom you refuse to forgive, your message of reconciliation is hypocrisy. The evidence that you are a disciple of Jesus is that you love your fellow Christian (John 13:35). In each of your relationships, make certain that your actions share the love and forgiveness that reflect what you received from God. Then you will not only speak the message of reconciliation, but you will live it as well.

Motives

So Jesus answered and said to him,
"What do you want Me to do for you?"

MARK 10:51

It is hard to believe that the Lord would ask us what *He* could do for us. However, sometimes that is the question we must answer. Bartimaeus was blind, and he knew exactly what he wanted Jesus to do for him: restore his sight. Yet he received much more than physical sight! He received salvation, for Jesus knew Bartimaeus's heart was faithful. Bartimaeus immediately used his gift to become a follower of the Savior.

Jesus also asked James and John what they wanted Him to do for them. They requested the most prominent places in His kingdom. This time, Jesus answered that He could not give them what they asked. Their request was selfish, and it brought dissension among their fellow disciples (Mark 10:41).

Only when we pray according to God's will is He pleased to grant our requests (John 15:16). We will not see our prayers answered if we ask selfishly (James 4:3). If God refrains from giving us what we are asking, we should evaluate our prayers. Are our motives selfish? Are we asking for far less than God wants to give? (2 Kings 13:19; Eph. 3:20). Are our requests worthy of the God we approach? Do we lack the faith God requires to give us our desires? (Matt. 17:20). Is there unconfessed sin? (Isa. 1:15). God delights in responding to our requests (Matt. 7:7). If we will ask according to His will, we, like Bartimaeus, will receive far more than we anticipated! (Jer. 33:3).

If You Seek Him

The Lord is with you while you are with Him.
If you seek Him, He will be found by you;
but if you forsake Him, He will forsake you.

2 CHRONICLES 15:2

Our response to God greatly determines His presence in our lives. If we seek God with all of our hearts, then we will find Him (Jer. 29:13–14). The Lord wants to have fellowship with us, but He will not force a relationship upon us. We cannot reject fellowship with God and expect Him to remain near. He does not merely follow us throughout our day in case we need His assistance. If we continue to forsake Him, a time will come when we desperately need Him and He will not be near (Isa. 59:1–2).

It is an affront to sovereign God to treat Him like a servant who should wait upon us. God will relate to us on His terms, not ours. God desires a close walk with us. He will make His presence real and personal if that is our desire. If we repent of our sin and seek God on His terms, we can look forward to intimate fellowship with Him (James 4:8–10). We are to continually seek Him, not content to enter a new day without the assurance that God is walking beside us.

Do you say you want to experience God's presence while your actions reveal otherwise? If you say you want to know God better but neglect studying His Word, are you truly seeking Him? Have you regularly forsaken the place of prayer? If your actions reveal that you are genuinely seeking God, then He promises that you will find Him (Matt. 7:7).

Working Alone

So when Moses' father-in-law saw all that he did for the
people, he said, "What is this thing that you are doing
for the people? Why do you alone sit, and all the people
stand before you from morning until evening?"

EXODUS 18:14

In our zeal to please God and advance His kingdom, we Christians often take on responsibilities that God never intended us to have. One of the great challenges of the Christian life is determining what God does *not* want us to do! Our intentions are admirable: We love God, we love His people, and we see many needs around us. But sometimes our good intentions cause more harm than good.

Moses was aware of the need for someone to settle disputes among the Israelites. Someone had to help those former slaves learn how to live together as the people of God, so Moses took it upon himself to meet this need. Long lines of unhappy people, hoping to have their cases heard, stood before Moses each day. Moses spent day after day carrying the weight of his nation's problems on his shoulders. Finally his father-in-law, an outsider, witnessed what Moses was doing and challenged the wisdom of his actions. Moses was taking on more than he could handle. He was wearing himself out trying to do what was impossible for one person. In doing this service alone, Moses was robbing others of an opportunity to serve the Lord. He was also doing a disservice to his people, who otherwise could have had their issues resolved much sooner.

When you become aware of a need, do not automatically assume God wants you to meet it. The only reason to perform ministry is that God clearly tells you it is His will. If you are feeling overwhelmed by all that you are doing, you are probably doing more than God has asked. Pray carefully about the assignments you take on, so that you don't rob yourself and others of God's best.

Far Be It from Me!

Moreover, as for me, far be it from me that I should sin against the Lord in ceasing to pray for you; but I will teach you the good and the right way.

1 SAMUEL 12:23

It can be tempting at times to give up on God's people! They are so imperfect and can be so sinful, yet they are His people. Samuel had thoroughly warned the Israelites of the dangers in appointing a king over Israel. Yet they wanted to be like the nations around them, insisting that they were willing to pay any price. Almost as soon as the people were granted their desire, they recognized their sin. But it was too late. What was Samuel to do? They had ignored his warnings. Now they wanted him to continue to minister to them. It would seem appropriate for Samuel to abandon them and allow them to suffer the consequences of their actions.

Samuel knew, as Jesus knew, that God sends His servants to the sick, not the healthy (Matt. 9:12). Samuel did not take the people's response as a rejection of him but as an indication of their walk with God. Samuel was serving God, not the Israelites. When God commanded him to minister to them, he could do nothing else, despite their resistance to his message.

At times people will not respond as they should to the message God speaks through you. Don't become discouraged; it is a reflection of their relationship with God. You are God's servant; if Jesus spent His time with the spiritually needy, you can expect Him to ask you to do the same. Don't lose your patience with God's people. Keep in mind that God loves them as much as He loves you.

The Key to Prosperity

*And in every work that he began in the service of the house of
God in the law and in the commandment, to seek his God,
he did it with all his heart. So he prospered.*

2 CHRONICLES 31:21

There is a way to ensure that you prosper in what you do:
serve the Lord with all your heart! Hezekiah, king of
Judah, lived in a dangerous and tumultuous time. He faced powerful enemies. Idolatry was the popular religion of the day. His
parents had rejected God and encouraged people to worship
other gods (2 Chron. 28). Hezekiah had the opportunity to
reject God as well, yet he chose to serve God with all of his heart.
He did everything in his power to promote worship of the true
God. He diligently followed God's commandments. As a result
of Hezekiah's determination to serve God, God blessed him.
Hezekiah thrived in an unsettled time because he resolved to follow God despite popular opinion.

God will honor the heart that commits to follow Him
(2 Chron. 26:5). In times when worshiping God is not in vogue
and when the forces of the day oppose Him, it takes courage and
resolve to seek after God. God is pleased to prosper those who
strive to please Him rather than to seek the approval of people
(1 Sam. 2:30). Hezekiah stands in stark contrast to Rehoboam,
an earlier king of Judah. It is said of Rehoboam that "he did
evil, because he did not prepare his heart to seek the Lord"
(2 Chron. 12:14). When you do not set your heart to seek the
Lord, calamity is the inevitable result. The surest way to prosper
in your endeavors is to diligently pursue the will of God.

Freely Give

"Freely you have received, freely give."
MATTHEW 10:8b

There is no room for misers in God's kingdom. When we begin to struggle in giving what we have to others, we have forgotten where we received our possessions. Every good thing we have ever received has come from God (James 1:17). All that we have acquired has been dependent upon His grace (1 Cor. 4:7). Job accurately summarized our condition: "Naked I came from my mother's womb, / And naked shall I return there. / The Lord gave, and the Lord has taken away; / Blessed be the name of the Lord" (Job 1:21).

We easily assume a sense of ownership of our possessions, as if they were things we earned ourselves, thereby giving us a right to them. Jesus reminds us to be prepared to give our possessions as freely and joyfully as we received them. It should be a pleasure for us to give what we have to others (2 Cor. 9:7). We ought to be a conduit through whom the Lord can pour His blessings, knowing we will disperse them to everyone around us. Sometimes we claim we are trying to be good stewards of our resources when actually we are being selfish.

If you struggle to give freely to others, you have become more attached to the gift than to the Giver. The account of the rich young ruler shows the tragedy of becoming too attached to worldly treasures (Luke 8:18–24). Meditate on all that your Lord has given to you (John 3:16). Resolve to express your gratitude to Him through your giving.

Nothing Can Separate You

Who shall separate us from the love of Christ?
Shall tribulation, or distress, or persecution,
or famine, or nakedness, or peril, or sword?

ROMANS 8:35

Nothing you could ever experience, no matter how terrible or frightening, could *ever* separate you from the love of God. No tribulation and distress you might ever suffer could be so intense that God's love for you is not even more fervent. No persecution could be so painful that God's love cannot bring comfort. Famine might starve you of food, but you will never hunger for the Father's love. Poverty cannot strip you of God's compassion, just as even death itself is incapable of robbing you of your heavenly Father's infinite love.

If you base your view of God's love on your circumstances, you will become confused. There may be times when you will ask, "How could a loving God allow this to happen to me?" You may begin to question what you find clearly stated in the Word of God. God promised that you would *never* be separated from His love; He did not say that you would never face hardship, persecution, poverty, or danger. If you doubt that God could love you and still allow you to experience difficult experiences, consider the life of Jesus.

If you allow the death of Jesus on the cross to forever settle any questions you might have about God's love, you will approach difficult circumstances with confidence. Knowing that there will never be anything that could separate you from God's perfect love, you will watch to see how God expresses His love in each circumstance. Don't ever judge God's love based on your circumstances. Instead, evaluate your circumstances from the perspective of God's love.

Long Enough on the Mountain

The Lord our God spoke to us in Horeb, saying:
"You have dwelt long enough at this mountain."

DEUTERONOMY 1:6

If God allowed us to live on the "mountaintop," we would not experience trials, but neither would we achieve any victories. The Israelites had gathered at the foot of Mount Horeb while God spoke to them and gave them His law. It was a breathtaking experience! Fire and smoke covered that awesome mountain; lightning flashed, and loud trumpet sounds pierced the air in a deafening crescendo! The ground at the foot of the mountain shook, and the people trembled in fear (Exod. 19:16–25).

As important as it was for God's people to have this inspiring encounter with Him, their Lord had not rescued them from Egypt in order for them to settle around a mountain in the wilderness. God delivered them so that they could conquer the Promised Land. God wanted to demonstrate His power to the Israelites so that they would trust Him in their conquest of Canaan. Finally, God announced that they had been long enough at the mountain; it was time to go to battle.

The mountain is an enticing place to set up camp. Peter, James, and John were prepared to reside on the Mount of Transfiguration with Jesus, but their Lord knew that a demon-possessed boy needed their assistance down below (Matt. 17:4, 14–18). At times God will graciously provide you a mountaintop experience. These times come in many settings: during your time alone with Him, at a Christian conference, by reading a Christian book, or at a prayer meeting. You may wish you could spend the rest of your life basking in the glow of your encounter with God. But remember, these mountaintop encounters are God's way of preparing you for the battles that await you.

251

Not Lost in the Crowd

And when Jesus came to the place, He looked up and saw him, and said to him, "Zacchaeus, make haste and come down, for today I must stay at your house."

LUKE 19:5

In our large world it's easy to feel that we are nothing more than an insignificant speck in the midst of a multitude. Our world tends to depersonalize us, seeking to make us like everyone else, but God loves us in specific ways that are particular to us.

Jesus was on His way to Jerusalem to fulfill His assignment on the cross. The multitudes thronged around Him in such numbers that the diminutive Zacchaeus could not see Jesus unless he climbed a tree. Zacchaeus would have been satisfied simply to catch a glimpse of the great Teacher. But Jesus stopped, turned, and looked directly at him! In that moment, Zacchaeus was oblivious to the crowd around him. Thus began a special time with Jesus that radically changed his life.

Jesus will relate to you in ways that are unique to you. He knows your past; He knows what you will face in the future. Because He knows everything about you, His word to you will perfectly fit the circumstances of your life. You may be in a group of Christians who are listening to God's Word, and you may hear things from Him that no one else hears. Don't become frustrated with others if they are not as excited about a truth from God as you are. Don't be impatient with them if they are not implementing God's Word in their lives exactly as you are. God will personalize His word to you. He will relate to each of your friends in a way that specifically meets their needs as well.

Returning to Your Failure

*But Simon answered and said to Him, "Master, we have
toiled all night and caught nothing; nevertheless at
Your word I will let down the net."*

LUKE 5:5

No one knows how to help you in your times of failure as
Jesus does! He will not overlook your shortcoming or
simply encourage you to do better the next time. He will give you
victory in the midst of your failure.

Peter had fished all night without success. His was not just a
meager catch; he had caught nothing, even though he was a
skilled fisherman. Jesus could have said, "Peter, don't worry about
your empty net. You'll soon be in a different business anyway."
Instead, Jesus told him to launch out into the deep and to cast out
his nets for a catch. How humbling it must have been for Peter!
Here was a carpenter telling this outspoken fisherman how to fish!

Jesus often gets your undivided attention when you fail. He
sometimes takes you back to your place of defeat in order to build
something good into your life. You may assume He must not
want you to continue because you failed so miserably in your
attempt. Perhaps your problem was that you relied on your own
strength instead of the Master's. Maybe you failed in a relationship. Jesus will not allow you to abandon it; He will help you
learn from your failure and experience the difference He can
make when He guides your relationships. When you try in God's
strength, you may discover that success is indeed within your
grasp. If you have recently experienced failure, you may be on the
brink of receiving a profound revelation from God!

God Remembers

Go and cry in the hearing of Jerusalem, saying,
"Thus says the Lord: I remember you, The kindness of
your youth, The love of your betrothal, When you
went after Me in the wilderness, In a land not sown."

JEREMIAH 2:2

Even when our hearts grow cold toward God and our devotion to Him weakens, His love remains steadfast. We may forget God, but He remembers us.

God was concerned because the people of Judah had allowed their hearts to drift far from Him. In a powerful moment, God shared His heart with His people, recalling what it was like when they first began loving Him. He remembered how they had loved Him, as a new bride loves her husband, with excitement and enthusiasm for the future. He recalled the kindness they had expressed as they willingly followed Him wherever He led them. God reminded them of the love they had once had for Him, so that the memory might rekindle feelings of devotion and their hearts might return to Him.

If you do not guard your heart, you will grow cold in your love for Christ. A time may come when He approaches you and reminds you what your relationship was once like. Do you recollect the joy that permeated your life when you first became a Christian? Do you recall the youthful commitments you made to Him, pledging to do anything He told you to do? Do you remember the thrill you experienced each time you came to understand a new dimension of His nature? Spiritual memory is important. You may not realize how far you have drifted from God until you contrast the love you are expressing to Him now with that of earlier days.

God has not changed. He is the same Person you gave your heart to when you became a Christian (Mal. 3:6–7). If your love for God is not as intense as it once was, return to Him. He will restore the intimate fellowship you once shared with Him.

Go!

"Go therefore and make disciples of all the nations,
baptizing them in the name of the Father and of the Son
and of the Holy Spirit."
MATTHEW 28:19

Our Master commands us to "go." We need permission to stay! The gospel is the account of Jesus' leaving His Father's right hand to go to Calvary. Jesus instructed those who wanted to be His disciples to leave their homes and their comforts and follow Him. Some insisted that they could not go yet because they still had to care for elderly parents (Luke 9:59–60). Others wanted to make sure everything was in order first (Luke 9:61–62). Still others expressed willingness to follow but wanted to know the details of what they would be doing (Luke 9:57–58). Jesus never excused those who struggled to follow Him. He made it clear that to follow Him meant He set the direction and they were to follow.

We can convince ourselves that Jesus does not really want us to adjust our lives, pointing to the success we are enjoying right where we are. Yet Jesus often told His disciples to go elsewhere in spite of the success they were experiencing. Peter had just pulled in the greatest catch of fish of his entire career when Jesus invited him to leave everything (Luke 5:1–11). Philip was enjoying astounding success as an evangelist when the Holy Spirit instructed him to go to the desert (Acts 8:25–40). Success where we are can be our greatest hindrance to going where Jesus wants us to be.

If you become too comfortable where you are, you may resist Christ's invitation to go elsewhere. Don't assume that God does not want you to go in service to Him. He may lead you across the street to share the gospel with your neighbor or to the other side of the world. Wherever He leads, be prepared to go.

God's Design

*For whom He foreknew, He also predestined, to be conformed
to the image of His Son, that He might be the firstborn
among many brethren. Moreover whom He predestined,
these He also called; whom He called, these He also justified;
and whom He justified, these He also glorified.*

ROMANS 8:29–30

Your life is a part of God's grand design. God has known
about you and had a plan for your life since before time
began. He knew everything about you before you were even
born (Jer. 1:5). God predetermined that you would become like
His Son. Your life, therefore, has a destiny. Christ is the model
upon which the Father is developing your life. You are meant to
have a relationship with the Father that is as intimate as the relationship between Jesus and the Father (John 17:21). Every event
He allows into your life is designed to make you more like Christ.

God's call came when He invited you to join Him in the
process! His call was extremely personal, designed specifically for
your response. How wonderful to realize that at a particular
moment in history, almighty God spoke personally to you and
invited you to become His child!

Because of your sin, you could never live blamelessly. But God
forgave your sin and justified you, declaring you righteous. All
the spiritual debt you carried with Him was forgiven, and you
were freed to enjoy God and to serve Him for the rest of eternity. In biblical times, the glory of God's people was His presence.
You, too, are glorified because the fullness of God now dwells
within you, and you will one day be with Him (Col. 1:27; 2:9).
He invites you to join Him in working out His will in your life—
conforming you to His image (Phil. 2:12).

Prayer Is Preparation

When the Day of Pentecost had fully come,
they were all with one accord in one place.

ACTS 2:1

Prayer does not give you spiritual power. Prayer aligns your life with God so that He chooses to demonstrate His power through you. The purpose of prayer is not to convince God to change your circumstances but to prepare you to be involved in God's activity.

The fervent prayer of the people at Pentecost did not induce the Holy Spirit to come upon them. Prayer brought them to a place where they were ready to participate in the mighty work God had already planned.

Jesus told His followers to remain in Jerusalem until the Spirit came upon them (Acts 1:4–5). The disciples obeyed His command, waiting for God's next directive. As they prayed, God adjusted their lives to what He intended to do next. As they prayed, a unity developed among them. For the first time the disciples used Scripture as their guide in decision making (Acts 1:15–26). The day of Pentecost arrived, and the city of Jerusalem filled with pilgrims from around the world. When God released His Holy Spirit upon the disciples, He had already filled the city with messengers who would carry the gospel to every nation. Prayer had prepared the disciples for their obedient response.

Prayer is designed to adjust you to God's will, not to adjust God to your will. If God has not responded to what you are praying, you may need to adjust your praying to align with God's agenda. Rather than focusing on what you would like to see happen, realize that God may be more concerned with what He wants to see happen in *you*.

257

Life and Light

In Him was life, and the life was the light of men.
JOHN 1:4

When Jesus came to a world that was in bondage to darkness and dead in its sin, He came as light and life. His light dispelled sin's darkness wherever He went, for the forces of evil could not withstand Him. The life He brought was abundant and free, available to all who were dead in their sin (Eph. 2:1; John 10:10).

If you are a Christian, Jesus lives in you, and His light is within you. Christians are called to dispel darkness (Eph. 5:11). The light of Christ ought to shine so brightly through you that those practicing darkness are uncomfortable when they are around you. The light within you should dispel darkness from the lives of your friends, coworkers, and family members.

The fullness of life found in Christ dwells within you as a Christian (Col. 1:27). The life that Jesus offers is available to others through you. Don't discount what you have to give to those who are hurting. Christ's life within you is more than sufficient to meet every human need. When people encounter you, they encounter Christ within you. You do not know all the answers, but you have Someone within you who does! You will not carry the burden of the needs of others. Christ will. Be aware that just as many resisted Jesus, so there will be those who resist the truth that you offer (John 1:11). Be thankful, however, that God chooses to express Himself through you, giving light and life to those around you.

A Heart of Flesh

I will give you a new heart and put a new spirit within you;
I will take the heart of stone out of your flesh
and give you a heart of flesh.

EZEKIEL 36:26

From our hearts comes our response to God. Apart from the cleansing work of the Holy Spirit, our hearts are extremely deceitful (Prov. 17:9). David prayed that God would cleanse him from the ravages of his sin and purify his heart (Ps. 51:10). God's greatest desire is that His people love Him with all their hearts (Deut. 6:5). Jesus said we are blessed if our hearts are pure (Matt. 5:8).

Sin hardens the heart (Matt. 13:4, 19). The more sin we allow to pass over our hearts and through our lives, the more resistant we become to a word from God. The sin of unforgiveness stiffens our hearts. We cannot continue to resist the prompting of the Holy Spirit without becoming hardened against Him. Exposing ourselves to evil and ungodly influences desensitizes us to God and His word. Over time, our hearts become like stone, unreceptive to a fresh word from God. We become anesthetized to sin.

Has your heart grown hard toward God? Do you feel as though nothing could soften it? God has a solution. He will separate you from the influences that are destroying you (Ezek. 36:24). He will cleanse you from all filthiness and remove everything that has taken His place in your affections (Ezek. 36:25). He will remove your heart of stone and replace it with a heart of flesh, tender toward Him and His Word. If your love for God is not what it should be, ask Him to renew your heart and restore your devotion to Him.

Much Beloved

*At the beginning of your supplications the command went out,
and I have come to tell you, for you are greatly beloved;
therefore consider the matter, and understand the vision.*

DANIEL 9:23

"For you are beloved." Could there be any words from God more welcome than these? Daniel was in exile in Babylon as a result of his nation's utter defeat by the Babylonians. He desperately wanted to make sense of his circumstances. So he did what he had done so many times before: he prayed. God immediately dispatched the angel Gabriel. Gabriel revealed that God had sent him to Daniel at the *beginning* of his supplications. God did not even wait for Daniel to finish his prayer. Why? Because God loved Daniel greatly. What a marvelous testimony! There had been times when Daniel's love for God had been put to the test. Now, when Daniel was in need, God was quick to respond in love to him.

God wants to answer the prayers of those whose hearts are completely His (2 Chron. 16:9). God can accurately orient you to the events of your day. Media, public opinion, and political leaders cannot tell you the truth of your circumstances. Only God can. God loves you and will speak to you in His time. His answer may come immediately as it did in Daniel's case, or it may be delayed, but it will come (Dan. 10:13). If it seems as though everything is crumbling around you, and you wonder why you do not see God's activity, take comfort in knowing that you are loved in heaven. If you are genuinely seeking God's answers, you can go to your Father confidently with your questions. He will respond to you in love (Luke 11:5–13).

260

The Glory of the Lord

When Solomon had finished praying, fire came down from
heaven and consumed the burnt offering and the sacrifices;
and the glory of the Lord filled the temple.

2 CHRONICLES 7:1

The glory of the Lord is His presence. When God occupies
a place, His glory is unmistakably evident! God has high
standards for where He will make His presence known. He does
not respond to our whims or come on our terms.

Solomon longed for God's presence to be obvious in the temple that he had painstakingly built for Him. Solomon had spared
no expense or effort in building this magnificent temple as a
house for the Lord. Yet he understood that constructing a spectacular building was no guarantee that God would choose to
inhabit that place. So Solomon prepared himself and the people
in the hope that God would look upon them with favor. The
priestly choir sang and played instruments in reverent praise to
God (2 Chron. 5:11–14). The priests sacrificed so many animals
on the altar that they could not count them (2 Chron. 5:6).
Solomon prayed, and when he finished, fire came down from
heaven and consumed their offering. The glory of the Lord filled
the temple! God's glory was so overpowering in Solomon's temple that the priests could not carry on their normal activities
(2 Chron. 7:2).

There is no mistaking when God inhabits a place. God's glorious presence fills a place, and it is impossible to carry on business
as usual! The New Testament teaches that our lives are temples
because Christ abides in us (1 Cor. 3:16). We cannot assume by
this that our lives are pleasing to Him. Like Solomon, we must
thoroughly prepare ourselves so that God will choose to reveal
His presence in our lives. When He does, there will be no doubt
that it is God!

Divine Potential

*And when Saul had come to Jerusalem, he tried to join
the disciples; but they were all afraid of him, and did not
believe that he was a disciple. But Barnabas took him
and brought him to the apostles.*

ACTS 9:26–27

Only God knows the potential of each believer. We can pro-
ject what we think God might do in someone's life, but
we have no way of knowing. We see only outward appearances
and behavior, whereas God looks at the heart (1 Sam. 16:7).

The apostles were skeptical of some who professed to be
Christians. No one seemed more unlikely to become a dedicated follower of Jesus than Saul of Tarsus. He had been one of
Christianity's greatest enemies, even overseeing the murder of
Stephen (Acts 7:58–60). When Paul suddenly expressed an
interest in knowing the leaders of the Christian movement, it
was natural for the apostles to suspect devious motives and to
doubt his conversion. Nevertheless, despite the apostles' reluctance, Barnabas assumed the best in Paul and risked his own life
to be Paul's advocate.

You may identify with Paul. Perhaps you were an improbable
candidate to be a committed Christian. It may be that God
placed a Christian friend beside you to help you develop your
faith. Thank the Father for those He has sent to you who believed
in what God could do in you, even when others doubted.

Perhaps you stand with the apostles. There may be some around
you in whom you have little confidence, though they claim to be
Christians. Be assured that if God could turn the proud and murderous Saul into one of the greatest saints in history, He is equally
capable of redeeming those around you. Don't give up on your fellow believers. Look to see where God is working in their lives; then
join Him. It is a great privilege to be like Barnabas and to invest in
the life of a fellow Christian. This is the purpose of discipleship.

Evil, Good
and Good, Evil

Woe to those who call evil good, and good evil;
Who put darkness for light, and light for darkness;
Who put bitter for sweet, and sweet for bitter!

ISAIAH 5:20

It is Satan's practice to convince people that what God calls good is actually evil and what God declares evil is, in fact, good. Satan persuaded Adam and Eve that their disobedience, rather than their obedience, would guarantee a full life. They believed him and immediately began to experience sin's consequences! Despite the absurdity of Satan's logic, he continues to deceive people into doubting what God has clearly said.

King Saul sought Samuel's affirmation for the sacrifice he had offered, even though he had acted in direct disobedience to God's command (1 Sam. 15:13). Ananias and Sapphira expected praise from the early church for their offering, though they were blatantly lying (Acts 5:1–11). An Amalekite soldier sought David's gratitude for killing Saul, God's anointed king (2 Sam. 1:1–16).

We, too, will face the temptation to call something good that God has declared wicked. We may be persuaded that we can accomplish more good by lying than by telling the truth. We may claim that we are mobilizing Christians to pray for someone in sin when, in fact, we are spreading gossip. We may assert that we are following God's will in our job when, in fact, we are striving to pursue our own ambitions. We will also be tempted to call evil that which God declares is good. God says it is good to love our enemies, yet we might decide our task is to hold them responsible for their actions.

It is so important to hold ourselves accountable to God's Word. God does not need us to find exceptions for His commands. He requires our obedience.

A Pure Heart

Also I heard the voice of the Lord, saying:
"Whom shall I send, And who will go for Us?"
Then I said, "Here am I! Send me."

ISAIAH 6:8

It takes a pure heart to see God (Matt. 5:8). You can attend church services, read your Bible, and pray; but if sin fills your heart, you will not see God. You will know when you have encountered God because your life will no longer be the same.

Isaiah was concerned with the death of King Uzziah, the able king of Judah, but was disoriented to his heavenly King. Then something happened that forever changed Isaiah's life. God, in all His awesome majesty, appeared to him in the temple, surrounded by heavenly creatures. Instantly, God's presence made Isaiah aware of his sinfulness. One of the seraphim came to him with a burning coal and cleansed Isaiah of his sin. Immediately, Isaiah began to hear things he had never heard before. Now, he was aware of a conversation in heaven concerning who might be worthy to be God's messenger to the people. This prompted Isaiah's eager response: "Here am I! Send me." Now that God had cleansed Isaiah, he was aware of heavenly concerns and prepared to offer himself in God's service. Whereas Isaiah had been preoccupied with earthly matters, now his only concern was the activity of God.

If you have become estranged from God and His activity, you need to experience His cleansing. Sanctification prepares you to see and hear God. It enables you to serve Him. Only God can purify your heart. Allow Him to remove any impurities that hinder your relationship with Him, and then your service to Him will have meaning as you offer Him your consecrated life.

Instruments

Shall the ax boast itself against him who chops with it?
Or shall the saw exalt itself against him who saws with it?
As if a rod could wield itself against those who lift it up,
Or as if a staff could lift up, as if it were not wood!

ISAIAH 10:15

One of the dangers in the Christian life is to take credit for what God does. This was the Assyrians' problem. They were a weak nation until God chose to bless them in order to use them as an instrument to punish the Israelites. However, the more God blessed them, the more confident they became in their own strength. When the farmers had good crops, they credited their farming skills rather than God. When their army won a victory, their generals took the credit. When the nation experienced prosperity, the Assyrians attributed it to their military and political might. Finally, God pointed out the absurdity of their conclusions (Isa. 10:5–19).

It is sometimes easier to handle poverty or weakness than wealth or strength. Poverty causes us to recognize our need for God. Prosperity persuades us that we no longer require Him. Scripture holds several examples of those who assumed they were self-sufficient, only to realize their dire poverty apart from God. Samson was the strongest person alive, but he forgot that his strength came from God. Once God removed his strength, Samson was reduced to a pitiful slave. Saul was the first king of Israel; yet when God removed His Spirit from this proud monarch, he became a paranoid, petty man, seeking counsel from the occult.

Be careful how you handle the success God gives you! As you enjoy His blessings in your family, your business, or your ministry, keep in mind that you are an instrument in the hands of the Master.

Prepare Your Mind

Therefore gird up the loins of your mind, be sober, and rest your hope fully upon the grace that is to be brought to you at the revelation of Jesus Christ.

1 PETER 1:13

Your mind is a wonderful thing! You can memorize life-changing passages of Scripture that can undergird you in your daily life; you can meditate upon God's Word, discovering His magnificent truths; you can discern between truth and falsehood; you can recall God's past blessings.

Some of God's most effective servants were those who disciplined their minds for His service. Moses, educated in the best schools of Egypt, assembled the Books of the Law for the Israelites. Isaiah used his scholarly mind to write an exalted prophetic book in Scripture. Paul learned under Gamaliel, the outstanding teacher of his day, and it was through Paul that God presented much of the theology found in the New Testament.

Sadly, many Christians today do not exercise their minds to be of service to God. They allow others to do their spiritual thinking for them. If they can find their theology from a book, they will not bother to study God's Word themselves. If a speaker makes an authoritative statement, they readily accept it without verifying whether it is biblical.

Paul urged Christians to strive for maturity in their thinking (1 Cor. 14:20). He said there was a time when his spiritual thinking was immature, but he had prepared his mind to know and understand the great truths of God (1 Cor. 13:11). He had not allowed others to do his thinking for him. When you became a Christian, God renewed your mind (Rom. 12:2). Be certain to use your mind in a way that brings glory to God.

Revenge

Beloved, do not avenge yourselves, but rather give place to wrath; for it is written, "Vengeance is Mine, I will repay," says the Lord.

ROMANS 12:19

One of the hardest areas in which to trust God is in the matter of justice. When we perceive an injustice, we want to see the guilty party punished. We want justice to prevail, especially if we are the victim. We become impatient if we are not avenged quickly. Yet God warns us that vengeance is not our prerogative. We are to desire justice, but we are not to seek vengeance (Mic. 6:8). When someone offends us, our responsibility is to respond to the offense with forgiveness (Matt. 5:44). God takes the responsibility to see that justice is done. God loves people too much to allow sin to go unchecked.

Peter claimed that God is not slow about His promises to us, but He is patient and long-suffering before He brings about judgment (2 Pet. 3:9). Yet ultimately God has prepared for absolute justice. There will be no sin committed that He will leave unpunished. Either the punishment will fall on His Son or it will be charged against the sinner, but everyone will ultimately give an account for everything they have done (2 Cor. 5:10).

God is absolutely just, and only He can ensure that justice is fully carried out. If we are impatient and seek revenge, we presume that we are wiser than God, and we reveal a blatant lack of trust that God will do the right thing. Only by trusting God's sovereign wisdom will we be free from our anger and preoccupation toward those who have committed evil. If we refuse to trust God's justice, we become enslaved to bitterness and anger. We must guard our hearts and trust God to exercise His judgment against those who oppose Him.

A Living Sacrifice

*I beseech you therefore, brethren, by the mercies of God,
that you present your bodies a living sacrifice, holy,
acceptable to God, which is your reasonable service.*

ROMANS 12:1

God takes great pleasure in worthy sacrifices. In the Old Testament God gave detailed instructions for how His people were to give their offerings. He declared that these brought a "soothing aroma" to Him (Lev. 1:13, 17). When the Israelites gave an offering to God, it was no longer their own; it belonged entirely to God. God would accept only the best that people could give. It was an affront to almighty God to offer Him animals that were damaged or imperfect in any way. God Himself met the standard for sacrifices when He offered His own Son as the spotless Lamb. Only the death of His perfect Son was a worthy enough offering to atone for the sins of mankind.

Now, God asks us to lay down our lives on His altar as a living sacrifice. Just as it was in the Old Testament, our sacrifice, once offered, cannot be reclaimed. We belong entirely to Him. We cannot make a partial sacrifice of our lives; our offering must be wholehearted.

Therefore, if you are a Christian, your life is not your own. Rather than dying, however, God asks you to live for Him as a living sacrifice. Every day, you are to offer your life to Him for His service. You do not serve Him in your spare time or with your leftover resources. The way you live your life for God is your offering to Him. Relentlessly pursue holiness so that your offering to God is unblemished and acceptable to Him (Eph. 4:1; Phil. 1:27; 1 Thess. 2:12).

Believing God's Love

And we have known and believed the love that God has for us.
God is love, and he who abides in love
abides in God, and God in Him.

1 JOHN 4:16

The greatest truth in all of Scripture is this: God is love. Understanding this in its full dimensions will set you free to enjoy all that is yours as a Christian. But you must accept that God loves you. If you grew up experiencing unconditional love in your family, this may not be difficult for you. However, if your early years were void of love, this truth may be hard to accept. God loves you, not because you deserve His love, but because His nature is love. The only way He will ever relate to you is in love. His love for you gives you an inherent worth that nothing can diminish.

If you cannot accept the truth that God loves you, you will be limited in how you can relate to Him. When He disciplines you, you will not take it as an expression of His love. Rather, you may resent Him. When God says no to a request that is less than His best for you, you will conclude that He doesn't care about you. Without a clear understanding and acceptance of God's love for you, you will be disoriented to Him and to what He wants to do in your life. If you will accept God's love, however, you will be able to return love to God as well as to others (1 John 4:19).

Are you experiencing the profound sense of joy and security that comes from knowing you are dearly loved by God? Being assured of God's love for you sets you free to enjoy the numerous expressions of love He showers upon you each day.

No Sin

Whoever abides in Him does not sin.
Whoever sins has neither seen Him nor known Him.

1 JOHN 3:6

The Bible makes two things clear about sin. First, living a lifestyle of sin indicates that you are not walking in the power of the Holy Spirit, regardless of what you say about your spiritual condition. You cannot regularly spend time studying and meditating on God's Word, praying and walking in fellowship with the Holy Spirit, and persist in sin.

Second, if you do not hate sin the way God does, then you do not truly know Him. There are those who continue in their sin yet insist that they love God and belong to Him. John makes it clear: If you have a lifestyle of sin, you have not seen Him and do not know Him. You may have prayed a "sinner's prayer," or made a commitment in your church, or been baptized, but the evidence of the Holy Spirit's presence in your life is that you are defeating sin. This does not mean that you will never sin, but it does mean that you refuse to make sin a lifestyle and you immediately seek forgiveness when you sin (1 John 1:10). It means that you are opposed to sin, as God is, and you allow the Holy Spirit to eradicate every trace of sin in your life. It means that when you sin, you immediately confess it and repent of it and do whatever is necessary to avoid repeating your sin.

If you find yourself falling into sinful habits or not grieving over your sin as you once did, this indicates that you are not abiding in Christ. Return to Him in repentance; restore your fellowship with Him; and you will once again experience victory over your sin.

Casting Your Cares

Casting all your care upon Him,
for He cares for you.
1 PETER 5:7

As you've no doubt discovered, becoming a Christian does not make your problems go away. But it does give you an Advocate to whom you can take every concern. The Christians Peter addressed were facing persecution. They did not know whom they could trust; a friend, a neighbor, or even a family member could betray them, resulting in suffering and even death. But Peter had walked with the risen Christ, and he had personally experienced the love that Jesus had for His followers. He knew that Christ was in control, capable of handling every trial and that He wanted to do so as an expression of His love.

Casting our cares is a choice. It means consciously handing over our anxiety to Christ and allowing Him to carry the weight of our problems. At times this is the most difficult part of trusting God! We don't like turning over the responsibility for our problems. We have been taught that self-reliance is good and praiseworthy. We may even enjoy worrying. Yet if we are to be freed from the burden of our concerns, we must choose to cast them into the strong hands of our Father.

Peter does not distinguish between little cares and big cares. God does not differentiate between problems we should handle on our own and God-sized needs. He asks us to turn them *all* over to Him. One of our greatest errors is to assume we can deal with something ourselves, only to discover that we really can't.

God sees you as His frail child, burdened with a load that surpasses your strength. He stands prepared to take your load and to carry it for you. Will you let Him?

Confession

Confess your trespasses to one another, and pray for one another, that you may be healed. The effective, fervent prayer of a righteous man avails much.

JAMES 5:16

onfession is God's provision to clear obstacles that hinder our relationships with God and with others. Confession is not just for those who don't mind admitting their faults. Confession is a command, given to every Christian. James advised that when we sin, it is important for us to confess not only to God, but also to our fellow Christians. There is a tremendous freedom that comes as we openly acknowledge the sinfulness of our actions to others.

If confession does not come out of repentance, it is merely admission, and not true confession. It is important to confess your sins specifically and not hide behind generalities. It is one thing to pray, "O Lord, forgive my sin." It's quite another to identify your sin specifically in painful honesty. Whenever possible, confession ought to be made directly to those whom your sin has hurt. You are not to confess the sins of others but only your offenses. Confession is not a sign of weakness; it is evidence of your refusal to allow sin to remain in your life.

Significantly, James linked confession with prayer. Your prayers will be hindered if you hold on to unconfessed sin. When James promised that the "effective, fervent prayer of a righteous man avails much," he did so in the context of confession. If you wish to have a powerful prayer life, you must regularly confess your sin. Only when there are no obstacles separating you from God and others will your prayers be effective. Pride will discourage you from admitting to others the sinfulness of your heart. A desire to please God will compel you to confess your sin and rid yourself of its oppressive burden.

It's Not Difficult!

*For this commandment which I command you today
is not too mysterious for you, nor is it far off.*

DEUTERONOMY 30:11

The Christian life is not difficult. The same Christ who lived a perfect, obedient, and sinless life stands prepared to live it again through you (Gal. 2:20). God's will is not hard to discern. He has given us the Scriptures, which reveal His will, and He has placed His Holy Spirit within us to guide us to His perfect will in every situation (John 16:13). Our greatest challenge will be to wholly commit our lives to follow God's will obediently as He reveals it.

Moses gathered the Israelites around Mount Ebal and Mount Gerizim before they were to enter the Promised Land. There, God described what they had to do in order to obey Him. God gave detailed instructions so there was no mistaking what was expected of them. Then God asked them to make a choice. If they chose to disobey His commands, they would face His wrath. If they chose to obey, they would receive His blessing.

God's Word comes to you in the same way. It is not too complex to understand. You don't have to struggle to discern God's will about adultery or forgiveness or honesty. God's Word is perfectly clear. The question is, how will you respond? Nowhere in Scripture did God excuse disobedience because His instructions were too vague or complex. Condemnation came because they knew exactly what God wanted them to do, yet they chose not to do it! God, through His Holy Spirit, will always give you sufficient revelation and strength to take the next step with Him. If you are uncertain about what God is asking of you, make sure that you are obeying all that you do know; and through your obedience, God's next instruction will become clear.

Sympathy with God

Then Ananias, hearing these words, fell down and
breathed his last. So great fear came upon all those
who heard these things.

ACTS 5:5

When God brings judgment upon someone, our natural inclination is often sympathy toward the one being disciplined. Yet when God acts in judgment, our sympathies ought always to lie with Him. Only God knows all that is at stake, and only He knows the full circumstances that provoked His wrath upon the one He is judging.

Ananias and Sapphira's experience is one of the most perplexing stories in the New Testament. In a time when God's grace had provided salvation for all mankind, His response to this couple seems unusually harsh. Yet there was much at stake in their deception. The church was in its formative stages. Ananias and Sapphira had witnessed the miraculous power of God and had seen thousands of people being added to the church. Nevertheless, they showed little regard for the Spirit of God when they blatantly lied to God and the church. Such irreverence would have been devastating to a church whose very life depended upon the presence and guidance of God's Spirit. God left a sobering reminder that He would not tolerate sin.

Many times the sin of one Christian has a devastating effect on others. At times, God chooses to judge someone's sin severely, as a deterrent for others. Don't try to protect someone from the judgment of God. It is a terrifying thing to fall under His judgment (Heb. 10:31). Yet His judgment on one may ultimately save that person and many others. When God is judging others, take heed and examine your own life. God knows what is at stake; He loves His children enough to provide a stark warning of sin's dangers.

Painful Reminders

Then Jews from Antioch and Iconium came there;
and having persuaded the multitudes, they stoned Paul and
dragged him out of the city, supposing him to be dead.

ACTS 14:19

God has many ways to deter us from sin. One is to provide reminders for us so that we never take disobedience to Him lightly. Before his conversion, Paul assumed that he was righteous before God. In reality, Paul was so disoriented to God that he arrested and executed Christians in order to please Him! Paul was so blinded to God's will that when he watched Stephen being brutally murdered for his faith, Paul's heart was hardened, and he became even more determined to imprison other Christians.

It is significant that there are two occurrences of stoning mentioned in the New Testament—Stephen's and Paul's. Was it coincidence that God allowed Paul to be stoned in the same manner as Stephen had been? God had certainly forgiven Paul for his involvement in Stephen's death, but God also left him with a reminder of what his arrogance had led him to do. If pride could blind Paul to God once, pride could do it again. Perhaps Paul's "thorn in the flesh" was a direct result of this stoning. It may have served as a visible reminder to Paul, and to others, of the terrible consequences of sin.

God is absolutely just. He loves, and He forgives, but He does not compromise His righteousness. God deals with us uniquely. He draws upon our experiences to teach us about Himself. God will forgive us of our sin, but He may provide stark reminders of the ugliness of sin. Let us thank God that He loves us enough to remind us of the destructive consequences of sin in our lives.

While He Prayed

*When all the people were baptized, it came to pass that Jesus
also was baptized; and while He prayed, the heaven was
opened. And the Holy Spirit descended in bodily form like a
dove upon Him, and a voice came from heaven which said,
"You are My beloved Son; in You I am well pleased."*

LUKE 3:21–22

The greatest moments in a Christian's life come through
prayer. When Jesus prayed, heaven opened, and the Holy
Spirit descended upon Him. The Spirit came upon the disciples
as they gathered to pray on the day of Pentecost (Acts 1:14; 2:1).
When the disciples prayed together after Pentecost, their gather-
ing place was shaken, and they were emboldened to proclaim the
gospel throughout the city (Acts 4:31).

Prayer is not a substitute for hard work—prayer *is* the work!
God does things in and through our lives by prayer that He does
in no other way. As we pray and as our attention is turned toward
God, we become more receptive to aligning our lives with His
will. God will not equip us with His power while we are racing off
to our next appointment! His Spirit will not empower us if we are
oblivious to what He is saying. He requires our complete attention before He will fill us with the powerful presence of His Spirit.

If you want to learn how to pray, use Jesus as your model.
Jesus did not always receive what He asked for, but His prayers
were always heard and always answered (Mark 14:36; Heb. 5:7).
If you do not sense the Holy Spirit's power in your life, you may
not be spending adequate time in prayer. Perhaps you are pursuing your own agenda rather than seeking the Father's will. You
may have abandoned the place of prayer before God's answer
came. If you will commit yourself to spend sustained time in
prayer, asking for God's kingdom on earth, God will work in
your life just as He did in the lives of Jesus and His disciples.

Weak with Those
Who Are Weak

Who is weak, and I am not weak? Who is made to stumble,
and I do not burn with indignation?

2 CORINTHIANS 11:29

Christians do not live in isolation. When we sin, there are repercussions throughout the Christian community. When a brother or sister suffers, we are affected. Our calling is not to be solitary Christians but to be members of a priesthood (1 Pet. 2:9).

It was impossible for Paul to remain unmoved while there were believers in Corinth who were spiritually weak. When he learned that false teachers had caused Christians in Corinth to stumble in their faith, Paul burned with indignation. Paul told the church members at Corinth to rejoice when a church member rejoices and to weep when a fellow member weeps (1 Cor. 12:26). We depend on one another, and this influences everything we do. Jesus said that even when we pray, we are to begin by saying "*our* Father" (Matt. 6:9). We must do everything with our fellow Christian in mind (1 Cor. 14:12).

It's possible to become so preoccupied with your own spiritual journey that you do not get involved in your church. You can become so focused on what God is doing in your own country that you are oblivious to the suffering and persecution that your fellow Christians face in countries around the world. If other believers around you are rejoicing or hurting, and you are unaffected, you have become desensitized to the people of God.

Ask God to place a burden on your heart for fellow believers. Make yourself aware of their needs. Pray for them and adjust your life to God's activity in their lives.

Spiritual Optimism

*Then David said to the Philistine, "You come to me
with a sword, with a spear, and with a javelin.
But I come to you in the name of the Lord of hosts,
the God of the armies of Israel, whom you have defied.
This day the Lord will deliver you into my hand."*

1 SAMUEL 17:45–46a

David was certainly an optimist! Regardless of his circumstances, David could always see God's activity! A pessimist focuses on the problems, concentrating on the reasons why something cannot be done. The optimist sees those same problems, but he sees them from the perspective of God's presence.

David was just a young boy when he faced Goliath, an intimidating veteran warrior who frightened even the bravest Israelite soldier. As he prepared for battle, David saw that Goliath was a giant. He heard his boastful taunts. He could not fail to notice his enemy's weapons: a sword, a shield, and a javelin. David did not barge into the battle unprepared for a fight. He armed himself with five smooth stones. David was prepared for God to grant him victory with the first stone he hurled at the giant or the fifth. David was ready to accept God's victory, whether it came easily or with much effort.

Optimists do not ignore the difficulties; they are keenly aware of them. But the knowledge of God's presence prevents them from becoming discouraged or giving up. It is impossible to stand in the presence of God and be a pessimist!

The account of David and Goliath vividly pictures the source of the Christian's faith—not our own size, strength, or resources, but the power of almighty God. If we focus on our opposition and problems, they will seem gigantic. But as we focus on God, we will see our situation in the proper perspective and be assured that all things are possible with God (Phil. 4:13).

All Things Are Pure

*To the pure all things are pure, but to those who are
defiled and unbelieving nothing is pure;
but even their mind and conscience are defiled.*

TITUS 1:15

Your heart's condition will be expressed through your life. It will be evident by your attitudes, your words, and your behavior. Jesus said that you can clearly see others only when your own eyes are unobstructed (Mark 6:42). If your vision is hindered by sin, you will not look at others properly.

If your heart is pure, you will approach life without malice. You will not question the motives of everyone around you; you will not doubt the truth of everything others tell you; you will not look for fault in others. Instead, you will look for the good in others, finding what is praiseworthy. You will not be naive or gullible, but you will seek what is good rather than what is evil. If your heart is pure, you will see others the way God sees them (Matt. 6:22).

If your heart is defiled, everything with which you are involved will seem corrupt as well. You will assume evil motives in others because you know what you would do given the same circumstances. You will be cynical about what you hear because your own words are deceitful. You will be drawn to evil people and evil things.

How do you look at the words and actions of others? Are you critical of them? Are you judgmental? If so, ask God to purify your heart. Once He has, you will be free to see yourself and others as God does.

Prayer Changes You

*Yet now, if You will forgive their sin—but if not, I pray,
blot me out of Your book which You have written.*

EXODUS 32:32

Prayer is not designed to change God; it is designed to change us. Prayer is not calling God in to bless our activities. Rather, prayer takes us into God's presence, shows us His will, and prepares us to obey Him.

Moses climbed Mount Sinai and spent forty days communing with God. God showed him the wickedness of the Israelites (Exod. 32:7). Moses had not known their desperate condition; nor had he realized the imminence of God's judgment upon them until God revealed it to him. As God made Moses aware of all that was at stake, Moses felt the same compassion for the people that God felt. Moses became willing to sacrifice his own life for his obstinate people. In a compelling and selfless prayer of intercession, Moses offered to have his own name blotted out of the book of life if God would spare the people. In Moses' time with Him, God had formed a mighty intercessor for His people.

God will use your prayer times to soften your heart and change your focus. As you pray for others, the Holy Spirit will work in your heart so that you have the same compassion for them that God does (Rom. 8:26–27). If you do not love people as you should, pray for them. If you are not as active in God's service as you know He wants you to be, begin praying. You cannot be intimately exposed to God's heart and remain complacent. The time spent with God will change you and make you more like Christ.

Questioning God

Then the Lord answered Job out of the whirlwind, and said:
"Who is this who darkens counsel
By words without knowledge?
Now prepare yourself like a man;
I will question you, and you shall answer Me."

JOB 38:1-3

ob was a righteous man who, from a human perspective, did not deserve to suffer. He lived a blameless life and followed God's laws to the letter. As he was experiencing great tribulation, Job cried out in frustration and questioned why God was allowing him to suffer. God came to Job in the form of a whirlwind with His answer. As soon as God spoke, Job recognized that he should not have challenged God's wisdom. God turned to Job and asked him several sobering questions: "Where were you when I laid the foundations of the earth? Where were you when I set the oceans in their place? Where were you when I put the constellations of stars in position?" God's questions humbled Job and reminded him that his own wisdom did not begin to compare with God's.

When God finished asking His questions, Job replied, "I have uttered what I did not understand, / Things too wonderful for me, which I did not know" (Job 42:3). In a moment of despair and frustration, Job had challenged God's wisdom. God had firmly reminded Job that He was still sovereign and that this truth was enough for Job. Whether Job ever knew that his life had been the focus of a cosmic struggle is unclear. Perhaps Job never realized that his experience brought glory to God in the face of Satan's challenge (Job 1:8–12). But Job was satisfied to know that God's wisdom was flawless.

At times you may not understand why a loving Father would allow you to suffer as you are. You may question the wisdom of God's direction for your life. Learn from Job. Review the awesome power and wisdom of almighty God (Job 38–41). Have confidence that this same God is directing your path.

Trusting God's Wisdom

*Go and tell Hezekiah, "Thus says the Lord, the God of David
your father: 'I have heard your prayer, I have seen your tears;
surely I will add to your days fifteen years.'"*

ISAIAH 38:5

The fundamental premise of Christianity is that God knows what is best better than we do. When we are experiencing God's blessing, it is easy to believe that God knows what is best. But when God allows sickness and sorrow in our lives, we may be tempted to question His wisdom.

The Lord told King Hezekiah that his life was coming to an end. God advised him to prepare himself for death and to make arrangements to turn over the kingdom. Instead, Hezekiah pled for his life, begging God to spare him from death (Isa. 38:3). God loved the righteous Hezekiah and, in His grace, granted him an additional fifteen years to live. Those fifteen years would prove that God's wisdom far exceeds human wisdom. During those added years, Manasseh was born, and he eventually succeeded Hezekiah as king of Judah. Manasseh, who reigned for fifty-five years, was the most evil king ever to rule over Judah (2 Kings 21:1). Manasseh encouraged the worship of idolatry throughout the nation. He passed his own son through fire according to the abominable practices of idolatry. He shed much innocent blood during his reign; every part of the nation suffered from his cruelty. Manasseh's wickedness provoked God to anger, but Manasseh ignored God's warning (2 Kings 21:16; 2 Chron. 33:10). All these hardships were caused by Manasseh, a king who would never have been born if Hezekiah had accepted God's will for his life! Furthermore, Hezekiah's extended reign led to Judah's eventual defeat by the Babylonians (2 Kings 20:12–20).

So much suffering resulted from Hezekiah's unwillingness to accept God's will for him. God knows what is best. Whether your circumstances are easy or difficult, you can completely trust His guidance.

God's Sufficient Grace

*And He said to me, "My grace is sufficient for you,
for My strength is made perfect in weakness."
Therefore most gladly I will rather boast in my infirmities,
that the power of Christ may rest on me.*

2 CORINTHIANS 12:9

Human strength is a strong deterrent to trusting in Christ. When we rely on our own strength, resources, and knowledge, we assume we can handle situations without help from God. We tend to divide problems into two categories: problems that we know require God's help and problems we think we can handle on our own.

Paul had a tenacious personality and an exceptionally strong will. He courageously faced angry mobs as he traveled far and wide to promote the cause of Christ. He had spent the first half of his life serving God in his own strength. However, once God gained his attention, Paul had to learn to rely on God's strength and not his own.

Paul was afflicted with a thorn in the flesh (2 Cor. 12:7). Whatever this was, it humbled him. He had performed incredible miracles, even raising the dead; but he could not remove the affliction that God had given him, an affliction that made him depend on God. The world had seen what Paul could do in his own strength, and it was horrifying! Now God wanted to exercise *His* power through Paul's life. When Paul thought he was strong, he neglected to rely upon God's strength. Only in his weakness did Paul trust implicitly in God.

If you feel strong in an area of your life, beware! Often your strength, rather than your weakness, hinders you from trusting God. God will bring you to a point of weakness if that is what it takes to bring you to trust in Him. Do not despise your weakness, for it leads you to trust in God's strength.

Leaders and Managers

And the Lord said to Samuel, "Heed the voice of the people in all that they say to you; for they have not rejected you, but they have rejected Me, that I should not reign over them."

1 SAMUEL 8:7

The Israelites were to be a nation unlike any other. Every other nation had a king or ruler, but Israel's king was to be God Himself! Still, the Israelites complained that they wanted to be like other nations and have an earthly ruler! As we read about the Israelites, we marvel at their foolishness. Yet we are prone to make the same mistake, choosing our human wisdom over God's leadership.

There is much discussion these days about leaders and managers. According to popular teaching, leaders have the vision and set goals for people or organizations to follow. Managers handle the day-to-day marshaling of resources under their charge. In the Christian life, God is the leader of our lives, our families, and our churches. God sets the direction; He establishes the priorities; He provides the resources. We are the managers. We take what He gives us and do with it as He directs.

The biblical term for leader is *Lord*. As our Lord, Christ has the authority to reveal the direction for our lives. As Lord, He chooses our careers, leads us to our marriage partners, and helps us set our daily priorities. We are to be good managers of the mind, body, and spiritual life He gives. He is the Lord of our families. He knows what is best for our children. He knows how to make marriages strong. Our responsibility is to obey Him as He leads our families to Christlikeness. Christ is the Lord of our church. He takes responsibility for expanding it (Matt. 16:18; 1 Cor. 12:18). Only He knows what is best for our church. Our task is to faithfully perform the role He assigns us.

Do not foolishly trust in human wisdom and leadership as the Israelites did. Follow your Lord and trust Him alone.

Spiritual Preparation

And while they went to buy, the bridegroom came,
and those who were ready went in with him to the wedding;
and the door was shut.

MATTHEW 25:10

There is no substitute for spiritual preparation. Spiritual preparation equips you for unforeseen crises or opportunities. However, if you are unprepared you will be vulnerable in life's unexpected events.

Jesus told a parable that teaches this truth. Ten virgins were awaiting the arrival of the bridegroom so that they could celebrate with him and his bride. Five of them prepared in advance and brought an adequate supply of oil for their lamps. The other five were not prepared, so they rushed out to buy additional lamp oil. While they were gone, the bridegroom arrived. The five who had planned ahead entered into the house with him, but the door was closed against the five who were not ready, and they missed the celebration.

If you are spiritually prepared when a crisis comes, you will not have to try to develop instantly the quality of relationship with Christ that can sustain you. If you suddenly have an opportunity to share your faith with an unbeliever, you will be equipped to do so. If you enter a time of worship spiritually prepared, you will not miss an encounter with God. If you are spiritually filled when you meet a person in sorrow, you will have much to offer. If you have established safeguards in your life in advance, you will not give in to temptation.

Christians lose many opportunities to experience God's activity because they have not devoted enough time to their relationship with God. If you have not yet developed the habit of daily prayer and Bible study, why not begin now, so that you will be equipped for whatever life brings?

Godliness and Persecution

*Yes, and all who desire to live godly in Christ Jesus
will suffer persecution.*

2 TIMOTHY 3:12

L iving a godly life will not insulate you from hardship. Paul said that the more blameless your life, the more likely you will be persecuted. According to Paul, "evil men and impostors will grow worse and worse" (2 Tim. 3:13). As the world increasingly embraces sin, worldly people are becoming increasingly intolerant of godliness. Darkness cannot tolerate light; the more your life illuminates the presence of Christ, the more you should expect opposition from the forces of darkness. Your Christlike nature will be offensive to those in rebellion against Christ's lordship.

You may have recently repented of your sin and taken a new step of obedience to God. Perhaps you expected to experience God's blessing immediately as He demonstrated His approval of your obedience. Instead, you were met with opposition. The persecution may have come even from other Christians who misunderstood your motives. Perhaps you obeyed God, and still your actions were met with criticism instead of praise.

If you are sincerely following the Lord's direction, don't be discouraged. Paul warned that those who seek to live godly lives will suffer persecution. Do not be surprised when this happens to you. If the world crucified the Son of God, surely the world will be hostile to anyone who lives by the power of the Holy Spirit. Persecution may be the best evidence that your life is like that of Christ. Jesus warned that the world hated Him, the Savior, and so it would certainly misunderstand and mistreat His disciples (John 15:18).

No Secrets

"For nothing is secret that will not be revealed, nor anything hidden that will not be known and come to light."

LUKE 8:17

One of Satan's subtle deceptions is that you can do things in secret that will never be revealed. This is simply not so. The Bible stresses that everything done in darkness will one day be brought to light. So before you commit yourself to do anything questionable, seriously ask yourself, "Am I willing for those around me to know what I am about to do? Am I willing for God to watch me participate in this activity?"

The knowledge that God sees what we do, the certainty that we are accountable for every word and action, ought to dissuade us from sin (2 Cor. 5:10). But we can become so alienated from God that even this knowledge does not deter us. God promises that He will publicly expose our sin so that we must give an account to others for our actions. Ultimately, everything we do will be exposed on judgment day.

Still, some people believe they can sin against God, their families, their employers, or their friends and never be discovered. God has provided a safeguard against sin: the certainty of disclosure. Scripture commands us to expose the deeds of darkness as we become aware of them (Eph. 5:11). As Christians we are to be the light that dispels darkness in our world. Sin cannot continue in the Christian's experience, for light cannot dwell with darkness. The only insurance against having your sins exposed is living a blameless life.

Victory Versus Defeat

The Lord will cause your enemies who rise against you to be
defeated before your face; they shall come out against you one
way and flee before you seven ways. . . . The Lord will cause
you to be defeated before your enemies; you shall go out one
way against them and flee seven ways before them.

DEUTERONOMY 28:7, 25

As the Israelites were preparing to enter the Promised Land, God set before them a choice: Heed His voice, obey His commandments, and experience continued victory. Or turn from God, disobey His word, and experience repeated and resounding defeat. It was a simple choice. The choice they made would be evident by the results on the battlefield.

The assurance of victory did not mean that the Israelites would not have to strap on their armor and go to battle. It did not guarantee them effortless victory. At times their enemies fought fiercely, and the battles raged back and forth. Nevertheless, as the Israelites walked closely with God, they knew that their efforts would always result in victory.

God gives us the same choice He gave the Israelites. If we walk with Him, in obedience to His Word, He will stand with us and ensure victory over our challenges. We must face the battle, but God promises us victory if we remain in His will. However, if we choose to disassociate from God, we surely will be overtaken by difficulties. As with the Israelites, our decision will be evident by the outcome. If you are continually being defeated by everything you face, your heart has departed from God.

If you have been experiencing defeat in the challenges you face, examine your heart. When you are buffeted by the crises of life, your heart may have shifted away from God. Choose to listen to God. Then obey what He tells you, no matter what you face, and you will experience victory.

Discouragement

And he said, "I have been very zealous for the Lord God of hosts; because the children of Israel have forsaken Your covenant, torn down Your altars, and killed Your prophets with the sword. I alone am left; and they seek to take my life."

1 KINGS 19:14

Kingdom work can be challenging! You can give everything you have to God's service and come away exhausted. This is what happened to Elijah. God had just used Elijah to call down fire from heaven in a spectacular display of divine power. But Elijah's exhilaration was soon replaced by strenuous work followed by death threats, causing him to flee for his life. Now he was alone, exhausted, and discouraged.

Again, God came to Elijah. This time, He came not in fire or in a loud, spectacular way, but in a still, small voice. God's servant was tired, and God brought him comfort. Elijah's focus had shifted from God to God's enemies. He had allowed his circumstances to overwhelm him, leaving him disoriented to God and feeling alone. So God encouraged him. God provided Elisha for him as a helper, friend, and companion.

God removed Elijah from the activity for a time, so that he could rest and spend time with God. When the nation next saw Elijah, he was rejuvenated and refocused on God and His assignment.

If you are overwhelmed by kingdom work so that your focus is no longer on God but on all that there is to do, let Him comfort you. Listen to His gentle voice. He will encourage you and provide exactly what you need to prepare you for what comes next. If He needs to remove you from your work for a time, He will. He may place a friend or colaborer beside you to help carry the load. God knows exactly how to encourage you. Let Him do so.

Never Too Busy

But a certain Samaritan, as he journeyed, came where he was. And when he saw him, he had compassion.

LUKE 10:33

If anyone could understand the temptation to let busyness distract Him from the Father's activity, Jesus certainly could! He told a parable that clearly illustrated this danger: A certain Jewish man was on his way to Jericho when he was brutally attacked by thieves and left to die by the road. First a Levite, then a priest, passed by. These were religious leaders; surely they would show compassion to a wounded person! But they had places to go and appointments to keep, so they passed him by. Surely someone else would come along who had more time to help the wounded man! Then a Samaritan, despised by the Jews, came along. Of all people, this man had reason to look the other way, since the wounded man was his enemy. But wherever he was going could wait, for someone needed his help.

It's easy to become so busy that you are oblivious to those in need. Your schedule can become so full of accomplishing good things that you are of no help to the people around you. God is at work in the lives of your friends, your neighbors, your family members. He may ask you to interrupt your day long enough to join Him as He ministers to them. Nothing on your agenda, no matter how pressing, is reason enough to ignore the voice of God when He tells you to stop and help. If you have become too busy to minister to those around you, ask God to reestablish your priorities so that you do not miss opportunities to serve Him.

One Man's Sin

Get up, sanctify the people, and say, "Sanctify yourselves
for tomorrow, because thus says the Lord God of Israel:
'There is an accursed thing in your midst,
O Israel; you cannot stand before your enemies
until you take away the accursed thing from among you.'"

JOSHUA 7:13

Just as the obedience of one Christian can bring blessing to others, the sin of one Christian can bring harm to many others. The children of Israel were rapidly advancing into the Promised Land. They had experienced a miraculous victory over the city of Jericho, and they were continuing toward their next conquest. To their surprise they met decisive defeat as they attempted to capture the small town of Ai. They sought God's explanation for their failure, and He provided it. He revealed that someone among them had disobeyed His clear command not to keep any possession from Jericho. The disobedience of one man and his family had paralyzed an entire nation! Achan thought he could conceal his sin and it would not affect anyone else. God chose to demonstrate the destructive power of one sin to His people. One act of disobedience cost Achan and his family their lives. It caused his countrymen to lose the battle; innocent soldiers were killed. His sin had serious repercussions for others, denying them the blessing, power, and victory of God.

Your sin will have an impact on others. Choosing to disobey God may cost your family God's blessing. The power of God may be absent from your church because you are living in disobedience. Your friends may suffer because you are not living righteously. Diligently seek to obey every word from God, for you do not know how your disobedience could affect those around you. Scripture promises that if you will obey the Lord, your life will be a channel of blessing to others (Ps. 37:25–26).

Seeing with Your Eyes

I have heard of You by the hearing of the ear,
But now my eye sees You.

JOB 42:5

In his time, Job was the most righteous person on earth. He was so godly that the Lord took pleasure in pointing him out to Satan (Job 1:8). Yet, despite his love for God and his diligent obedience to His commands, even Job had not fully come to know God. The blessings God had given to Job had not revealed everything about God's character. There were characteristics that Job would come to realize only through adversity. So the Lord allowed Satan to test Job through suffering.

Although Job lost everything he had, even his seven children, Job discovered that God was still with him. Though he faced the most difficult and bewildering tribulations imaginable, Job came to understand that God was infinitely wiser than he (Job 42:1–4). As Job endured the insensitivity of his friends, he learned that God is the only One who is absolutely trustworthy. Job learned much about God through his anguish. Finally, he confessed that at first he had only heard about God, but now, through his suffering, he had come to see God (Job 42:5).

When you are in the midst of your trials, your Lord will reveal His character to you in ways you never knew. You will experience His strong and comforting presence. Like Job, you will learn that your Lord will remain, even when everyone else abandons you. You will see God more clearly as He takes you through the dark times. Then you will experience God in ways you had previously only heard about from others.

It Is Your Life!

For it is not a futile thing for you, because it is your life, and
by this word you shall prolong your days in the land
which you cross over the Jordan to possess.

DEUTERONOMY 32:47

It's puzzling that so many Christians try to live the Christian life without reading their Bible, except for sporadic perusals of God's Word, seeking a pithy thought for the day. The Word of God is not merely a source of helpful suggestions, preventive warnings, or inspirational thoughts: It is life itself!

God gathered the children of Israel at the edge of the Promised Land to review their pilgrimage with Him. They had spent forty years in a desert because their parents had not trusted God's Word. Their parents died without seeing the Promised Land because they had not believed God's Word. Even the revered Moses was soon to leave them because he had not shown proper reverence for God's Word. Many of them knew those who had been put to death as a consequence of their disobedience to God's Word. Over the years God's Word had become the most important thing in the life of the Israelites.

God commanded His people to bind His words on their hearts, to teach them diligently to their children, and to regularly discuss them in their homes (Deut. 6:4–9). So essential was His Word that it was to hold a prominent place in the daily lives of His people.

Our reverence for God's Word is revealed not only by what we say but also by what we do. Spending more time reading and studying the words of people rather than the Word of God reveals our hearts' condition. To blatantly disregard God's Word is to reject life itself. To obey God's Word is the surest way to experience all that God has in store for us.

Prepared for Worship

He will sit as a refiner and purifier of silver;
He will purify the sons of Levi, And purge them as gold
and silver, That they may offer to the Lord
An offering in righteousness.

MALACHI 3:3

The quality of our worship is not based on our activities but on our character. Churches can mistakenly assume that the better the music, the more impressive the building, and the more eloquent the preaching, the more worshipful the experience will be. Genuine worship, however, originates from within our hearts. If our relationship with God is not healthy, all these things are nothing more than religious pageantry.

The Levites were the worship leaders of their day. Their task was to offer sacrifices on behalf of the people. God declared that before they could worship Him in righteousness, He would first refine them with His refiner's fire, purging them of any impurities. Merely being members of the religious profession, having official responsibilities in the temple, and going through the rituals of worship did not guarantee that their religious activities would be acceptable to holy God.

Today, we tend to look to external things to enhance our worship. The true quality of our worship, however, rests within us. If we have not allowed God to purify us first, our worship will be void of His presence. If we do not have a pure heart, we may give offerings, but they will be unacceptable to God. Attending a religious service will not automatically ensure an encounter with God.

If you are not satisfied with the quality of your worship, don't be too quick to blame your environment. Look first to your own heart. Allow God to refine your heart until it is pleasing to Him, and you will be free to worship God as He intends.

Bringing People to Jesus

He first found his own brother Simon, and said to him,
"We have found the Messiah"
(which is translated, the Christ).

JOHN 1:41

People become known for many things. Noah is known as a righteous man in an evil age. David is known as the man after God's own heart. Peter is known as the outspoken disciple. John is known as the disciple whom Jesus loved. Judas is known as the betrayer. Paul is known as a fearless proclaimer of the gospel. Andrew is known for bringing others to Jesus.

The first person Andrew brought to Jesus was his brother Peter. As soon as Peter joined the disciples, he became the spokesperson for the Twelve, while Andrew remained in the background. It was Peter, not Andrew, who rose to prominence as one of Jesus' inner circle of three. We do not read of Andrew resenting Peter; it seems he was satisfied to bring others to Jesus and leave the results to Him.

It is not surprising that Andrew found the boy with the loaves and fishes and brought him to Jesus (John 6:8–9). Andrew brought Greeks to Jesus, even though they were despised by pious Jews (John 12:20–22). There is no record of Andrew ever preaching a sermon, performing a miracle, or writing a book of Scripture. He is remembered for those whom he brought to Jesus.

Andrew is a good role model for us. Our job is not to transform people into Christians nor to convict them of their sin. It is not our responsibility to make people do what they ought to do. Our task is to bring them to Jesus, and He will perform His divine work in their lives.

Hidden from the Wise

In that hour Jesus rejoiced in the Spirit and said, "I thank You, Father, Lord of heaven and earth, that You have hidden these things from the wise and prudent and revealed them to babes. Even so, Father, for so it seemed good in Your sight."

LUKE 10:21

One hindrance to hearing a word from God may be our own wisdom. Wisdom, like success, can delude us to think we should take the role of teacher rather than student. Our knowledge lulls us into thinking we have sufficient wisdom to meet any challenge. Believing we are wise tempts us to evaluate the shortcomings of others, yet be unaware of how much growth is still required in ourselves.

The Pharisees were the religious experts of their day. They possessed much information about God, but they had no personal relationship with Him. Their knowledge clouded their view of their condition before God. Jesus thanked His Father that it was not to these "experts" that the Father had revealed spiritual truth, but rather to those who were humble and who recognized their need for God's revelation.

When religious leaders experience spiritual failure, their downfall is often met with surprise. It shouldn't be. Religious people with the most knowledge are sometimes the ones least responsive to God's Word. Knowledge can easily lead to pride, and pride impedes us from seeking God.

How do you know if you are a "Pharisee"? When you do not have a teachable spirit. When you become defensive if a fellow Christian shares a concern about your spiritual condition. When you do not seek to hear from God, believing you already know what He thinks. When you feel that you are capable of helping others in their spiritual lives, but no one can teach you anything. Don't allow the limited knowledge you now have to blind you to the great truths God still wants to reveal to you.

A Second Time

Now the word of the Lord came to Jonah the second time.

JONAH 3:1

Jonah didn't like the assignment God gave him. God directed him to leave his homeland and go to the enemy city of Nineveh, a hostile and evil center of idol worship. There Jonah was to warn the people of God's impending judgment and urge them to repent. The Hebrews hated the people of Nineveh, so the rebellious prophet fled in the opposite direction, hoping for a different word from God that was more to his liking. Instead, God was determined that his word to Jonah would be obeyed (Isa. 55:11). He spoke to Jonah again. His second message was the same as the first. However, during the interval, Jonah had been buffeted by storms and had traveled in the stomach of a fish for three days. This time, he was prepared to hear God again and do His bidding.

God also spoke to the prophet Jeremiah two times (Jer. 33:1–3). But Jeremiah accepted God's Word to him the first time. The second time God spoke to him was to give him a fuller revelation of what He had first told him.

What God says to us next will depend on how we responded to His previous word to us. If, like Jonah, we disobeyed His earlier instructions, God will give them a second time. If we obeyed His first directive, as Jeremiah did, He will give us a fresh and deeper expression of His will (Matt. 25:23).

If you have not received a fresh word from God, return to the last thing God told you and examine your obedience. Is the Lord still waiting for your obedience? Seek to be like Jeremiah, and properly respond to your Lord's instructions the first time.

I Will Rejoice!

Though the fig tree may not blossom,   *Though the flock may be cut off from the fold,*
Nor fruit be on the vines;   *And there be no herd in the stalls—*
Though the labor of the olive may fail,   *Yet I will rejoice in the Lord,*
And the fields yield no food;   *I will joy in the God of my salvation.*

HABAKKUK 3:17–18

At times it seems that everything around you is collapsing. Endeavors you invested in may fail. People to whom you minister may disappoint you. The business or career you worked hard to build may crumble. These times, as difficult as they are, are opportunities to stop and examine what is truly important to you.

Habakkuk witnessed the collapse of most of what mattered to him. Yet through the loss, failure, and disappointment, he was able to distinguish between what was precious to him and what was transitory and empty. He came to the point where he could sincerely say that even if *everything* around him failed, he still would rejoice in God. If the fig tree bore no fruit; if the vine produced no grapes; if the flocks and herds stopped reproducing; he would still praise God. His praise might not come easily, as he watched everything fall short of his expectations, but he would praise God nonetheless. Habakkuk could not make fig trees produce figs. He could not control the productivity of the flocks and herds, but he could control his own response to God. He chose to praise the Lord.

Do things seem to be falling apart around you? You can still praise God. Your praise for Him does not depend on the success of your endeavors but on God's nature and His love and faithfulness to you. Ask God to help you look past worldly concerns to understand the reasons you have to praise Him.

God Speaks through His Activity

Look among the nations and watch—Be utterly astounded!
For I will work a work in your days
Which you would not believe, though it were told you.

HABAKKUK 1:5

Christians habitually seek God's voice through prayer, through His word, or through His messengers. Yet sometimes we fail to hear God speak through His activity, even though He is working all around us. Unbelievers see God's activity without understanding what they see. God encourages His people to watch for His activity so they will know how they should respond and adjust their lives.

The disciples discovered much about God's power by witnessing Jesus calming a raging storm with a command. Seeing Jesus dine with the notorious sinner, Zacchaeus, taught them a poignant message about God's love for sinners. Watching Jesus hang upon the cross communicated a compelling message of what God was willing to do to free people from sin. Discovering the empty tomb revealed an astounding truth of God's victory over death. To those with spiritual discernment, God's activity is a significant revelation about His heart and His will.

If you are sensitive to what God is doing around you, He will clearly speak to you through His activity. You will know that God is at work, because what you see will astound you, and human power and wisdom will not explain it. If things happen that are direct answers to your prayers, God is speaking to you. When you experience events that surpass your understanding and ability, it may be that God is communicating a critical message to you.

If you want to hear God's voice, look around you to see what He is doing. When you are watching for God at work, what you see will reveal His character, and you will have a fresh understanding of how to respond to Him.

Revival

O Lord, I have heard Your speech and was afraid;
O Lord, revive Your work in the midst of the years!
In the midst of the years make it known;
In wrath remember mercy.

HABAKKUK 3:2

Only God can restore life to something that has died. If you find that your heart has grown cold to God, that the spiritual life of your family or church has waned, call out to God to revive you, for only He can give life. It is not your activity but your relationship with God that brings life!

Spiritual fervor can ebb if left unattended. We all begin our walk with the Lord enthusiastically, with an excited sense of anticipation. But over time, busyness creeps in. We become distracted and let our sin go unchallenged. We may take our relationship with God for granted and not notice the gradual decline until we find ourselves drained of spiritual vitality.

This descent can happen in your church just as it does in your personal life. Do you remember a time when the Holy Spirit was moving mightily in your church, and the members sensed God leading in an exciting direction? Are the services now lifeless and the power of God only a memory?

At a time like this it is futile to try to bring back life yourself. You can organize many activities and exhort those around you, but only God can resurrect what is dead. If God has initiated something in your life, or family, or church, only He can sustain it or revive it. If you sense that the spiritual vigor has gone out of your life or the life of your church, this is God's invitation to pray. He wants you to intercede with Him so that He might revive His work. Jesus said that He *is* Life. It is unnecessary to remain spiritually lifeless when He has promised vibrant, abundant life if you will claim it.

Are You Coming to the Celebration?

So he answered and said to his father, "Lo, these many years I have been serving you; I never transgressed your commandment at any time; and yet you never gave me a young goat, that I might make merry with my friends."

LUKE 15:29

God is concerned with bringing people from death to life. His heart rejoices over each person who returns to Him from a time of rebellion. If your heart is like God's, you, too, will rejoice when a sinner returns to the Father.

Jesus' parable about the prodigal son is as much about the older son who remained as it is about the wayward son or the father. Year after year the older son labored for his father, waiting for a future reward. He had seen the brokenness his brother's rebellion had caused his father. Yet when his brother returned, the older son did not rejoice with his father. He felt no pleasure in seeing his father happy. His concern was for himself and the injustice he perceived he'd been dealt. He felt like a martyr and totally missed the blessing of celebrating with his father.

It is possible to serve God year after year and yet have a heart that is far from Him. You might be one of the hardest workers in your church and yet be filled with bitterness because others do not share your load. You can become so preoccupied with your spiritual labors that when God works miracles in the lives of those around you, you cannot rejoice.

If you serve the Lord out of duty or habit, but not out of joy and gratitude, you will feel like a martyr. You will envy those who are experiencing joy in the Lord while you feel weighed down by the work you are doing. This is not the abundant life your Father has planned for you. Come to the celebration, spend time with the Father, and share in His joy!

History

Listen to Me, you who follow after righteousness,
You who seek the Lord:
Look to the rock from which you were hewn,
And to the hole of the pit from which you were dug.

ISAIAH 51:1

As Christians, we ought never to overlook our heritage. An awareness of our Christian heritage helps us to understand our identity, and it gives us a sense of where God is leading us.

The Israelites had a rich heritage. Their nation began as a result of Abraham and Sarah's faithfulness. The generations that followed included Isaac, Jacob, and Joseph as their faithful leaders. God richly blessed His people and made them prosper. God continued to show favor on the Israelites by leading them out of Egypt into a prosperous land of their own. God established His nation through some of the most awesome miracles in history. God continued to provide strong leaders, such as Moses, Joshua, Gideon, Deborah, Samuel, David, and Solomon. He sent mighty prophets such as Elijah, Isaiah, and Jeremiah. Unfortunately, in Isaiah's day, God's people had reached a point where they had forgotten their heritage. They lived as spiritual paupers rather than as heirs to a rich heritage and members of a royal priesthood.

Your spiritual heritage is even richer than that of Isaiah's generation. Your spiritual ancestors include Mary the mother of Jesus, John the Baptist, the disciples, the apostle Paul, and a host of saints down through the ages. Even more important, you look to Jesus as the author and finisher of your faith (Heb. 12:2). You may have a family history of faithfulness that goes back several generations.

Do you see the full picture of God's redemptive work? God's plan involves you, just as it has included each Christian throughout the centuries. God wants you to participate in His continuing work to redeem a lost world. *Your* obedience today will provide a legacy of faithfulness to the generations that follow.

The Lord Hears

Then those who feared the Lord spoke to one another,
And the Lord listened and heard them;
So a book of remembrance was written before Him
For those who fear the Lord
And who meditate on His name.

MALACHI 3:16

God has designed His kingdom so that Christians with kindred spirits join together. It is exciting when you find another Christian who shares the same concerns and burdens that you do! Often, God will graciously bring another believer alongside you who will undergird you in the work and concerns God has placed on your heart.

God releases a powerful dimension of His presence to His children when they unite in heart and mind regarding His kingdom. The Bible says that when two or more Christians meet and reverently discuss matters concerning the Lord, God is pleased to listen to them and to respond to their concerns. When two or three believers agree in prayer, God chooses to respond to their unity by making His powerful presence known in their midst (Matt. 18:19–20). When two people walked together and discussed the confusing events of Christ's crucifixion, Jesus joined them and helped them understand the events of their day (Luke 24:13–32).

If you are carrying concerns about your family or your church or your friends, ask God to bring like-minded believers around you to share the burden with you in conversation and in prayer. Don't attempt to bear your load of cares on your own. You may pray about them, but you will miss the blessing of uniting together with a group of believers who join together to intercede for one another and to enjoy God's presence. Everything God has woven into the fabric of His kingdom promotes interdependence, not individualism. As you face your concerns, deliberately seek out other believers with whom you can stand and share your load.

Spiritual Enemies

*For we do not wrestle against flesh and blood, but against
principalities, against powers, against the rulers of the
darkness of this age, against spiritual hosts of wickedness
in the heavenly places.*

EPHESIANS 6:12

In a battle, it is imperative to identify your enemy. If you are not aware of the point of your attack, you are vulnerable. Paul had many enemies. Some resented him, others hated him, and others wanted to kill him. Some, who were supposedly on his side, sought to harm him and his ministry (Acts 9:23; Phil. 1:17; 2 Tim. 1:15; 1 Tim. 1:20; 2 Tim. 4:14). In spite of the persecution he faced, Paul never lost sight of his real enemy. Paul was wary of Satan. When people attacked him, he knew they were not his real opponents. They were simply unwitting instruments of the spiritual forces of darkness.

When you meet opposition to your faith, your first reaction may be anger toward your antagonist. This may divert your attention from the deeper, spiritual dimensions of your conflict. Your adversary may be hopelessly in bondage to sin. Rather than retaliating, you should immediately and earnestly intercede for that person. Your opponent's hostility is your invitation to become involved in God's redemptive work to free him or her from spiritual bondage.

Be alert to the spiritual warfare around you. It is real and potentially destructive to you and those you care about. Knowing your real foe will protect you from bitterness and unforgiveness. Your hope lies in the reality that "He who is in you is greater than he who is in the world" (1 John 4:4). Do not place your hope in humanity, but steadfastly trust in the One who has already defeated your enemy.

A Defeated Enemy

*Having disarmed principalities and powers,
He made a public spectacle of them,
triumphing over them in it.*

COLOSSIANS 2:15

Christians are not called to defeat Satan. God has already done that in Christ! Nor is it our mandate to "bind" Satan. Jesus has already set limits on the extent and duration of Satan's freedom. Satan, "our ancient foe," was decisively and completely defeated by Christ's sacrifice on the cross and in His resurrection. With regard to Satan, our assignment is to trust in the victory that Christ already achieved and daily resist him with the truth of his defeat, as Jesus did.

Satan is the father of lies and a master deceiver (John 8:44). If he can convince you that God has not defeated him, then you will not experience Jesus' victory. You will find yourself fighting battles that Christ has already won! You will fear Satan though he has already been utterly and humiliatingly defeated. Your responsibility is to resist Satan, and he will flee from you (James 4:7). When you resist him, you are acknowledging that Jesus has defeated him and given you victory over his influence. God has provided you with spiritual armor that is more than sufficient to withstand any assault by Satan (Eph. 6:10–20).

Christians can become preoccupied with battling Satan. This deceives them to invest their time and energy attempting to do something that Christ has already done for them. If Satan can divert you to wage a warfare that has already ended in surrender, he will have eliminated your effectiveness where God wants you. Fearing Satan is fearing a prisoner of war. You have no need or calling to defeat Satan; you need only to apply Christ's victory in every area of your life and to live the victorious Christian life. As you go about sharing the gospel message with others, Satan and his forces face the reality of their defeat in each life that is claimed by the kingdom of God (Luke 10:17–20).

Grace, Mercy, and Peace

*To Timothy, a true son in the faith: Grace, mercy, and peace
from God our Father and Jesus Christ our Lord.*

1 TIMOTHY 1:2

How you pray for your family members and friends is important. There is no better way to pray for someone you love than by following the example found in Scripture. Paul often asked for specific gifts from God for those He cared about. On Timothy's behalf, Paul requested grace, mercy, and peace.

Grace is the unearned gifts the Father bestows on His children. The Lord relates to us only by His grace. His grace provided salvation though we deserved destruction (Eph. 2:8). His grace blesses us with the riches of heaven. His grace brings us peace in troublesome times. His grace brings us good things every day (1 Tim. 1:14).

Mercy is God withholding the punishment we deserve because of our sinfulness. The consequences of our sin is death, yet Jesus paid this penalty for us (Rom. 6:23). God is long-suffering and will delay giving us our just punishment in order for us to have every opportunity to repent and to receive His gift of salvation (2 Pet. 3:9).

Peace is the state of mind and heart we experience when we are confident of God's grace and mercy toward us. Peace comes in knowing that God's grace will sustain us, even in our most difficult crises (Phil. 4:7). God assures us that even when we fail miserably in our commitments to Him, He will show mercy upon us. This assurance gives us peace.

The peace God gives is fundamentally different from the peace the world offers (John 14:27). The world seeks to sedate us from the problems we face through counseling or drugs or temporary pleasures. The peace that God gives goes right to the soul, relieving the heart and mind.

How are you praying for your loved ones? There could be no better request than asking the Lord to give them an abundance of His grace, His mercy, and His peace.

Have You Done What You Know to Do?

*Therefore, to him who knows to do good
and does not do it, to him it is sin.*

JAMES 4:17

It is never a minor thing to know God's will and not do it. God calls this sin. We can make excuses for our lack of obedience: "I'm just not ready yet" or "I'll do it later!" or "I don't think it will make a difference" or "I can't afford to!" We rationalize, we procrastinate; yet, in God's eyes, rationalization and procrastination are nothing more than disobedience. At times we deceive ourselves into thinking that good intentions equal obedient actions. They do not. A good intention without corresponding activity is disobedience. When we encounter God and He gives us a direction, it is not enough to write down the date in our spiritual journal, or even to tell our friends and church of our "decision." God's call is not to "make a decision" but to obey! Deciding to obey is not equal to obeying (Matt. 21:28–31)! Loudly affirming the necessity of obedience is not the same as obeying (Luke 6:46). Making commitments, even publicly, is not the same as obeying our Lord. Substituting our own good works is not the same as obeying.

God told King Saul to wait until the prophet Samuel arrived. Instead of waiting, Saul took matters into his own hands and offered a sacrifice. Saul discovered, to his deep dismay, that other acts of supposed piety do not take the place of obeying a clear command from God (1 Sam. 15:22). As with Saul, God expects you to obey everything exactly as He tells you. Only obedience satisfies God's desire for obedience!

Counted Faithful

And I thank Christ Jesus our Lord who has enabled me,
because He counted me faithful, putting me into the ministry.

1 TIMOTHY 1:12

From a human perspective, the apostle Paul's record as a zealous persecutor of Christians should have precluded him from being used in God's service. Paul was known as the "chief of sinners," a blasphemer, persecutor, and violent aggressor (1 Tim. 1:13–15). Everything changed when God saved Paul. He embraced the Christian life with the same fervency in which he had opposed it. Paul labored to be faithful in every assignment, no matter how small or large. Ultimately, because of Paul's faithfulness, God entrusted him to be one of His foremost promoters of the gospel.

Paul understood that everything he ever accomplished for God's kingdom was due to the enabling power of God. He was not deceived into thinking that his own intelligence or personal drive brought about God's will. Rather, Paul was grateful for the opportunity to be tested and found faithful in any assignment, regardless of its size.

Your ability to serve God is not based on your past, but on your faithfulness today. If you are faithful with the task God entrusts to you, God will enable you to accomplish it. Don't distinguish between big and small assignments from God. Paul saw every one as a privilege he did not deserve. Whether God has asked you to pray for someone, to minister to a person in need, to lead a Bible study, or to care for those who are sick, strive to be faithful. You will experience His enabling as you serve Him. If you are faithful in a little, God will entrust you with more. You will be able to join Paul in praising God for having counted you faithful, putting you into His service (Luke 16:10).

Let No One Look down on You

Let no one despise your youth, but be an example to the believers in word, in conduct, in love, in spirit, in faith, in purity.

1 TIMOTHY 4:12

Timothy was a sincere young man who earnestly desired to serve the Lord. Yet certain weaknesses in Timothy's life hindered him from serving God confidently. Timothy was very young to be a religious leader, and apparently some doubted his abilities. Timothy had a tender nature and was sickly (1 Tim. 5:23). His was an inauspicious beginning for a young minister of the gospel in an age of persecution!

Paul urged Timothy not to allow his youthful insecurity to blunt his zeal and faithfulness in doing what God had told him. Rather than arguing with those who criticized Timothy, Paul urged him to live as an example of godliness. Paul advised Timothy to live a life that was so spotless in word, conduct, love, spirit, faith, and purity that his life could serve as a model for others in the church to follow. Timothy's life was to be the evidence that God had called him. God looked beyond Timothy's youth, timidity, and physical weakness and saw his sincere heart.

As you seek to follow God's will, you may identify with Timothy. Perhaps some things about you seem to disqualify you from serving the Lord effectively. You may be sensitive because you are a new Christian or because you come from a sinful past. Perhaps you have little education or money or social status. You may have previously experienced failure in your service for God. Don't allow this to intimidate you from following God's will. Your area of weakness may be God's means of demonstrating His strength (2 Cor. 12:9). Allow God to demonstrate His call upon you by transforming your life into a model of godliness.

Wisdom Justified

But wisdom is justified by all her children.

LUKE 7:35

The world is full of "experts." There are people everywhere who want to convince you of the wisdom of their opinion. Yet God says that it is not the one who declares his viewpoint the most loudly or vociferously who is the wisest, but the one who is vindicated over time.

Wisdom is not proven by argument or debate. Wisdom is proven over time. Some people adamantly proclaim that their opinion is best. Regardless of how convincingly these people defend their viewpoint, time is the best judge of their wisdom. The result of a practice proves its validity, not how loudly it is promoted.

When you seek to obey what God has told you, you will sometimes meet resistance and criticism from others who disagree with the wisdom of your actions. Your immediate response may be the urge to vindicate yourself. However, if you wait patiently, time will reveal the wisdom of your actions far better than you could through argument.

Through the ages, the wisdom found in God's Word has been tested and proven true. It is critical that you measure everything you hear against the Scriptures. Trends in psychology and philosophy come and go, but God's Word is timeless. Whenever you share an opinion in counseling someone else, make sure that it comes from the Scripture and not merely from your best thinking. As long as you base your life choices on the Word of God, time will be your defender and will validate the wisdom of your choices. If, over time, you clearly see you are wrong, ask God's forgiveness and seek a fresh word from God through the Scripture. Then obey that word and watch to see God confirm His wisdom in your life.

Don't Avoid
the Impossible

But Jesus said to them, "They do not need to go away. You
give them something to eat."

MATTHEW 14:16

Jesus asked His disciples to do something that clearly was impossible. There were five thousand men, along with their families, and they were famished. There were only five loaves of bread and two small fish—obviously not enough to feed a multitude. The cost of food for even a portion of the crowd would have far exceeded the disciples' small budget. It may have seemed absurd to the disciples that Jesus should ask them to distribute the paltry amount of food to the massive crowd. Yet that is exactly what Jesus asked them to do. Because Jesus had given the command, the disciples obeyed and witnessed an incredible miracle.

Christ will lead you into many situations that will seem impossible, but don't try to avoid them. Stay in the middle of them, for that is where you will experience God. The key difference between what appears to be impossible to us and what is actually possible is a word from our Master! Faith accepts His divine command and steps out in a direction that only God can complete. If you attempt only things that you know are possible with the visible resources you possess, those around you will not see God at work. You will be the one who receives the credit for a job well done, but God will have no part in it.

Take inventory of your life and the decisions you are presently facing. Have you received a word from the Master that awaits your next step of faith? If you will proceed with what He has told you, no matter how incredible it might seem, you will experience the joy of seeing your Lord perform a miracle, and so will those around you.

Tempted by Shortcuts

*Then Abishai said to David, "God has delivered your enemy
into your hand this day. Now therefore, please, let me strike
him at once with the spear, right to the earth; and I will not
have to strike him a second time!"*

1 SAMUEL 26:8

You will sometimes be tempted to take shortcuts to your
destinations in life. David faced this temptation numerous
times before he finally assumed the throne. Samuel, God's
prophet, had anointed David and prophesied that he would be
the next king of Israel (1 Sam. 16:12–13). Yet, while David waited on God's timing, he watched in frustration as a crazed King
Saul brought the kingdom into jeopardy. Saul pursued David to
murder him, forcing David to flee for his life.

Then an incredible opportunity presented itself to David.
David found Saul in a vulnerable position, sleeping with his
army. Abishai, one of David's warriors, offered to kill Saul. It
seemed to make perfect sense. Saul had tried to kill David on
numerous occasions. God had said He intended for David to be
the king. By taking matters into his own hands, David could
bring an end to his exile and assume the throne as God's anointed servant. Yet he refused to compromise his integrity in order
to become king, even though he wanted the position and it was
rightfully his. Accomplishing God's will in any manner other
than the way God prescribed was unthinkable.

At times you may face similar temptations. Well-meaning friends
advise you to hasten God's will for you rather than waiting upon
Him. You may be sorely tempted to take control of your situation,
assuming the end will justify the means. These are the times when
you must trust God's perfect timing. God may plan for you to
attain a certain position or take a new direction, but the timing may
not be right. Watch over your heart. Don't allow others to persuade you to compromise your integrity as you follow God's will.

Steadfast in Your Resolve

*Now it came to pass, when the time had come for Him
to be received up, that He steadfastly
set His face to go to Jerusalem.*

LUKE 9:51

It is easy to become distracted in the Christian life! The
moment you understand what God wants you to do, it
will seem as though everyone around you requires your time and
attention! When the time came for Jesus to go to the cross, He
"set His face" toward Jerusalem, so that nothing would prevent
Him from accomplishing His Father's will. So obvious was His
resolve to go to Jerusalem that the Samaritans, who hated the
Jews, rejected Him because they recognized that He was a Jew
traveling through their village to the hated city of Jerusalem.

Jesus determined not to digress from His mission, but He took
time to minister to many people along His way. He sent out seventy disciples into the surrounding towns (Luke 10:1). He healed
lepers (Luke 17:11–19). He cured a man of dropsy (Luke 14:1–4).
He brought salvation to the home of Zaccheus (Luke 19:1–10).
He continued to teach His disciples (Luke 15:1–32). Jesus did not
refuse to minister to others as He went to Calvary, but ultimately
He refused to be deterred from His Father's will.

If you know what God wants you to do, set your sights res-
olutely toward that goal with full determination to accomplish it
(Prov. 4:25). Your resolve to go where God is leading ought to be
evident to those around you. Beware of becoming so sidetracked
by the opportunities around you that you lose sight of God's ultimate goal for you. Do not succumb to the temptation to delay
your obedience or to discard it altogether. Once you have received
a clear assignment from God, your response should be unwavering obedience.

New Strength

But those who wait on the Lord
Shall renew their strength;
They shall mount up with wings like eagles,
They shall run and not be weary,
They shall walk and not faint.

ISAIAH 40:31

A t times you may feel so worn out and stressed that you are not sure you can take another step. You may seem to spend all your time running from crisis to crisis and to be constantly giving your time and energy to others. Your Lord wants to renew your strength and enable you to enjoy the abundant life He intends for you. The key is to *wait* upon Him to do so.

Our generation does not enjoy waiting. We are harried by all the commitments we have made and the many responsibilities we hold. We rush through our lives without stopping to evaluate our activities. Sometimes in our haste to get on with our work, we race ahead of God. Part of God's restorative process is to slow us down and make us listen to Him. As we wait on Him, God will remind us of our utter dependence upon His strength. When we slow down and seek His will, He will reveal *His* plans.

Biblically, waiting on the Lord is never passive; it is always active. Waiting requires us to cease our own pursuits and give God our complete attention. We may have to give up some of the activities we have allowed to inundate our lives. We may need to take an entire day to sit quietly before the Lord. If we ask Him, God will show us the resources He has provided to help with the work we have been attempting on our own. God may address feelings of guilt that have motivated us to do things that He has not asked us to do.

Jesus carried more responsibility than you do. More people needed Him than will ever need you. Yet He was never overwhelmed or inadequate for the task. Now Christ offers to guide you so that you will fulfill your heavenly Father's will and gain the strength necessary for each day (Matt. 11:28).

Press On

Brethren, I do not count myself to have apprehended;
but one thing I do, forgetting those things which are behind
and reaching forward to those things which are ahead.

PHILIPPIANS 3:13

The world will tell you that the dominating influence in your life is your past. If you came from a difficult home life, that will determine the direction of your life. If your culture was treated unfairly, that will dictate the condition of your life today. If you were hurt or abused or if your youth was spent in rebellion, the remainder of your life will be spent struggling with your past. The world is preoccupied with the past because it faces an uncertain future.

Christians, on the other hand, live in freedom because Christ has overcome our past. The "old things" have been done away with and "new things" have come (2 Cor. 5:17). God has so totally forgiven the Christian's sin that He chooses not to remember it (Isa. 43:25). Christians do not forget the past, but we are not controlled or motivated by it. The Christian looks to the future with hope.

The people of the world focus on what they are overcoming. Christians focus on what they are becoming. Christians know that the Holy Spirit is conforming them into the image of Christ. Christians know that ultimately they will stand before Christ to give an account of their actions and will spend an eternity in the presence of God. Christians know that eventually every injustice will be addressed and every hurt comforted. They know that Satan, and death itself, will finally be brought to an end. The Christian's future is so full and rich and exciting that it supersedes whatever happened in the past.

If you are preoccupied with your past, ask God to open your eyes to the incredible future that awaits you and begin, like Paul, to press on to what is ahead.

Losing Your Life

For whoever desires to save his life will lose it,
but whoever loses his life for My sake will find it.

MATTHEW 16:25

Christians are commanded to lose their lives. This means they ought to deliberately release their lives to God and His kingdom. One of the greatest hindrances to your being on mission with God will be your view of what constitutes your "legitimate rights"—that is, those things that you feel you have a right to experience and enjoy. It's not difficult to turn over to Christ those things that are not a sacrifice or that you would prefer to do without anyway. Rather, it is the things that are good and that are dear to you that may stand between you and God's will.

It's good to be near your grown children and grandchildren, for example, but God may want you to go to another city or continent on mission with Him. It's good to get adequate rest, but you may receive a call of distress in the middle of the night. You may assume that you have a right to certain material things, yet God may ask you to release all of your possessions to Him and His purposes (Matt. 19:21).

Jesus modeled perfectly this attitude toward life. He had a legitimate right to enjoy the comforts of heaven. Yet, He did not look at it as a right He should hold on to; nor did He see leaving all that was His as a sacrifice too costly to make (Phil. 2:5–11). As a result, God highly exalted Him and brought salvation to a broken world.

Has the world convinced you that there are certain rights that you must protect? Are you trying to save your life? Have you noticed that in so doing, you are actually losing the life God wants you to have?

A Part of Something Bigger

Moreover He said, "I am the God of your father—the God of Abraham, the God of Isaac, and the God of Jacob." And Moses hid his face, for he was afraid to look upon God.

EXODUS 3:6

God always speaks to you in the context of what He has done in the lives of those who have gone before you. When God encountered Moses, He did not give him an assignment independent of what He had done through those who had preceded him. God had made promises to Abraham, Isaac, and Jacob hundreds of years earlier, and He was now going to involve Moses in His ongoing activity to fulfill the covenant He had made with Moses' forefathers.

The God who led Moses, who worked through Elijah, who directed Paul, who guided each man and woman of God through the centuries, is the same God who approaches you to become involved in His work. Do you sense the significance of that? You are a vital part of something much bigger than yourself!

We tend to think only of the present. We want immediate results and lack a sense of eternity. We often act as if God had not been working at all where we were before He approached us. We expect that anything God does through us will be completed while we can see the results. We become impatient if God intends to complete what He began in us through another person or even another generation.

Moses came to understand that his involvement in God's work was in the context of hundreds of years of divine activity. When Moses came face to face with the same God who had guided his forefathers, he was deeply humbled. Do you sense that your life is a part of God's eternal purposes?

Not Sorrowing as Others

*But I do not want you to be ignorant, brethren, concerning
those who have fallen asleep, lest you sorrow
as others who have no hope.*

1 THESSALONIANS 4:13

Christians do not grieve as the world grieves. The world experiences sorrow without hope. The Christian also has sorrow, but the Christian's sorrow is accompanied by hope.

In Jesus' day, a funeral was a time for an impassioned demonstration of grief. It was a sign of respect for the deceased to wail loudly at a funeral. A person grieving the loss of a loved one had no power to change what had happened. There was probably no time in human experience when people felt more helpless or vulnerable than at a funeral.

Jesus, too, wept at the funeral of a close friend, but His sorrow did not come from a lack of hope (John 11:35). Jesus knew that soon Lazarus would be alive again. He also knew that at His second coming, Lazarus and all of Jesus' followers would be resurrected from death to spend eternity with Him in heaven. Jesus wept because He saw the hopelessness felt by the people He loved. His friends had the Resurrection and the Life right in their midst, yet they were grieving! (John 11:25).

When Jesus conquered death, He forever changed the way Christians view death. Christians still experience the sorrow of losing someone we love, but we have hope because we know that God can bring good out of any situation (Rom. 8:28). We have hope in the knowledge that nothing, not even death, can separate us from God's love (Rom. 8:38–39). We have hope because Jesus will bring us to join Him in heaven so that we might enjoy eternity in unhindered fellowship with Him (John 14:3).

Even though you are a Christian, you cannot escape life's sorrows. But you can temper your grief with the hope that Christ is risen, for He is your hope and your comfort.

God Is Faithful

He who calls you is faithful, who also will do it.

1 THESSALONIANS 5:24

God never calls us to do anything without faithfully keeping His word and enabling us to do it. We are not always faithful to do what God tells us, but He remains faithful and stands by His word to fulfill what He has promised (Isa. 46:11).

When the children of Israel reached the Red Sea, they might have concluded that God had abandoned His promise to them. The sea was barring their advance, and the murderous Egyptian army was racing to overtake them! Yet God proved then, as He has ever since, that He is absolutely faithful to every word He speaks to His children.

God may have spoken to you about something in particular—a ministry in your church, the way to raise your children, or what you should do in your job. You have obeyed Him, but now you face a Red Sea experience. It seems that what you thought God wanted to accomplish is not happening. Perhaps your ministry has not been well received, or your children are rebelling, or those at your workplace are criticizing your actions. Trust in the character of God. It is His nature to be faithful. The testimony of His people throughout the ages is expressed by the psalmist, who declared: "I have been young, and now I am old; / Yet I have not seen the righteous forsaken, / Nor his descendants begging bread" (Ps. 37:25).

Regardless of how bleak your present circumstances are, do not lose hope. No one has ever experienced unfaithfulness on God's part! Allow time for God to reveal His faithfulness to you. Someday you will reflect on what God has done and praise Him for His absolute faithfulness to you.

Christian Anger

"Be angry, and do not sin":
do not let the sun go down on your wrath.

EPHESIANS 4:26

Few things are more destructive to Christians than anger. Anger causes us to lose our self-control and to say and do things we would otherwise never consider. Anger, if allowed to remain, turns into bitterness that eats away at our hearts. Scripture consistently commands believers to put away anger and lists it as one of the sins of the flesh (Eph. 4:31).

At times, we try to defend our anger by citing Ephesians 4:26. As additional proof we argue that Jesus cleansed the temple in "righteous indignation." Ephesians refers to anger that does not lead to sin. Jesus was capable of being angry without sinning. When Jesus cleared the temple, Scripture does not indicate that He was angry (Matt. 21:12–14; Mark 11:15–18; Luke 19:45–46).

We must be careful not to justify our anger with Scripture. Ephesians 4:31 commands us to put away *all* anger. That does not mean that we cease to have strong convictions or lose our desire for justice. It does mean we refuse to allow the sins of others to cause us to sin. Anger does not bring about God's redemptive work; far more often it hinders what God is working to accomplish.

If you feel that you have a righteous anger because of something that has happened, see if you are holding anger in your heart without sin. Is your anger turning into bitterness? Is your anger causing you to speak in an unchristian manner to someone or to gossip about them? Is your anger causing you to make excuses for your own ungodly behavior? Is your anger preventing you from acting in a loving, redemptive, and Christlike way toward someone? You must examine any anger within you and allow God to remove any sinful attitudes that your anger may have produced.

Judge Not

Judge not, and you shall not be judged. Condemn not, and you shall not be condemned. Forgive, and you will be forgiven.

LUKE 6:37

There is a significant difference between judgment and discernment. God sees people's hearts and knows their motives (Prov. 16:2). Only God can accurately judge those who deserve punishment. Ultimately, Christ will sit in judgment upon us all in the day of judgment (2 Cor. 5:10).

Our problem is that we like to sit in the judgment seat and pronounce condemnation upon those whom we think have sinned! Scripture commands us not to judge or condemn others, for we cannot be judgmental and redemptive at the same time. It is difficult to pray sincerely for someone while we are judging them. At times our judgmental attitude can seem to provide us an excuse not to become involved in God's redemptive work in someone's life. Scripture reminds us that God will treat us with the same grace or severity with which we treat others (Luke 6:38).

God commands us not to judge others, but He does want us to be discerning. Jesus said we would know people's spiritual condition by the fruit of their lives (Matt. 7:16). He said grapes are not produced by thorn bushes. If a person's life produces thorns, we can assume that person is not a grapevine! Are we being judgmental? No, we are being discerning. Scripture commands us to avoid associating with scoffers or fools (Prov. 22:10; 17:12). Unless we are able to identify scoffers and fools, we cannot obey God's command. That is not being judgmental; it is being discerning. As Christians, we have been instructed to observe the lives of others so that we can help them while avoiding any sinful influence.

You will be helpful to others only if you see them as God does. If you have been judgmental of others, ask forgiveness and pledge yourself to let God use you as His minister of reconciliation (2 Cor. 5:18).

The Day of the Lord

For you yourselves know that the day of the Lord so comes as a thief in the night.

1 THESSALONIANS 5:2

In the Scriptures, the exhortation to prepare for the day of the Lord is usually given to God's people, rather than to unbelievers. Christians must be prepared for Christ's return, so that they can properly respond to Him. The most important thing about the day of the Lord is clear: it comes unexpectedly.

In Scripture, there are several references to the day of the Lord. Often this refers to Jesus' first coming or His second coming, but it can also refer to any time God comes to His people, either in salvation or judgment (Isa. 13:6; Joel 2:11; Mal. 3:2). Amos had predicted that the day of the Lord would be far different from what the people expected (Amos 5:18). The people of his day thought it would come with joy and singing, yet Amos said there would be grieving and judgment of sin. When Jesus came the first time, His coming caught people by surprise. Because they were expecting the Messiah to come in a different way, many did not recognize Him.

The final day of the Lord will be at Christ's second coming. Meanwhile, there will be times when God will come to you, your family, and friends. You need to be watching for the signs of God's convicting work in your children, your friends, and your coworkers. You must take notice when God begins to do a special work in the lives of the people in your church. It may be that you have an unusual sense of God's presence in a worship service and you begin to intercede for those who are present. Prepare yourself now and pay attention to what is happening in the lives of those around you. You may discover that the day of the Lord is at hand.

Sitting at Jesus' Feet

But Martha was distracted with much serving, and she
approached Him and said, "Lord, do You not care that my
sister has left me to serve alone? Therefore tell her to help me."

LUKE 10:40

Martha loved Jesus dearly and would have done anything for Him. Her struggle came in being still! Martha spent so much time serving Jesus that she had no time to enjoy His company or to get to know Him better. The harder Martha worked, the more frustrated she became with her sister Mary. Mary was sitting at Jesus' feet while Martha scurried around the house to make sure everything was in perfect order for Jesus. Martha's service, though it started out with gladness, deteriorated into resentment and envy.

It is good to want to serve Christ as an expression of love for what He has done for you. Yet when your activity consumes your time and energies so that you have no time for Him, you have become too busy! You may think, as Martha did, that if you don't do the work, it won't get done. That may be true, but Jesus taught that your highest priority must be your relationship with Him. If anything detracts you from that relationship, that activity is not from God. God will not ask you to do something that hinders your relationship with Christ. At times, serving God and carrying out His mission is the best way to know and experience God. At other times, it is more important to sit quietly at His feet and listen to what He is saying.

We are not called to continually sit at the feet of Jesus; otherwise our service for Him would cease. Neither are we called to serve Him incessantly, without taking time to find restoration in His presence. Have you been serving God so diligently that you have not had time to spend with Him?

Thanksgiving

*And one of them, when he saw that he was healed, returned,
and with a loud voice glorified God, and fell down on his face
at His feet, giving Him thanks. And he was a Samaritan.*

LUKE 17:15–16

Thankfulness is foundational to the Christian life.
Thankfulness is a conscious response that comes from
looking beyond our blessings to their source. As Christians, we
have been forgiven, saved from death, and adopted as God's children. There could be no better reason for a grateful heart!

Lepers in Jesus' day were social outcasts. Their highly conta-
gious condition ostracized them from those they loved. When ten
lepers encountered Jesus, they desperately implored Him to show
them mercy. Jesus sent them to the priest. As they obeyed, they
were healed! These ten men had been forbidden to enter their
own villages, to live in their own homes, to work in their own jobs,
or even to touch their own children. Imagine what unrestrained
joy must have filled them as they ran back home again!

One of the lepers, a Samaritan, stopped and ran back to thank
Jesus. Samaritans were normally shunned by the Jews, but Jesus
had healed him! Jesus asked him, "Where are the others?" Ten
lepers had been healed. Ten lepers were reveling in their new-
found health. Ten men were joyfully rushing to share the good
news with those they loved. But only one considered the Source
of that blessing and stopped to thank and worship the One who
had given him back his life.

We, too, have been healed and made whole by the Savior. We
are free to enjoy the abundant life the Savior has graciously given
us. Could we, like the nine lepers, rush off so quickly to glory in
our blessings without stopping to thank our Redeemer? God
looks for our thanks. Our worship, prayers, service, and daily life
ought to be saturated with thanksgiving to God (Phil. 4:6).

Overtaken by Blessings

And all these blessings shall come upon you and overtake you,
because you obey the voice of the Lord your God.

DEUTERONOMY 28:2

When you walk in fellowship with God, you do not have to ask Him to bless you. He *wants* to bless you! Just as you enjoy surprising someone you love with unexpected gifts, God delights in giving you His gifts in times and ways that you might never expect. God's blessings often come in the midst of your everyday life—an encouraging telephone call in the middle of a busy morning or a letter you receive at the end of a hard day. A friend may drop by to help when you are overwhelmed, or you may receive unexpected financial help at a time of need. Often, God's blessings do not come in spectacular ways but in the ordinary busyness of your life. They come just when you most need an expression of God's love.

Blessings come as a result of obedience. When you walk closely with the Lord, blessings will come, regardless of whether you seek them. Blessings from your obedience will also come to those around you—to your children and to your grandchildren. Solomon enjoyed vast wealth during his reign, but God's blessing upon him came largely as a result of his father David's obedience in the previous generation. God promised Abraham that his obedience would bring blessing to all the families of the earth (Gen. 12:2–3).

Do not take God's gifts for granted. When you receive an unexpected blessing, thank God for His continuing love and be alert to recognize the next time His blessing overtakes you!

When God Blesses Others

*Therefore, when Saul saw that he behaved very wisely,
he was afraid of him.*

1 SAMUEL 18:15

J ealousy is a destructive attitude that poisons the way you view life. It is so harmful that God condemned coveting in two of the Ten Commandments. King Saul was a jealous and insecure man. He had been elevated to the highest position in Israel. He had been blessed in numerous ways. But Saul saw that David was gaining the attention and praise of the Israelites. The Israelites recognized Saul's accomplishments, but they also praised David, whom God was using to accomplish even more (1 Sam. 18:7). Rather than rejoicing that God had empowered another to defeat their enemies, Saul became murderously jealous and sought to destroy David.

Jealousy is an abomination in the life of a Christian. God has made us His children. None of us deserves to be God's child, so there is no need to compare our blessings with those of other children of God. Jealousy is self-centeredness at its worst. Jealousy robs us of joy and chokes out contentment. Jealousy hardens the heart and stifles gratitude. Jealousy assumes that God's resources are too limited for Him to bless another and still bless us.

Saul grew so preoccupied with his jealousy toward David that he neglected important things, bringing suffering and pain upon his people. Because of his jealousy, Saul's family was destroyed.

Watch over your heart! If you find yourself unable to rejoice in the success of others, beware! Do not let jealousy taint your heart. Repent before it robs you of any more of the joy and contentment God desires for you. When you are tempted to compare your success in life to that of another, ask God to remind you of all the ways He has blessed you undeservedly.

Standing with Others

Two are better than one, Because they have a good reward for
their labor. For if they fall, one will lift up his companion.
But woe to him who is alone when he falls,
For he has no one to help him up.

ECCLESIASTES 4:9–10

From the beginning of time, God made it clear that it is not good for His people to be alone (Gen. 2:18). God designed us to cooperate. Throughout the Scriptures He speaks of His people as a community that accomplishes more together than separately. God did not create us as isolated individuals, each seeking to achieve our own goals. Rather, the success of our endeavors depends upon our interdependence. This is why He established the Church and released His Holy Spirit to empower the community of believers to spread the gospel. We are to be a kingdom of priests (1 Pet. 2:9).

During difficult times it is critical that we are walking in fellowship with other Christians. When a crisis hits, it is overwhelming to face it alone. But if we have cultivated supportive friendships, we will find strength in the comfort and encouragement of those who care about us. Interdependence is also a safeguard for us when we are lured by temptation. The consistent testimony of those who have fallen to temptation is that they isolated themselves from other believers and were not held accountable by Christian friends.

If you are not a part of a caring community of believers, you are missing out on what God designed you for. You are also in danger of falling into sin. You must link your life with others who are seeking God's will. Seek to be a person who willingly joins others in carrying out God's assignments. Strive to be the source of support and encouragement that those around you need.

327

Crouching at the Door

If you do well, will you not be accepted?
And if you do not do well, sin lies at the door.
And its desire is for you, but you should rule over it.

GENESIS 4:7

When temptation enters our hearts and minds, we either deal with it and gain mastery over it, or it eventually leads us to sinful actions. The time between the initial temptation and the chosen response is critical. Much hangs in the balance.

Cain knew that God was displeased with him but pleased with Abel. Feelings of jealous anger crept into Cain's heart, and thoughts of murder pervaded his mind. As Cain considered what to do, God's Word came to him. God warned him that sin was waiting at the door of his life, looking for an opportunity to enter. Now was not the time to treat temptation lightly, not the time to assume sin would never cause any harm. Now was the time to master the sin and renounce it before it overcame him. Tragically, Cain did not master his sin; instead, sin overtook him and destroyed his life.

Temptations come at unexpected moments. Sinful thoughts may cross your mind. Selfish feelings may begin to invade your heart. The promptings of the Holy Spirit will warn you that God is not pleased with the direction your thoughts and feelings are taking you. At that moment of conviction, you must master the sin that crouches at the door of your life. Sin destroys. Sin brings death. Sin is not something to toy with or take lightly. God's Word to you is the same warning He gave to Cain: Master the sin at the door of your life before it brings its inevitable and disastrous consequences. Heed His caution, and you will avoid unnecessary hardship for yourself and others.

Not in Word
But in Power

For the kingdom of God is not in word but in power.

1 CORINTHIANS 4:20

Christianity is not moral platitudes, lofty intentions, and noble thoughts. The fundamental characteristic of God's kingdom is power. Paul faced constant criticism about his work among the early churches. Some of his detractors would travel to cities such as Corinth and speak extensively about all that Paul was doing incorrectly. At times, people in the churches were enticed to believe the slanderous criticisms against the apostle.

Paul responded with a reminder that the test of a kingdom citizen's authenticity was not the persuasiveness of his words, but the spiritual power of his life. Paul candidly acknowledged that some did not find him eloquent in speech (2 Cor. 10:10). Yet they could not question God's power in his life. He had seen many people converted, and many churches were started through his ministry. He had been used to heal the sick and raise the dead through God's power. Regardless of whether his words were eloquent, they carried spiritual power and authority that came from God.

You will encounter many people who seek to convince you of their opinions concerning the kingdom of God. They may speak passionately. They may even bring charts and graphs to prove their points! But the test of the validity of their words is the spiritual power of their lives. If a person speaks forcefully about a point of doctrine but is habitually sinning, his words are discredited by his life. If a person talks of the power of God but gives no evidence of victory in her life, her words are empty. It is much easier to talk about the victorious Christian life than it is to live it.

If you only have the appearance of godliness without any corresponding spiritual power (2 Tim. 3:5), ask God to cleanse you of your sin and to fill you with His Spirit so that your life is characterized by power.

Quenching the Spirit

Do not quench the Spirit.

1 THESSALONIANS 5:19

We cannot prevent God from accomplishing His work in the world around us, but we can quench His Spirit in our lives. God has given us the freedom to withstand the Holy Spirit's activity in our lives. When we ignore, disobey, or reject what the Spirit is telling us, we quench His activity in us. The prophet Isaiah described the result: "Hearing you will hear and not understand, and seeing you will see and not perceive; For the hearts of this people have grown dull. Their ears are hard of hearing, and their eyes have closed, lest they should see with their eyes and hear with their ears, lest they should understand with their hearts and turn, so that I should heal them" (Isa. 6:9; Matt. 13:14–15).

When you sin, the Holy Spirit will convict you of your need for repentance. If you habitually ignore Him and do not repent, your heart will grow hardened to God's Word. If the Spirit speaks to you about God's will for you, and if you refuse to take action, a time will come when the Spirit's voice will be muted in your life. If you continually reject the Spirit's promptings, a day will come when you no longer hear a word from God. If you repeatedly stifle God's Word to you so that you are no longer sensitive to His voice, He will not give you a fresh word. Be wary of resisting the voice of the Spirit in your life. You may not always be comfortable with what the Spirit is saying to you, but His words will guide you to abundant life.

Taking Responsibility

Then the man said, "The woman whom
You gave to be with me,
she gave me of the tree, and I ate."

GENESIS 3:12

Adam and Eve did everything they could to avoid taking responsibility for their sin. Adam blamed his wife: "*She gave me of the tree.*" He even pointed an accusing finger at God, saying it was "the woman, whom *You* gave me." Eve blamed the serpent saying: "The *serpent* deceived me, and I ate." God ignored their excuses and announced the judgment they would face as consequences for their disobedience.

One of the dirges of mankind is that we refuse to take responsibility for our actions. We want to blame others for our problems: Our parents did not raise us well; our friends let us down; our pastor was not a good enough preacher; our children are rebellious; our employer is not sensitive enough; our spouse is not understanding; there is not enough time in the day . . . the excuses are plentiful! Yet forgiveness and restoration cannot happen until we accept full responsibility for our actions.

An obvious indication that we have not genuinely repented is that we make excuses for our sinful behavior. Nowhere in Scripture does God excuse one person's sin because of someone else's actions. If we make a habit of blaming others for our failures, we will not reach a point of honest repentance. God will hold us accountable for our own actions, not others (2 Cor. 5:10). Strive always to acknowledge and take responsibility for your own sins. It will free you to receive God's forgiveness and to press on to spiritual maturity.

God Is with You

*Thus says the Lord of hosts: "In those days ten men
from every language of the nations shall grasp the sleeve of a
Jewish man, saying, 'Let us go with you,
for we have heard that God is with you.'"*

ZECHARIAH 8:23

God's desire is to fill His people with His Spirit so that others recognize His powerful presence in them. The presence of the Lord in a believer's life ought to be obvious. When the Spirit of almighty God fills a believer, the believer cannot go on living as before. Others will see God.

God told His people through the prophet Zechariah that His presence ought to make a difference in their lives. If God's people walked closely with Him, people from every language and every part of the world would hear that they were a people who knew God. People would come from every nation on earth to find the true God among His people. If the people saw a child of God, they would long to be with him or her because in so doing they would be with God. God gave the vivid picture of ten people clinging to one believer, hoping to find God.

Christ's presence ought to be so evident in your life that the people around you are drawn to you. They should want their children to be with your children because your children are being raised with a godly influence. Employers ought to want you in their workplace; people should seek you for their leader because they know you as someone of integrity before God. Your life and your home ought to be a magnet for people as they sense God's presence with you and your family. The more you allow Christ to make His presence evident in your life, the more people will draw near you and find Him.

The Gift of Encouragement

Yet I considered it necessary to send to you Epaphroditus,
my brother, fellow worker, and fellow soldier,
but your messenger and the one who ministered to my need.

PHILIPPIANS 2:25

Some people know just what to say and do to encourage others who are going through difficult times. Their words give strength to those who are discouraged and comfort to those who are grieving. These people are sensitive to God's voice. They are not self-centered or unaware of the struggles of those around them. They are the ones we immediately seek when we enter a crisis. They are welcome visitors when we are in distress, for their presence sustains us.

Scripture testifies of many whom God enabled to encourage others. When Moses was overwhelmed by his work, Jethro went to him and encouraged him. Jethro gave Moses wise counsel that eased his strain (Exod. 18:1–27). When Paul was imprisoned far from those who loved him, Epaphroditus risked his health and safety in order to go to Paul and minister to him (Phil. 2:25–30). Later, Paul urged Timothy to come and visit him, for Paul found strength and encouragement in Timothy (2 Tim. 4:9; Phil. 2:19–20). Paul asked Timothy to bring Mark also. Mark was the kind of friend Paul needed when he was enduring hardship (2 Tim. 4:11; Philem. 24). Paul also relied on Luke for encouragement. When everyone else was absent or preoccupied, Luke could be found with Paul (2 Tim. 4:11). Paul experienced trials throughout his life, but God sustained him by placing godly friends around him who provided support in practical and sacrificial ways.

God wants to develop you into the kind of friend who can strengthen others. The words you share and the things you do can bring comfort and encouragement to your family, your friends, your neighbors, and your coworkers.

Birth Pangs

But all these things are merely the beginning
of birth pangs.

MATTHEW 24:8 (NASB)

When will Christ return? This question has been pondered much through the generations. The imminence of His coming provides the backdrop for everything the Christian does. Christ has not revealed exactly when He will come, but He has told us signs to watch for. The time of His coming is unclear; the fact of His coming is certain.

Jesus said that certain events would signal the nearness of His coming: There will be wars and rumors of wars; there will be famines and earthquakes; Christians will suffer persecution for the sake of Christ; false prophets will come and teach heresy, leading many astray; lawlessness will abound as people do what is right in their own eyes; the authorities will be unable to control crime. Because of lawlessness, people will become cynical and fearful, and their love for others will grow cold (Matt. 24:6–12).

Jesus said that the signs of the end times will be like birth pangs. The pain of childbirth increases in frequency, and it increases in intensity. Jesus said that the presence of war or famine or false teachers does not mean that His coming is upon us. These things, He said, are merely the beginning. He said that the *frequency* of wars, earthquakes, and crime will increase until finally Christ's return brings everything to a finish. The *intensity* of wars and famines and other human crises will also escalate.

Our day has seen everything Jesus spoke of reach unprecedented proportions. If there were ever a time Christians should be alert to Jesus' coming, it is today.

Weariness

"Come to Me, all you who labor and are heavy laden,
and I will give you rest. Take My yoke upon you and learn
from Me, for I am gentle and lowly in heart,
and you will find rest for your souls."

MATTHEW 11:28-29

If you find that Christianity exhausts you, draining you of your energy, then you are practicing religion rather than enjoying a relationship. Jesus said that a relationship with Him would bring rest to your soul. Your walk with the Lord will not make you weary; it will invigorate you, restore your strength, and energize your life.

Hard work or lack of sleep can make you tired. This fatigue can usually be remedied by a good rest. But there is a deeper fatigue that goes beyond physical tiredness. There is an emotional exhaustion that comes from experiencing heavy burdens and draining crises. There is a tiredness deep within your soul that comes from carrying the weight of the needs of others. You can go on a vacation, but your soul will not be restored. This condition can only be rectified by finding rest in Christ.

Some zealous Christians want to do all they can to serve Christ, and they exhaust themselves in the process. It was to these that Jesus extended His invitation to go to Him and learn from Him. Jesus spent most of His earthly ministry surrounded by needy multitudes. He faced relentless opposition, He often prayed throughout the night, and He rarely had any privacy; yet He always received the rest and strength that came from His Father. It was not that Jesus did not work hard but that He knew the path to spiritual rest. Are you weary? Go to Jesus and let Him give you His rest. His rest will restore your soul as nothing else can.

Not Quarrelsome

And the servant of the Lord must not quarrel but be gentle to all, able to teach, patient.

2 TIMOTHY 2:24

There should be no quarrelsome Christians. The truth of God is within us; we need never be intimidated or frustrated by those who do not accept God's truth.

At times people may disagree with you regarding God's Word. Perhaps they question the way you say He is leading you, or they may challenge your faith in God. At times like these it is never helpful to argue. You will never debate anyone into the kingdom of God. You will never persuade someone that God has spoken to you by outarguing them! Only God can convince others of the veracity of His word to you. If you will allow God to vindicate you in His time, and in His way, a time will come when the wisdom of your choice will be evident (Luke 7:35). If you find yourself often quarreling with others, you need to ask God to clearly reveal your motives and to forgive you for your disobedience to His clear command.

If your motivation for arguing comes from your desire to be right, or to be exonerated, or to gain the esteem of those listening to you, you are acting selfishly, and God will not honor you. God is not interested in how right you are. He is interested in how obedient you are. God's command is not that you win arguments, but that you are kind and forgiving when others mistreat you. You bring God no honor by winning a dispute in His name, but you reflect a Christlike character when you demonstrate patience to those who mistreat you or misunderstand your motives. Arguing may never win people to your view, but loving them as Christ does will win you many friends over time!

Profitable

All Scripture is given by inspiration of God, and is profitable
for doctrine, for reproof, for correction, for instruction in
righteousness, that the man of God may be complete,
thoroughly equipped for every good work.

2 TIMOTHY 3:16–17

All Scripture is profitable! Knowing this, we cheat ourselves when we do not access every book, every truth, every verse, and every page of our Bibles for the promises and commands God has for us. Because every verse of Scripture is inspired by God and gainful to us, we should not pick and choose which verses we will read and study. We should not claim verses we like and ignore those that convict us! If we are to become mature disciples of Jesus, we must allow every Scripture to speak to us and teach us what God desires us to learn. Scripture enables us to evaluate the soundness of doctrines that are being taught. Scripture ought to be the basis for any reproof or correction we bring to another.

If you are not firmly grounded in God's Word, you will be bombarded with an assortment of doctrines, lifestyles, and behaviors, and you will have no means to evaluate whether or not they are of God. You cannot develop a righteous life apart from God's Word. Righteousness must be cultivated. As you fill your mind with the words of God, and as you obey His instructions, He will guide you in the ways of righteousness. Scripture will equip you for any good work God calls you to do. If you feel inadequate for a task God has given you, search the Scriptures, for within them you will find the wisdom you need to carry out His assignment. Allow the Word of God to permeate, guide, and enrich your life.

Wishing to Be Healed

When Jesus saw him lying there, and knew that he already had been in that condition a long time, He said to him, "Do you want to be made well?"

JOHN 5:6

Jesus asked a man a question that appears to have had an obvious answer! He came upon a man who had been lame for thirty-eight years and who was sitting beside a pool of healing. Jesus asked him if he wanted to be healed. Why would Jesus ask such an obvious question? Perhaps the answer was not so clear. Bartimaeus was blind, yet when he cried out for Jesus to have mercy on him, Jesus asked what he wanted Him to do (Mark 10:51). It would have seemed apparent that the foremost concern of a blind person would be to receive sight. There were times, however, when Jesus considered it important for people to verbalize their need and specifically ask Him to heal them.

Just because we are spiritually sick, or just because we are near a place of healing, does not necessarily mean we want to be made well. We may attend church regularly, but choose to remain sinful. Our generation has taken many of the activities that the Bible identifies as sin and has labeled them as addictions or character flaws or the result of an abusive upbringing. We act as if having an addiction is sufficient excuse for disobeying God's commands. As Christians, we are no longer helpless victims of our sin. There is no sinful habit or past hurt that is beyond the healing touch of our Lord.

Have you gone year after year without receiving spiritual healing? God is capable of freeing you, but you may have become comfortable in your sin. You may not want to be healed. If you really want to receive spiritual health, God can give it today. He wants you to ask Him.

A Tender Plant

For He shall grow up before Him as a tender plant,
And as a root out of dry ground.

ISAIAH 53:2

The coming of Jesus was like a tender plant in the midst of a parched ground. Parched ground offers little hope for survival; it is dry and too hardened to allow most plants to penetrate its crust. Yet Jesus was prophesied as a tender plant that would break through the hostile soil and overcome the dry and lifeless environment in order to bring life.

When Jesus was born, His people were hardened to God's Word. There is no written record of God's having spoken to His people for four hundred years. The religious leaders of Jesus' day had studied and memorized the Scriptures, but the words were lifeless to them. So hostile had they become to the truth that when God's Son came to them, they killed Him. Nevertheless, despite the enmity of the people, Jesus brought life to all who believed in Him.

Jesus is capable of bringing life to any person, society, or culture no matter how hardened or hostile they have become to the gospel. Even the most calloused sinner will discover that Jesus knows how to penetrate the heart and bring life where there was only bitterness. The work of Jesus in a person's life may seem fragile at first; but like the mustard seed, it will eventually grow into something strong.

As you pray for someone you care about, don't be discouraged if this person has not responded to Jesus. Just as a tender plant finds a way to grow in a hard and unreceptive environment, so the love of Jesus has the ability to emerge in a life that seems completely unresponsive.

Hold Fast

Test all things; hold fast what is good.
Abstain from every form of evil.

1 THESSALONIANS 5:21–22

Hold fast to what is good, or the world will take it away. Satan is the relentless enemy of good. When he saw that what God gave Adam and Eve was good, he set about to take it away from them. When he saw that King David was pleasing to God, he attempted to destroy David's relationship with God. Never take the good in your life for granted. If you do not hold on to it firmly, it may be lost.

People will challenge the good that you are practicing. They may criticize you for your moral stand, your child rearing, your use of money, or your involvement in church. Time pressures will attack the good in your life. Your time to pray, study Scripture, be with your family, and serve in your church will all be pressured by the many other time demands you face. You may give generously to your church and other Christian causes, but you will be tempted to spend your money selfishly and minimize the good you are doing with your finances.

Scripture reveals the solution for holding on to what is good—abstain from every form of evil. Evil robs you of what God intends for you. A spouse and family are great blessings, but the evil of adultery can rob you of the good that God has given. Prayer is a wonderful gift from God. Yet sin robs the power of prayer (Isa. 1:15). If you will not abstain from evil, it will rob you of the good things God has given. God's commandments do not restrict you: they free you to experience God's best. Diligently abstain from every form of evil, and you will be free to enjoy every good thing God has for you.

A Heart That Loves God

*For I desire mercy and not sacrifice,
And the knowledge of God more than burnt offerings.*

HOSEA 6:6

No amount of activity for God will ever take the place of a heart that is right with Him. Through the ages God's people have been persuaded that they could please Him through their service and their offerings, regardless of their heart condition. King Saul offered generous sacrifices, hoping God would overlook his disobedience (1 Sam. 15:22–23). David may have assumed that after all he had done on God's behalf, God would overlook his sin (2 Sam. 12:7–15). Ananias and Sapphira thought that their generous gift to the church would compensate for their deceitfulness (Acts 5:1–11). Paul was certainly one who had thought his zealousness would please God. After his conversion, however, he concluded that even if he had faith to remove mountains, gave all he had to feed the poor, and offered his body to be burned for the sake of God, and yet had a heart that was not right, it would all be for nothing (1 Cor. 13:1–3).

We are susceptible to the same misunderstanding as all of these people were. We can be deceived into assuming God is more interested in our activity for Him than He is in the condition of our hearts. God has consistently made it clear that He will not be pacified by even the most generous offerings and zealous service if our hearts are not right with Him (Mic. 6:6–8). No matter how much we do in God's service, regardless of how active we are in our church, no matter how honorable our reputation in the Christian community, He will not overlook a sinful heart. His desire is that we devote ourselves to knowing Him and loving Him with all of our hearts.

341

Raining Righteousness

Sow for yourselves righteousness;
Reap in mercy;
Break up your fallow ground,
For it is time to seek the Lord,
Till He comes and rains righteousness on you.

HOSEA 10:12

The people of Hosea's day had become hardened to God's Word. They had heard it many times before and had grown apathetic to what God required of them. God's solution was for them to break up the fallow ground of their hearts. They were to allow Him to soften their hardened hearts. When the earth was dry and crusty, the farmer would plow to loosen the soil so it was receptive to the seeds and the rains that would give life to the crop. Likewise, God's people were to break up the sinful barriers in their lives that prevented God's Word from penetrating their hearts. Then, said Hosea, God would give life and refresh them by raining down on them in righteousness.

As Christians, we must continually cultivate our hearts and minds so that they are receptive to whatever God tells us. John the Baptist exhorted those around him to prepare for Jesus' coming. We, too, can remind others to prepare their lives so that God's righteousness will penetrate and fill their lives. We can urge them to repent when we see sin sinking into their lives. We can share the joy that God's Word brings us and encourage our friends to seek God's will also. We can model obedience for our children. We can tell of the blessings that have come to us as a result of our obedience. We can help to break up the fallow ground in the hearts of those around us.

Hosea admonished God's people to seek the Lord until His righteousness rained down upon them. We should immediately cultivate our heart whenever it starts to become hardened toward God. If we keep our hearts prepared, we will be ready when God's Word comes to us.

Small Things Are
Not Despised

For who has despised the day of small things?

ZECHARIAH 4:10a

The world loves the spectacular. God has proven that He is certainly capable of the extraordinary, but He often chooses to work through the ordinary and seemingly insignificant. In this way He demonstrates His love and His power.

Throughout history, God's answer to a critical time was to send a baby. Isaac, Moses, Samuel, John the Baptist, and Jesus were all born as answers to a time of need. When God delivered the Israelites from the Midianites' oppression, He intentionally used an army of merely three hundred men to defeat a vastly larger army. He had more soldiers available, but He preferred to demonstrate His power in the way He accomplished His purposes. When Jesus selected His first disciples He could have enlisted a multitude to follow Him, but He chose twelve. It was not the number of disciples but the quality of their walk with Him that would determine how they affected their world. When Jesus fed a multitude, five loaves of bread and two fish from a boy's lunch were sufficient in the hands of the Lord.

Jesus compared the kingdom of God to a mustard seed (Matt. 13:31–32). The mustard seed was the smallest seed known to the Jews, yet it grew into an enormous tree. He also likened God's kingdom to leaven that is hardly noticeable but raises the entire batch of dough (Matt. 13:33). When children came to Jesus, His disciples assumed they were an annoyance and chased them away (Matt. 19:13–15). But Jesus said that in order to enter His kingdom, people must approach God as a child.

Christians often accept the adage "the bigger the better." We measure success by the number of people involved in our ministry. We seek spectacular displays of God's power. We must learn to view success as God does. God is interested in the heart; He is pleased with obedience.

343

Not by Might

This is the word of the Lord to Zerubbabel:
"Not by might nor by power, but by My Spirit,"
Says the Lord of hosts.

ZECHARIAH 4:6

God's word came to His people at a critical time. They were a despondent, disillusioned people who faced a daunting task. They had been exiled in Babylon for seventy years. During this time they had witnessed the strength of the most dominant military power in their world. They had watched the Babylonian army marching off to conquer other nations. They had seen the wealth and splendor of the Babylonian king. When Babylon was in turn conquered by the Persians, the Israelites saw an even greater superpower emerging on the world stage. They lost heart when they compared their own weakness and captivity with the enormous strength and wealth of the superpowers of their day.

As the Israelites returned to Jerusalem after seventy years in captivity, they found their city in ruins. Their magnificent temple had been destroyed. The city walls had been torn down. They had no resources to rebuild their splendid city. As these former refugees looked at the mammoth task before them, they realized their poverty and weakness, and they became greatly dismayed. Then came God's Word! He promised that they would, indeed, rebuild their city. But, He told them, the rebuilding would not be accomplished by their own power and resources but by His Spirit. As long as they had God's Spirit, they had everything they needed.

There will be times when obeying God will lead you to impossible situations. If you look at your own skills, knowledge, and resources, you will become discouraged. However, when you became a Christian, God placed His Spirit within you. You now have the resources of heaven at your disposal. The success of your endeavors will not depend on the way you use your own resources but on how you obey the Spirit of God.

All Things
Pertaining to Life

As His divine power has given to us all things that
pertain to life and godliness, through the knowledge of Him
who called us by glory and virtue.

2 PETER 1:3

As a Christian, you have everything you need to live a holy and abundant life (2 Pet. 1:3–11). Your intelligence, your education, or your family background do not determine the holiness of your life. Everything you need to live a victorious, joyful, and abundant life is found in the Holy Spirit who resides within you (Gal. 5:22–23).

According to Peter, each Christian, by faith, has access to these qualities: goodness, knowledge of God, self-control, perseverance, godliness, brotherly kindness, and love. It would be of no use to inherit a fortune if you did not know it was yours. Likewise, it is of no benefit to inherit everything necessary to become like Christ if you do not claim it.

If we continue to lack self-control when God has made it available, we rob ourselves and those around us. If God is willing to instill brotherly kindness into our behavior, but we never display it, people will suffer needlessly as a result.

The key to all that God has made available to us is our faith. We must believe that God wants to build these qualities into our lives. In the Gospels, Jesus related to people according to their faith (Matt. 8:13; 9:29; 15:28). He rewarded genuine faith by granting salvation and healing. If He met unbelief, He did not reward it (Mark 6:5–6).

Review the qualities that Peter said God wants to instill in you. If you lack any of these qualities, ask God to work them into your character, so that you will be more like Christ.

Three Temptations

Now when the tempter came to Him, he said, "If You are the Son of God, command that these stones become bread."

MATTHEW 4:3

Jesus was tempted in every way that we are, yet He never sinned (Heb. 4:15). Jesus began His public ministry with His baptism. As John the Baptist raised Him from the water, Jesus heard His Father's affirmation, "Well done!" Immediately afterward, Jesus spent forty days fasting in the wilderness. There Satan met Him and presented three temptations.

First, Satan enticed Jesus to use His divine power to transform stones into bread. It seemed a logical thing to do. Jesus was hungry, but He had a much greater need to follow His Father's leading. The Father had led Him to fast; Satan sought to persuade Him to eat.

Next, Satan tried to convince Jesus to use *Satan's* means to accomplish the *Father's* ends. "If You are the Son of God, throw Yourself down" (Matt. 4:6). Jesus understood that this would be presumption, not faith. It would be attempting God's work in the world's way. The world looks for spectacular displays; God uses a holy life.

The final temptation Satan proposed for Jesus to achieve God's will was by worshiping Satan (Matt. 4:8–9). In return, Satan offered to give Him all the kingdoms of the world. By compromising, Jesus could gain a powerful ally and achieve His mission without suffering the cross. Jesus knew that only God was to be worshiped, and to worship Satan would not bring instant success, as Satan promised, but devastating failure.

As you seek to follow God, temptations will inevitably come. Sometimes they will come to you immediately after a spiritual victory. Jesus relied on God's Word to see Him through the temptations that could have destroyed Him and thwarted God's plan. He has modeled the way for you to meet every temptation.

Enlarge Your Tent!

Enlarge the place of your tent,
And let them stretch out the curtains of your dwellings;
Do not spare; Lengthen your cords,
And strengthen your stakes.

ISAIAH 54:2

When God comes to a life in power, it is always a time of rejoicing and expectation for the future! Isaiah described this experience as similar to that of a child born to a previously barren woman. The child's arrival changes everything! Life cannot continue as usual! Whereas the dwelling place might have been large enough for two, it must now be made bigger. The child's presence causes the parents to completely rearrange the way they were living.

Isaiah proclaimed that when God comes, you must make room for Him in your life. You must "enlarge the place of your tent" because God's presence will add new dimensions to your life, your family, and your church. You do not simply "add Christ on" to your busy life and carry on with business as usual. When Christ is your Lord, everything changes. Whereas before you may not have expected good things to come through you or in your life, now you should have a spirit of optimism. You ought to expect your life to become richer and fuller. You can anticipate God blessing others through your life. You can look for God to demonstrate His power through your life in increasing measure.

As a Christian, how do you make room for Christ in your life? You repent of your sin. You allow Christ the freedom to do what He wants in you. You watch eagerly for His activity in your life and in your family and in your church. You live your life with the expectancy that Christ will fill you with His power in the days to come and will "stretch" you to do things in His service that you have never done before.

God's Revelation
Is His Invitation

Surely the Lord God does nothing,
Unless He reveals His secret to His servants the prophets.

AMOS 3:7

Christians spend much time talking about "seeking God's will," as though it were hidden and difficult to find. God does not hide His will. His will is not difficult to discover. We do not have to plead with God to reveal His will to us. He is more eager to reveal His will than we are willing to receive it. We sometimes ask God to do things He has already done!

The people in Amos's day became disoriented to God and to His desires. God had revealed His will; the problem was that they had not recognized it or obeyed it. Amos declared that God does *nothing* in the affairs of humanity without seeking one of His servants to whom He will reveal His activity. Tragically, there are times when no one is walking closely enough with Him to be receptive to His word (Isa. 59:16; 63:5; Ezek. 22:30–31).

Jesus walked so intimately with His Father that He was always aware of what the Father was doing around Him (John 5:19–20). Jesus said that if our eyes are pure, they will see God and recognize His activity (Matt. 6:22). If we are not seeing God's activity, the problem is not a lack of revelation. The problem is that our sin prevents us from noticing it.

When God is working in your child's life or when He is convicting your coworker, He may reveal His activity to you. His revelation is His invitation for you to join Him in His redemptive work. Be alert to God's activity around you. He will reveal His activity to His servants. If your spiritual eyes are pure, you will be overwhelmed by all that you see God doing around you!

The Race

I have fought the good fight, I have finished the race,
I have kept the faith.

2 TIMOTHY 4:7

There is much satisfaction in finishing something you have begun! The success of a race is determined not only by how well you begin but also by how well you end. Many athletes can begin a race impressively, but if they stumble or are injured or lack the stamina to finish, their good start is useless. Paul rejoiced that he had not only begun the race; but he had also finished it. His prize was a robust faith in God and a life filled with God's powerful presence.

The Christian life is not easy. Some mistakenly assume that once they become children of God, their struggles are over. Many Christians begin their walk with Christ enthusiastically; but as the pressures mount, they lose heart and abandon their pilgrimage.

Paul described his Christian life as a battle. There were times when he struggled, and only through perseverance could he continue. It may surprise us to know that the great apostle had to struggle at times to be faithful to God. Paul faced persecution, misunderstanding, betrayal, and death threats. His Christian life was anything but easy, yet he persevered.

Your faith in God is not proven by beginning the race but by enduring to the finish. Publicly announcing your commitment to Christ in your church does not compare with a lifetime of devotion to His cause. Use Paul as your model. Live your life in such a way that you can one day conclude, "I have fought the good fight, I have finished the race, I have kept the faith!"

He Has Shown You

He has shown you, O man, what is good;
And what does the Lord require of you
But to do justly, To love mercy,
And to walk humbly with your God?

MICAH 6:8

God never conceals His expectations from us. We never have to guess how we should live. In response to the misguided ways in which people sought to please God, the prophet Micah clearly explained what God does and does not expect. The people asked: Should we come to God with many offerings? Should we bring a thousand rams and ten thousand rivers of oil? Would God be pleased if we gave our firstborn child to Him to express our devotion? (Mic. 6:6–7). Micah's response was straightforward: "He has shown you, O man, what is good."

Micah listed three things God desires. First, He wants us to show justice. The desire to receive justice is not enough. We must also be absolutely just in the way we treat others. If we have given our word, we should keep it with complete integrity. If we have people working for us, we should treat them as fairly as Jesus would. We should act justly in every relationship.

Second, we are to love mercy. The knowledge that we have received undeserved mercy from God should motivate us to show mercy to others. We must resist the temptation to retaliate against those who have wronged us, choosing to show them mercy instead.

Finally, God requires us to walk humbly with Him. God does not ask us for spectacular acts of service—He asks for humility. At times we try to make the Christian life far more complicated than it is. We may hide behind questions about the Bible or uncertainty about the second coming of Christ. We can allow ourselves to become distracted in order to avoid confronting what God has clearly told us to do today. If we strive to be completely obedient in the basics, the more complex assignments will become clear.

Built on a Rock

*Therefore whoever hears these sayings of Mine,
and does them, I will liken him to a wise man
who built his house on the rock.*

MATTHEW 7:24

The Christian life is hard work. Christianity involves systematically striving to implement the truths of God's Word into your life. Spiritual depth and maturity do not come without consistent effort.

Jesus had just concluded the Sermon on the Mount, which sets forth some of the most profound truths ever spoken. The Son of God had clearly explained the kind of life that is pleasing to the Father. Yet Jesus knew, even as He was concluding His sermon, that some of His listeners would leave and never apply a word they had heard.

Jesus said that a man who takes the words of God and builds them into his life is like a wise man who builds his house on a rock. Rocks are hard to build on. It takes great effort to attach a foundation to a rock. A house built on sand provides instant comfort; building on a rock is laborious and tedious. Yet building on sand leaves the builder in a vulnerable position, while the one building on the rock is secure.

How can you tell what kind of foundation a life has been built on? Watch to see what happens when a storm comes. A life built upon the Word of God will withstand the very storm that sweeps away the life that did not heed God's Word.

There are no shortcuts to spiritual maturity. Maturity comes only through hard work and obedience to what God says. The next time you hear Jesus speaking, begin immediately to firmly build His truth into your life, so that no storm can unsettle you.

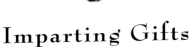

Imparting Gifts

For I long to see you, that I may impart to you
some spiritual gift, so that you may be established.
ROMANS 1:11

Your life affects those you have contact with, whether you intend it or not. It may be a positive experience for them or a negative one, but your life _will_ affect others.

Paul wanted to leave a spiritual blessing with other believers. He had heard of the Christians in Rome, and he longed to go to them to build them up in their faith. Paul always mentioned the Roman believers in his prayers, even though he had never met them (Rom. 1:10). While he waited for an opportunity to visit Rome, Paul wrote a letter to the church. His letter to the Romans is one of the most cherished and challenging books in the New Testament.

We should share Paul's goal of leaving a spiritual blessing with everyone around us. We have opportunities to strengthen our parents, our children, our friends, our coworkers, and our fellow Christians. Spiritual blessings are not given haphazardly, but by choice. Our self-centeredness may cause us only to seek blessings from others rather than to impart them. Only when we are determined to focus on _giving_ a blessing rather than _receiving_ a blessing will we have the quality of ministry to others that God gave to Paul.

You may not realize it, but your life has the potential to bless everyone you encounter. Are others strengthened and encouraged in their faith because of their relationship with you? Do you usually look at others in terms of what they can do for you or in terms of how you can encourage them? As you go about your day, strive to be a positive influence on everyone you encounter!

Who Are You?

And the evil spirit answered and said, "Jesus I know,
and Paul I know; but who are you?"

ACTS 19:15

There is no secondhand spirituality. No one else can develop Christian maturity on your behalf. A strong Christian heritage is an asset, but it cannot take the place of your own vibrant, growing relationship with Christ.

Paul had a powerful walk with God. God used him so mightily that extraordinary miracles occurred through his life. Cloths that touched Paul were taken to the sick, and the sick were healed (Acts 19:10–12). Evil spirits were cast out. Paul's preaching and teaching were instrumental in building a strong church in Ephesus. Paul's ministry was so impressive, in fact, that others tried to duplicate it.

Seven sons of the chief priest, Sceva, attempted to cast out demons the way Paul did. They confronted an evil spirit and attempted to exorcise it "by the Jesus whom Paul preaches." These men were trying to use a spiritual power that Paul had acquired after years of walking closely with his Lord. They could imitate Paul's words, but they could not duplicate the power that was his through his personal relationship with God. The evil spirit retorted, "Jesus I know, and Paul I know, but who are you?" The demon then viciously attacked them and humiliated them. The evil spirits were fearfully aware of Jesus (James 2:19); they were familiar with Paul's influence over the powers of darkness. But the demons had no knowledge of the seven sons of Sceva.

You can duplicate the words and deeds of a spiritually mature Christian, but you cannot inherit his or her walk with God. Christian maturity takes effort; it comes over time. If you ignore the place of prayer and if you neglect your relationship with Christ, you will not grow in your faith. Imitating the faith of others will not give you victory. Only as you nurture your own relationship with Jesus will your life be filled with spiritual maturity and power.

Dethroning Idols

So the word of the Lord grew mightily and prevailed.

ACTS 19:20

Paul's world worshiped idols. No idol was more revered in Ephesus than the goddess Diana. The great statue was housed in a magnificent temple and was recognized as one of the wonders of the world. An idol-making industry, providing a livelihood for many people, developed in Ephesus to support the widespread idolatry of the day.

Paul did not go to Ephesus to condemn those worshiping idols but to unashamedly proclaim the good news of Jesus Christ. As Paul shared the truths of God, and as people were set free from sin's bondage, idol worship began to decline. The contrast between stone carvings and God's power to change lives became obvious. The righteous lives of the Christians stood in stark contrast to the hedonistic practices of the idol worshipers. The victorious Christian witness was so compelling that the economy of the entire city was thrown into upheaval as idolatry diminished in favor of Christianity.

An idol is anything that diverts our devotion from God. Our society is as idolatrous as Paul's was. Rather than worshiping statues, we choose possessions, pleasures, or careers as our gods and pour our time, finances, and energy into these things.

Each of us is called, as Paul was, to live a victorious, joyful, and purposeful Christian life in the midst of an idolatrous society. We do not have to seek out and condemn today's idols. Rather, as we live out our Christianity, enjoying the abundant life God gives, our lives will discredit the idols around us. We may face opposition and hostility from those who are angered at the contrast between our God and theirs. People do not like to have their idols dethroned! Yet as we uphold Christ, others will see a difference and be drawn to Him and the life that He offers.

Opposition!

*An angel of the Lord appeared to Joseph in a dream, saying:
"Arise, take the young Child and His mother, flee to Egypt,
and stay there until I bring you word; for Herod will seek the
young Child to destroy Him."*

MATTHEW 2:13

Whenever God clearly speaks to you and you obey His will, you can expect to face opposition. Spiritual assaults and attacks by the ungodly are not always signs that you are out of the will of God; they may even indicate that you are in the very center of God's will. Mary's husband, Joseph, was a righteous man who feared God, yet his obedience to God forced him to flee for his life to a foreign country. Joseph's hardship came, not because of his sin, but because of his obedience. Although Joseph and Mary were forced to move to another country, they remained in the center of God's will.

Jesus warned His disciples to expect persecution from the world as they obeyed the Father. He reminded them that they would not face persecution alone, for Jesus, too, had faced the hostility of the world and had been victorious (John 16:33).

Don't become discouraged when you face opposition. Opposition may indicate that you are acting in obedience to God. Do not let opposition cause you to doubt God's will. Examine your heart. If you have done what you know He has asked you to do, trust Him to see you through the antagonism that comes from those who are not walking with Him. When they encountered persecution, the disciples did not ask God to remove their opponents, but to give them boldness as they faced opposition (Acts 4:24–31). God's will for you may involve hardship, as it did for His Son (John 15:20), but He loves you and will not allow you to face more than you are able to handle.

Faithfulness in Prayer

Now there was one, Anna, . . . a widow of about eighty-four
years, who did not depart from the temple, but served God
with fasting and prayers night and day.

LUKE 2:36–37

Your faithfulness allows God to reveal greater insight to you than to the less faithful. Faithfulness brings opportunities to you that are not given to the unfaithful. God takes pleasure in answering prayers that come from a faithful heart.

Anna had been a widow for many years. In her day, a widow had little status in society and was virtually helpless on her own. Anna spent her time, day and night, in prayer and fasting in the temple. As she prayed, she yearned to see the Messiah. God chose few people to encounter the Savior when He was born, revealing His Son only to those whose hearts were faithful and pure. Anna was one of those few. Jesus would later say to His followers, "Blessed are your eyes for they see, and your ears for they hear . . . it has been given to you to know the mysteries of the kingdom of heaven, but to them it has not been given" (Matt. 13:16, 11).

Anna continued faithfully in prayer until her prayer was answered. The answer to her prayers did not come immediately. In fact, it came near the end of her life. But God honored her faithfulness. God's redemptive plan to send the Messiah included answering the prayers of a humble widow.

Faithful praying may mean a lifetime of waiting to receive an answer. God is looking for intercessors who are willing to continue to pray and to believe until they see God's answer.

Preparing for the Presence of God

"Prepare the way of the Lord;
Make His paths straight. . . .
And all flesh shall see the salvation of God."

LUKE 3:4,6

If we are to receive the powerful presence of God, we must prepare ourselves. John the Baptist was God's messenger to help people prepare to receive the Savior of the world. John preached unwaveringly: "Repent, for the kingdom of heaven is at hand!" (Matt. 3:2). Those who heard John's message and prepared their lives recognized Jesus when He came, and they left all to follow Him. This was especially true of the disciples, whose hearts God Himself prepared (Matt. 16:17). Preparation must precede God's presence!

God's instruction for preparation is specific: repentance! This involves a complete change of mind, heart, will, and behavior toward Him. He is *Lord,* and your life must be prepared to receive Him as your Lord. Anything less is inadequate. Some were obviously unprepared to follow Jesus and missed the opportunity (Luke 9:57–62). The religious leaders of Jesus' day were largely unprepared for His arrival. They knew the Messiah was coming. They even knew where He would be born (Matt. 2:4–6). Yet when word came that the Savior had been born, they made no effort to join Him, preferring instead their religious ritual.

If you are unprepared, you, too, will miss the opportunity to experience Jesus. You may practice religion, but you will miss God. While others encounter the Lord personally in worship, your heart will remain unmoved. As others receive a fresh word from God, you will experience a painful silence. Religious activity can never substitute for a heart that is pure before Him. Purity comes only through repentance. Pray, as the psalmist did, that God will examine your heart and reveal your need to repent of your sin (Ps. 139:23–24).

The Wisdom of Spiritual Checking

*And Jesus increased in wisdom and stature,
and in favor with God and men.*

LUKE 2:52

We are accustomed to having our progress measured in many ways. We are given tests in school, evaluations at work, and physical examinations by our doctors. Yet we may never measure our spiritual or social growth. As Jesus grew from an infant to a child to a youth to an adult, he "increased in stature" with God and men. The better people knew Jesus, the more they trusted Him. They admired His wisdom and appreciated His compassion. Likewise, as Jesus grew in His relationship with His heavenly Father, He continued to please Him.

The apostle Paul said that when he was a new Christian, he behaved as a spiritual child, but as he matured in his faith, he began to act like a spiritual adult (1 Cor. 13:11). There is nothing wrong with acting like a baby when you are an infant, but it is the obligation of every believer to strive for maturity (Heb. 6:1).

When you are a new believer, you will not always know how to relate to others in a spiritually mature way. You may battle with envy, anger, or unforgiveness. But the longer you walk with Christ, the more you should relate to others as He does. As you are conformed to the image of Jesus Christ, your heavenly Father will become increasingly satisfied with your obedience to Him, as the Father was with His Son. It is helpful for you to measure the progress in your spiritual life from time to time. A good way to evaluate your spiritual growth is to ask mature Christians around you if your actions reveal spiritual maturity. It is imperative that you ask God to evaluate your spiritual maturity and that you never become satisfied with less than a fully developed relationship with God.

Blessed in Believing

"Blessed is she who believed, for there will be a fulfillment of
those things which were told her from the Lord."

LUKE 1:45

In the kingdom of God, believing is a prerequisite to receiving. God spoke to Mary and gave the assurances He always gives when He assigns the impossible to His people. Everything was in place for God to act. Everything waited on Mary to believe Him. Once she believed, it was done! It takes an undivided heart to believe under such circumstances and a pure heart to see God (Matt. 5:8; Heb. 12:14).

This has always been God's way with His people. Mary could not see all that had been arranged and assembled in the courts of heaven. She could not see the legions of angels prepared to protect her and her baby. She was unaware of the future and all that she and her child would face. All she knew was that God had spoken to her, and that was enough. So she responded: "Behold the maidservant of the Lord! Let it be to me according to your word" (Luke 1:38).

When God speaks about His plans, He does so with everything already in place to fulfill His word. God never speaks hypothetically. He knows exactly what will come to pass. He simply asks you to believe Him. You will experience great blessing when you place your absolute trust in Him. Mary could not have dreamed all that would result from her faithful obedience. Likewise, you cannot possibly imagine all that God has in store for you when you trust Him. He knows exactly what He will do to bring salvation to someone you have prayed for or to heal your friend or to provide for your needs. God has everything in place. Will you believe Him?

Spontaneous Praise

And Mary said,
"My soul magnifies the Lord,
And my spirit has rejoiced in God my Savior."

LUKE 1:46–47

Praise is the spontaneous response of a grateful child of God in His presence. The person who knows God and experiences Him intimately sings to the Lord with deepest praise! Mary was overwhelmed by the Lord's goodness to her. In response, she sang one of the most beautiful and profound songs of praise found in Scripture. Trying to stop the praise of a thankful heart would be like trying to arrest the flow of a mighty waterfall! God created us to praise Him; praise will be our activity when we are gathered around His throne in heaven.

You should never have difficulty thinking of reasons why God deserves your praise. You should enjoy the times you have to praise your Lord, both privately and publicly, in worship. If your life is not filled with praise, it may be that you have lost your appreciation for God's merciful activity in your life. Never forget what God has saved you from. Never take for granted what it means to have the assurance of eternity with God. Do not disregard the spiritual kinship you enjoy with other believers. Take time often to recount the blessings He has poured out upon you and your family. As you contemplate the boundless love and mercy God has shown you, you will want to sing His praises as Mary did. Spontaneous praise is authentic praise. It does not have to be manipulated or orchestrated. It is a real and personal expression of a grateful heart and wonder-filled life that has encountered holy God!

Nothing Will Be Impossible

For with God nothing will be impossible.

LUKE 1:37

The angel Gabriel told Mary that God was planning to do something humanly impossible. All human logic would agree that a virgin could not give birth to a child. It was impossible. Yet this is exactly what was to happen. When God speaks of doing the impossible, it is no longer absurd. When was the last time God did the impossible in your life? When was the last time God spoke to you about what He wanted to do and you were scared to death by its magnitude?

God still does the impossible! Too often we acknowledge our belief that God can do whatever He wants; then we add a safety clause: "But I just don't think God will do that with me!" We become practical atheists, believing that God can perform miracles but never expecting a miracle in our own lives.

God wanted to bring salvation to all of humanity. It is critical that Mary not only believed God could perform a miracle, but also adjusted her life to the awesome work He planned to do through her. The difference between a Christian and a moral person is the divine. The difference between a church and a social club is the miraculous. Some can duplicate the morality of a Christian, but no one can reproduce the miraculous that should be a part of the Christian experience. Do you believe that nothing is impossible for God?

Have This Mind in You

Let this mind be in you which was also in Christ Jesus.

PHILIPPIANS 2:5

Attitudes do not just happen; we choose them. Paul urged believers to have the same attitude that Jesus had. Jesus was the Son of God. His place was at the right hand of His Father, ruling the universe. No position could be more glorious or honorable than the right hand of the heavenly Father. Jesus' relationship with the Father gave Him the right to this honor.

Jesus chose not to hold on to this right. Nothing, not even His position in heaven, was so precious to Him that He could not give it up if His Father asked Him. His love for His Father compelled Him to make any sacrifice necessary in order to be obedient to Him. When the Father required a spotless sacrifice for the redemption of humanity, Jesus did not cling to His rights; nor did He argue that He should not have to suffer for the sins of rebellious creatures of dust (Isa. 53:7). Rather, He relinquished the glory of His heavenly existence in order to become a man. He was born in a cattle shed; He slept in a feeding trough. His life was spent preparing for the day when He would suffer an excruciating execution. All of this He did willingly.

We are tempted to hold tightly to things God has given us. We say, "I would be willing to give up anything God asked of me, but I just don't think He would ask me to give anything up!" The Father asked His Son to make radical adjustments in His life. Can we not expect that He will ask us to sacrifice privileges and comforts as well?

If you find yourself resisting every time God seeks to adjust your life to His will, ask the Spirit to give you the same selfless attitude that Jesus demonstrated.

Commended by God

For not he who commends himself is approved,
but whom the Lord commends.

2 CORINTHIANS 10:18

It is common for all of us to seek approval for our actions. As children, we longed for the affirmation of our parents. As we grew older, we also valued the opinions of our friends, colleagues, and employers. At times, the esteem of others can claim such importance that it becomes our way to measure our worth as a person.

Paul said that he was not striving to obtain the approval of people. Some of his critics thought their criticisms could determine what he did. Yet these same people were praising themselves for their own opinions and behavior. They were seeking the approval of others, and they were receiving it.

Jesus said that those who seek to gain the approval of others "have their own reward" (Matt. 6:2–5). Paul, too, realized that achieving the praise of others is not difficult, but earning God's approval is a far greater accomplishment. The affirmation "Well done!" that Jesus received from the Father became Paul's goal as well (2 Tim. 2:3–5). Paul knew that self-approval is not hard to attain. Paul himself had once been pleased with his own life, until he came to realize that the righteousness he was so proud of was mere rubbish in the kingdom of God (Phil. 3:8). After his conversion, Paul understood that God's evaluation of his actions was what mattered, not his own opinion of himself.

Whose opinion matters most to you? Have you become complacent, enjoying the approval of those around you? Have you become satisfied with your estimation of the way you are living? The commendation that matters most is the one that comes from God. The pleasure that your life gives to God should be your motivation to live righteously.

True Worship

*But the hour is coming, and now is, when the true worshipers
will worship the Father in spirit and truth; for the Father is
seeking such to worship Him. God is Spirit, and those who
worship Him must worship in spirit and truth.*

JOHN 4:23–24

We are designed to worship God in spirit and in truth. As Jesus spoke to the Samaritan woman at the well, He sought to help her do this by imparting to her God's living water (John 4:13–14).

Jesus sought out this woman personally to give her abundant life. In the same way, the Father seeks an encounter with each of us that is real and personal. The Samaritan woman had *heard* about God; Jesus said true worship must be "face to face" with God. Worship is not religion or ritual; worship is an intimate and vital encounter with a Person. True worship includes the full recognition of who God is: Holy, Sovereign, Almighty, Loving, Merciful. This recognition brings about the realization of our own sinfulness.

True worship is life-changing! It creates within the worshiper's heart a hatred for sin. True worship results in repentance, obedient submission, and a desire for holiness (Isa. 6:1–8). True worship generates a desire to show mercy and to express forgiveness. It includes a joyful acceptance of all that God has provided by His grace. True worship is not exclusive. Just as the Samaritan woman rushed off to tell others of her encounter with the Lord, so true worship will compel the worshiper to include others. As a result of this woman's encounter with Jesus, many others from her village came to know Him as well. The one who has truly worshiped will have a sense of peace and a confident expectation of what God is about to do. True worship produces a transformed life, reflecting the One who has been worshiped.

Food

Jesus said to them, "My food is to do the will of Him who sent Me, and to finish His work."

JOHN 4:34

Throughout Jesus' ministry, we see a marked difference between His priorities and the concerns of His disciples. The disciples were often preoccupied with how to meet their physical needs (Matt. 14:15–17; John 4:8; Luke 18:28). Jesus repeatedly assured them that the Father knew their needs and would provide (Luke 11:11–13). Jesus stressed that their priority was to "seek first the kingdom of God and His righteousness"; the necessities of daily life would be provided (Matt. 6:33).

When Jesus spoke to the woman at the well, His disciples had gone into a nearby town to get food. While His disciples were seeking earthly nourishment, Jesus was giving this woman "living water" that would satisfy her soul for eternity. When they returned, the disciples urged Jesus to eat. He replied that His "food" was to do the will of His Father. Since their attention was on earthly matters, His disciples misunderstood His reply. Jesus' very life came from obeying His Father. Because of Jesus' obedience that day, the woman received eternal life. In her excitement, she brought many others to Jesus to hear for themselves, and many believed that He was indeed the Christ, the Savior of the world (John 4:39–42).

The apostle Paul understood what Jesus had been teaching His disciples. When Paul wrote to the believers in Rome, he stressed that "the kingdom of God is not eating and drinking, but righteousness and peace and joy in the Holy Spirit. For he who serves Christ in these things is acceptable to God and approved by men" (Rom. 14:17–18).

When Satan tempted Jesus to turn stones into bread, Jesus quoted the Scriptures, summarizing the focus of His life and ministry: "Know that man shall not live by bread alone; but man lives by every word that proceeds from the mouth of the Lord" (Deut. 8:3).

It Is Finished!

So when Jesus had received the sour wine, He said,
"It is finished!" And bowing His head,
He gave up His spirit.

JOHN 19:30

God always finishes what He begins (Phil. 1:6). God never speaks a word without ensuring that it comes to pass (Isa. 55:11). Christ is both the Alpha and the Omega, the beginning and the end (Rev. 1:8, 17). Christ is as much at the *end* of His work as He is at its *beginning*.

Jesus was given an enormous mandate. He was to live a sinless life, remaining absolutely obedient to His Father. Even the manner of His death was to fulfill numerous prophecies that had been foretold in Scripture (Matt. 26:24, 31, 54, 56; 27:9, 35; 46; John 19:28, 36–37). Yet, despite the extremely complex assignment Jesus received from His Father, He could shout triumphantly from the cross, "It is finished!"

Christ now resides within each believer. His assignment today is to complete God's will in each Christian. He is just as determined to do this in us as He was to complete God's will for Himself. You will have to resist Christ in order to remain out of the will of God. What is it God wants to do in you? Have you allowed Him to complete what He has begun? He will not *force* you to receive all that He has for your life. If God's work has not been brought to fruition in you, it is not that Christ has not been diligently working toward that end. Rather, you may need to release areas of your life to Him and be as determined to see God's work in you completed as Christ is. Review the things God has said to you over this last year. Are there promises God has made to you that you have refused to allow Him to complete? If so, commit to yield your will to God today.

Index of Readings

Index of Readings

Index of Readings

Index of Readings

Index of Readings

Index of Readings

Index of Subjects

Index of Scriptures

Index of Scriptures